CHASING GIDEON

CHASING GIDEON

The Elusive Quest
for
Poor People's Justice

KAREN HOUPPERT

THE NEW PRESS

Earlier and shorter versions of the chapters "A Perfect Storm" and "Death in Georgia" were first published in *The Nation*.

"American Bar Association's Ten Principles of a Public Defense Delivery System by the Standing Committee on Legal Aid and Indigent Defendants" copyright © 2010 by the American Bar Association. Reprinted with permission. This information or any or portion thereof may not be copied or disseminated in any form or by any means or stored in an electronic database or retrieval system without the express written consent of the American Bar Association.

Requests for permission to reproduce selections from this book should be mailed to: Permissions Department, The New Press, 38 Greene Street, New York, NY 10013.

Published in the United States by The New Press, New York, 2013
Distributed by Perseus Distribution

LIBRARY OF CONGRESS CATALOGING-IN-PUBLICATION DATA

Houppert, Karen, 1962-
 Chasing Gideon : the elusive quest for poor people's justice / Karen Houppert.
      pages cm
 "Earlier and shorter versions of the chapters "A Perfect Storm" and "Death in Georgia" were first published in The Nation."
 Includes bibliographical references.
 ISBN 978-1-59558-869-2 (hardcover : alk. paper) -- ISBN 978-1-59558-892-0 (e-book) 1. Legal assistance to the poor--United States. 2. Right to counsel--United States. I. Title.
 KF336.H68 2013
 345.73'056--dc23

                        2012047464

The New Press publishes books that promote and enrich public discussion and understanding of the issues vital to our democracy and to a more equitable world. These books are made possible by the enthusiasm of our readers; the support of a committed group of donors, large and small; the collaboration of our many partners in the independent media and the not-for-profit sector; booksellers, who often hand-sell New Press books; librarians; and above all by our authors.

www.thenewpress.com

Book design by Bookbright Media
Composition by Bookbright Media
This book was set in Adobe Caslon

Printed in the United States of America

2 4 6 8 10 9 7 5 3 1

For Zack Houppert-Nunns

CONTENTS

Introduction ix

Chapter 1: *Due Process Theater: A Case of Vehicular Homicide* 1

Chapter 2: *"I Have No Counsel": The Man Behind Gideon v. Wainwright* 57

Chapter 3: *A Perfect Storm: Looking for Justice in New Orleans* 103

Chapter 4: *Death in Georgia: A Capital Offense* 179

Conclusion 249

Afterword by David J. Carroll 253

Acknowledgments 261

American Bar Association's Ten Principles of a Public Defense Delivery System by the Standing Committee on Legal Aid and Indigent Defendants 263

Notes 265

INTRODUCTION

March 2013 marks the fiftieth anniversary of the landmark U.S. Supreme Court decision *Gideon v. Wainwright*, which established the constitutional right to free counsel for the poor. Most Americans have a glancing knowledge of this basic right from popular TV shows such as *Law and Order* or *CSI*. We recognize it from the arresting officer who announces as he snaps on the handcuffs, "You have a right to an attorney. If you cannot afford an attorney, one will be provided for you."

A half century has passed since the Supreme Court ruled in the *Gideon* case and since *New York Times* reporter Anthony Lewis penned his award-winning book recounting Clarence Earl Gideon's request for a lawyer to help him fight his burglary charge. Lewis's book, *Gideon's Trumpet*, was hopeful and optimistic about a future where effective legal assistance is provided for all criminal defendants, regardless of their ability to afford it. But a look at the state of indigent defense today reveals instead a situation in which citizens are routinely being denied their basic constitutional rights.

Enormous changes have taken place in the U.S. criminal justice system since the Supreme Court ruled in the *Gideon* case, including an explosion in the number of prosecutions, and in particular drug arrests, which swelled from fewer than 50 per 100,000 people in 1963 to 750 per 100,000 people by 2000.[1] The advent of mandatory minimum sentences and other harsher approaches to law enforcement, applied broadly through the so-called War on Drugs, have raised the stakes and changed the dynamics of criminal defense. Plea bargaining, which now resolves more than 90 percent of all cases, positions the lawyer in particular constraints, as does the overwhelming caseload that so many criminal defense lawyers carry.[2]

This book focuses on the stories of four defendants in four states—Washington, Florida, Louisiana, and Georgia—that are emblematic of contemporary problems with providing lawyers to poor people throughout the country. In Washington, where teenager Sean Replogle hit another car and the driver later died, crushing caseloads in the public defender's office regularly compromise the quality of representation that poor and working-class defendants receive—with devastating consequences for the accused. In Florida, where Clarence Earl Gideon brought his original case and where Miami-Dade County's chief public defender for thirty-two years, Bennett Brummer, appealed to the courts themselves for relief from accepting more clients and providing inadequate representation a new chapter in the Gideon case unfolds. In Louisiana, Gregory Bright served twenty-seven years for a crime he didn't commit and Clarence Jones has sat in jail for more than sixteen months on a burglary charge, waiting for a lawyer to be appointed to him; here, the interplay of race, poverty, cronyism, high incarceration rates, and antiquated funding mechanisms create a dysfunctional indigent defense system in which innocent people are routinely jailed and denied basic access to an attorney. And in Georgia, where a jury sentenced Rodney Young to death in 2012 as valiant but underfunded defenders explained his mental retardation, disparate funding levels for prosecutors and public defenders can tip the balance between life and death.

Taken together, these four stories point to fundamental flaws in the way we provide legal representation to the poor in America. They also hint at solutions for reform, and this book documents some creative efforts to fix a broken system, as well as telling the stories of committed lawyers steadily working to deliver on the promise of *Gideon*.

These cases raise questions about how we as a nation will choose to define "justice." By justice, do we mean that we will pay lip service to the notion that everyone has a lawyer to represent them in court? That we will provide a warm body in a suit and tie to stand next to a defendant? Or do we mean to equate justice with fairness—and actually provide folks who are accused of crimes with meaningful representation? Are we, in fact, committed to a level playing field, the adversarial system of justice in which both sides are properly armed to argue and from which truth emerges? Are we committed to making the system work as it is designed to? Back in the 1800s, Mark Twain joked that "the law is a system that protects everybody who can afford a good lawyer." In many ways, that remains true.

CHAPTER 1

Sean Replogle in 2012. He is now twenty-nine, works in a fast-food restaurant, and recently served the cop who testified against him: "You tried to put me in prison at eighteen and sat next to me for eight days of a trial and you don't even recognize me?" Photo by Barbara Smith.

DUE PROCESS THEATER:

A CASE OF VEHICULAR HOMICIDE

Sean Replogle was a blond, rail-thin senior in high school when he turned eighteen on September 16, 2001. He describes himself as a "happy-go-lucky kid" with a lot of friends. Aside from catching it for occasionally skipping, he had never been in trouble at school. He'd certainly never been in trouble with the law. Indeed, it had been his wish since childhood to work in law enforcement; he hoped to be a cop someday. For now, though, he was flipping burgers at McDonald's after school. He worked hard and saved his wages. A few weeks after his eighteenth birthday, he used the $1,700 he had accumulated to buy a thirteen-year-old red Mustang.

His dad, Chuck Replogle, was proud of the fact that Sean had earned the money for his own car. And, in any case, he could not have helped. Chuck Replogle was a widower barely scraping by financially. He taught in a before- and after-school program at a local public elementary school. By working an early morning shift at the school, doing some carpentry in the afternoons, and then returning for a second shift at the school in the afternoons, he had been able to support Sean and his younger sister. Years ago, he made better money as a journeyman carpenter. But his wife took ill when Sean was very young. Disease sucked the life out of her; the hospitals sucked the savings out of the family's bank account. She died when Sean was a preschooler. Then Chuck was injured on the job and

3

had to find new, less physically demanding work. He loved his work with children, but his meager salary certainly precluded buying a car for his teenage son.

He couldn't even afford to help Sean cover insurance costs for the car. In fact, when Chuck took his son to the insurance office shortly after Sean bought the car and the agent changed the quote he'd given over the phone—upping the amount by $40 due to Chuck's credit rating—they were stuck.[1] Sean was paying for the insurance from his McDonald's earnings and he didn't have the extra money either. He would get his paycheck the next day, Sean told the agent, and come back to settle things.

That, anyway, was the plan.

McDonald's paid Sean on Friday. On Saturday, the boy drove his new Mustang with a friend to the Moneytree to cash their respective checks. On the way home, Sean traveled the same route he had taken to his house hundreds of times before, driving his father's car. He turned onto Garland, a two-way street that ran ruler straight through a mixed-use neighborhood. It cut past a post office, past a slew of squat, sixties-era single-story ranches with flat green patches of lawn and cement drives, past the campers and faux-barn sheds and misshapen shrubs that distinguished the otherwise identical homes, past the Garland Avenue Alliance Church, past the low-slung brick Spokane Guild School & Neuromuscular Center. As Sean approached a cross street, he noticed a Toyota inching out beyond the stop sign to make a left turn. Sean had the right of way and, he says, assumed that the car would see him and brake. It did not.

Sean tried to stop. As the Toyota slid into the intersection directly in front of him, Sean slammed on the brakes. His friend yelled. Both wrenched the wheel. The brakes froze. Tires screeched. Time slowed—the sound of metal eating metal—and then sped. After clipping the end of the Toyota, the Mustang careened away. The two cars came to a stop on opposite sides of the street. Clambering out, Sean tore across Garland and found himself staring into the 1997 Toyota Camry at a woman whose head had shattered the window and was covered in blood.

Sean couldn't think. "Oh, my God. Oh, my God. Oh, my God," he moaned.

The woman, Judy Rodeen, was unconscious. . . . Or dead.

Life changes in an instant. For Sean Replogle, Judy Rodeen, and Spokane public defender Carol Dee Huneke, that moment occurred at 3:51 P.M. on October 20, 2001, when their lives inexplicably converged on the corner of the city's Garland and Belt streets. The consequences of the car crash and the ensuing trial would spin out over the decade, coincidentally paralleling the story of another local boy in trouble with the law, a twelve-year-old accused of sexually molesting a neighbor child, whose overworked lawyer would make decisions about the nature of the boy's representation that would spark radical reforms in the way public defenders work in the state of Washington. Sean's careening car set in motion a series of events that would unfurl over many years: one person died; a teen's life was ruined; a lawyer was radicalized and her career was destroyed; a working family was pushed deep into $450,000 debt; taxpayers footed tens of thousands of dollars in court-affiliated costs; and a victim's family was shattered, with a trial bringing little consolation. Meanwhile, justice for the poor in Spokane County, Grant County, Washington State, and the nation was put under the microscope.

On this fine October day in 2001, Judy Rodeen had been sipping a cup of coffee with her elderly parents at the Starbucks in Spokane's Five Mile Shopping Center as she had done every Saturday afternoon at 3 o'clock for the past four years. Her mother and father were getting up in years—her dad, Lowell Stack, was 85; her mom, Frances Stack, was 83 and had Alzheimer's. Judy, who lived just up the street, kept a close eye on them.[2]

After coffee, the three of them climbed back into Lowell Stack's 1997 Toyota Camry and started home, taking a route that Lowell Stack, too, had driven hundreds of times before as he returned from the shopping center. He traveled down North Belt Street, past Shadle Park, past the ball fields, past the Messiah Lutheran Church, past the Second Church of Christ, Scientists, past the brown-, tan-, and white-brick ranch homes. As they approached Garland Street, Judy recalls, her parents looked to the right and left in unison. "That was just something they had done all their time together when riding in a car," she says. "And then we proceeded straight across Garland onto Belt."[3]

That much, Judy remembers. After that, things get blurry.

"The only part in my mind that I thought I saw was the two headlights on the car [coming toward us]. And I don't remember anything from then on. I don't even know if that was real or in my mind or not. It . . . I can't recall it."

Four months after the accident, an insurance investigator would push her: "Do you have any recollection of seeing the Mustang as it was maybe a block away or half a block away?" the investigator pushed.

"No, I really can't say that. I just can't bring anything . . ."

"Do you have any recollection as to the speed of the Mustang?"

"No."

"Did you hear any sound of the engine of the other vehicle, the Mustang?"

"No, I don't even remember the crash. . . . My first recollection was when the ambulance were [sic] there and they were. . . . I was on the board. They evidently had gotten me out of the car. That was my first recollection, of coming to."

"Did you hear anything said by the driver of the Mustang at any time?"

"No."

"I want to also ask you if you have any recollection at the impact. Were you belted in?"

"No."

A senior in high school, money in his pocket, a new Mustang, cruising the streets of Spokane, Sean Replogle, like all eighteen-year-olds, believed himself so invincible that he didn't even wear a seatbelt that afternoon in October 2001.

Since then, he has parsed this moment over and over, trying to make sense of it—possibly trying to alter the course of events. "Me and Chuck weren't buckled up," Sean says today, toggling between past and present tense, between putting this behind him and re-living it. "We're stupid eighteen-year-olds." The old man driving the Toyota heads right into the intersection. "He never looks over," Sean says. "I look over at Chuck for a split second and say to him,

'Do they not see me?' I slam on the brakes. At the last second I see them notice me." But it is too late.

After the crash, Sean couldn't get out of his wrecked car. "I panicked, trying to open the door and I couldn't." He yelled at his friend Chuck to get out and then clambered over the passenger seat. "I get out, run over to their car. It was like something out of a horror scene. The driver was dazed and confused. I say, 'Are you okay?' He wouldn't answer. Couldn't answer."

Then Sean saw the woman in the backseat with her head through the glass. "I thought she was dead."

Someone called an ambulance—no one recalls who it was. EMTs arrived within minutes. They moved the elderly driver of the Toyota, Lowell Stack, from the car. Stack, according to witnesses, was bleeding from the head and excoriated himself, repeating "Oh, my God. Oh, my God. What have I done?"[4] Asked if he was okay, he nodded. "I think I'm alright." But he was worried about his daughter in the backseat: "How's Judy?"

Officer Erin Raleigh, one of the first cops on the scene, spoke to Sean. "Sean appeared to have been crying and was currently teary eyed and very upset at the time," Raleigh wrote in a contemporaneous report.[5] "Sean told me he was driving his Mustang when the collision occurred. Sean explained to me he was driving westbound on Garland and was travelling 'a little fast,' but stated he never made it out of second gear. . . . Sean told me he was just worried about the other people involved in the collision, to make sure they were ok." Another officer on the scene, Bryan Grenon, put it differently in his report: "Replogle appeared to be distraught and somewhat distant."[6] Another witness, Yvonne Belcourt, who'd been driving the car behind him and was furious at "the speed of this child," ascribed different motives: "After the wreck, the only thing I remember is jumping out of the car, screaming at the kid. . . . And then I remember him jumping up and down screaming, 'Oh, God, oh, God,' and I swore at him. I said, 'What the f— do you think you're doing?' Only I didn't say 'F,' I said the bad word. I'm not normally a swearer. . . . I don't remember what else he said. I wasn't concerned about him. I was concerned about the old people in the car." (With echoes of Albert Camus's *L'Étranger*, in which the protagonist's behavior after his mother's death was studied and recast as indicative of his guilty conscience, Sean's affect at the scene would later be dissected, analyzed, characterized, and re-characterized as lawyers and witnesses searched for telltale signs of guilt or innocence.)

Officer Raleigh asked about insurance and Sean admitted he had none. Raleigh went to speak with Officer Grenon about the folks in the other car. "Officer Grenon stated that all three motorists were going to be transported to Providence Holy Family Hospital Emergency to be treated for their injuries. Grenon stated none of the parties in the vehicle had sustained life-threatening injuries, but did need to be viewed by the medical staff at the hospital to be treated." Another cop measured skid marks from both vehicles and took photographs of the scene.

Sean was "pretty freaked out" but remembers a cop comforting him, assuring him that the family in the Toyota was okay. He went home thinking the others would be all right, that he himself was "stupid for speeding," and that cops would be ticketing the Toyota's driver "for blowing a stop sign." Sean found out the Stack family's address and sent a Hallmark card, telling them how sorry he was.

Later that evening, at 9:30 P.M., Officer Raleigh noted in his written report that the cop measuring skid marks had done his calculations and determined the speed; Sean had been going 45 mph prior to impact, he said. The speed limit was 30 mph.

The next day, Officer Raleigh went by the Replogles' house and gave Sean a ticket for reckless driving and issued a Notice of Infraction for Liability Insurance Required. "I released Sean on his signature promising to contact the court within 15 days," Officer Raleigh noted.

On Monday, Sean went to school but felt terrible. Judy Rodeen, the woman in the backseat of the car, turned out to be the office manager at his high school. "She was the main office lady, so the office people all hated me after that," Sean said. Everyone at school knew what had happened. He walked down the halls. People stared. Pointed. He was a monster.

Doctors put fifteen staples in Judy Rodeen's left ear and head, five stitches near her left eye, and treated her for pain in the left side of her body.[7] Judy's mother, Frances Stack, suffered cervical injuries, contusions, and lacerations. After examining Lowell Stack and running some tests and x-rays, an emergency room doctor decided he needed surgery to treat his wounds. He hospitalized the elderly man and operated immediately.

Then, seven days after the accident, Lowell Stack took a turn for the worse. He rapidly deteriorated. At 6 P.M. on October 28, eight days after the accident, Lowell Stack died in the hospital. The preliminary cause of death was "from complications arising out of the injuries sustained in the crash," a police report noted.[8]

Sean would learn about the death in a roundabout way. A friend of his who worked as a student assistant in the high school office overheard a conversation among staffers and slipped out to find Sean. Sean was sitting in class when his friend motioned him out into the hall. "The guy died, dude," his friend said. "They're all talking about it in the office."

Horrified, Sean turned, walked out of school, and went home. "Oh, my God!" he recalls thinking. "What the heck? Oh, my God!"

Two days later, the police showed up at the door to the Replogles' home. "I was in my bedroom playing video games with my friend," Sean says. "Dad came in my room and said there are a couple police officers here that need to talk to you."

Corporal Tom Sahlberg broke the news. "I . . . advised him that the #2 driver had passed away, and now he was involved in much more serious charges that included Veh[icular] Homicide and Assault," Sahlberg wrote in his official report.[9] "He was fully cooperative and asked how the Stack family was doing, and that he had sent them a card. In addition, he had set up a court date for the Reckless Driving citation, which I advised him had been dismissed because of the more serious charges now pending. . . . I told him to be careful answering any official questions until he had an attorney, but that he was free to contact me with any questions he had."

Sean didn't know what to say. "I'm so sad that this person had to die," he thought. "But this was an accident." It was hard for Sean to comprehend that he was being charged with murder. As his father stood beside him, Sean listened, trying to make sense of what the cops were saying. Sahlberg told Sean that he would be back to formally arrest and book him in a few days.

Then, two days later, police arrived at the house with a minivan, put cuffs on Sean, and took him downtown to book him. He was released on his own recognizance—but he was terrified. How would he survive prison? he wondered. What would they do to him—a skinny kid who had no idea how to defend himself? Who played video games and cried when he was in a car accident? What would happen to him? How could he mentally or physically prepare for life behind bars?

Like many Americans, neither Sean nor his family had given much thought to "public defenders" or "indigent defense" prior to his car accident. Likely the terms were entirely unfamiliar to them. Legal services for the poor and the working class was not an issue for them. Why would it be? They had never been in trouble with the law.

But they were about to get a lesson, via immersion in the criminal justice system. Sean was assigned an attorney, Carol Dee Huneke. This was a small stroke of luck in a slew of bad news.

When Huneke first met Sean Replogle in October 2001, she had been working as a Spokane County public defender since 1998 (with earlier stints as a public defender in western Washington and then Idaho). At thirty-three, she was the mother of a one-year-old and the wife of a prominent federal public defender, Roger Peven.

She never intended to be a public defender—or even a lawyer for that matter. The way she describes it, she was a rolling stone who washed up on the shores of a public defender's office in western Washington and discovered that "these were her people" and she loved the work. Born and raised in Texas, she went to the University of Texas School of Law because she couldn't think of anything better to do after college.

She didn't love it. And, after interning one summer for Texaco's legal department, she liked it even less. She decided to continue with law school since she'd already attended for a year. But since she had no intention of ever practicing law, she didn't bother enrolling in any practical courses. Instead, she took an eclectic assortment of classes on topics that interested her, like Ethics, Women and the Law, and Maritime Law. (Huneke's experience is fairly typical; a 2008 study by the Center for the Study of Applied Legal Education reported that only 2 percent of law schools require practical clinical training for students.)[10]

Then, in 1993, a year after she graduated from law school, she found herself unemployed, broke, and struggling after following a love interest to Washington State. "I needed money," she recalls today, and a slight smile plays around her lips as she describes a newspaper ad that she answered for a public defender. She showed up for her interview and walked into the office's chaotic reception area. One client snoozed on a chair; the receptionist was AWOL; a basket of condoms sat on the front desk where there might ordinarily be, say, a bowl of mints. Down the hall, a disturbed and disheveled client with his hair in Einstein-like disarray stormed around ranting at the top of his lungs: "Fuck those fucking fucks!"

Huneke took a seat in the lobby and watched, bemused, as drama unfolded all around her. Eventually, someone called her name and led her into a back office. Behind the desk waiting to interview her was the "disturbed" man—not a client at all, but the director of the agency.

He grilled Huneke, asking her everything from philosophical questions to hypotheticals about trial decisions, then offered her the job. Afterwards, he took her on a tour of the building, introducing her to her colleagues in the misdemeanors department where he told her she would start out. This was a Thursday and one of the attorneys, shaking her hand, joked that he had three trials all starting on Monday. Might she be persuaded to take one? She blithely agreed.

He wasn't joking.

He came by her cubicle the next day with a folder that he plopped on her desk. He explained that this was a DUI case. But Huneke, fresh out of law school, had never tried a case before. "I had never even watched a trial," she says, "unless you count TV." But they seriously expected to send her into court on Monday. So she went. "The first trial I ever watched was myself doing it," she says.

Huneke spins a good yarn—a useful trait for a trial lawyer, and one she has clearly honed over the years as she built complex narratives to sell her clients' perspectives in court. There are the facts, and then there are the facts-woven-into-story, and Huneke clearly understands the superior power of the latter. Her life, too, as she spins it, is a series of cautionary tales and comeuppances with herself as the hapless, accidental hero forced into serious reckoning by the end. Her first trial falls in this tradition.

"At the time, I thought what you read in a police report was true," she begins. "I don't think that now." The police report said that her client, an elderly fisherman, had caused an accident by turning onto a road in front of an oncoming car. Her client admitted having several glasses of wine but said he wasn't drunk. The officer on the scene made her client do three tests to see if he was intoxicated. He made the man walk a straight line and then turn. The man walked a crooked line. He made the man stand on one leg. The man could not perform this simple task; he listed to one side. He made the man use his right thumb to touch and count all the fingers on his left hand. The man got no higher than three. He refused a Breathalyzer test.

Huneke knew she had a lousy case and figured she would suggest to her client that he simply plead guilty. Then, the "funny, crusty old character" came into her office. She explained what the police report said and as she spoke, the guy struggled with his pant legs, trying to pull them up to show her something. He couldn't manage to get his trouser legs high enough to show her what he wanted. Finally, right there in the office, he dropped his pants. The sight of his leg shocked her. It was bent at an odd angle and horribly disfigured, full of scars from multiple surgeries. He explained that he had fallen into the machinery of a conveyor belt on one of the fishing vessels he worked on and was disabled. When she questioned him about the finger test, he raised his hand for her to inspect. He'd lost two fingers in a fish guillotine. Later, when she asked him a final question in the courtroom—"Why had he refused the breath test?"—he referred to his past machinery-related accidents. "I don't like machines," he said. "I don't trust 'em."

The jury laughed. They loved him.

Huneke won the case, but she knows now she was simply lucky.

And she knows now that any system that would allow her to try a case like this is ridiculous. Back then, she had spent her weekend cramming, reading two books, one about the law in the state of

Washington, one about how to try a DUI case. A colleague had to talk her through the basic structure of a trial by sketching out the standard sections on a legal pad—"first you have the prosecutor give his opening argument, then it is your turn for an opening argument," etc.—and then she was thrown in a courtroom to sink or swim, defending clients for whom the stakes were much higher.

"I remember so specifically sitting next to this old fisherman as the jurors were coming in," she says. "I was thinking, 'Somebody has to stop this from happening. I don't know what I'm doing.'" Huneke shakes her head. "You learn some basic rules at school and then you get this job being someone's lawyer," she says. "You understand, I'm supposed to do the best for this person. Court, the law, nothing was how I thought it would be."

Then Huneke got another client, and another and another until, like public defenders across the city, the state, the nation, she had hundreds of clients in a year and way more than she could reasonably handle. "It didn't shock me, but it was more like, 'How do I do this job that is so overwhelming and crazy and all these people are relying on me?'" She was profoundly aware that she was getting a legal education on the backs of clients who deserved better. "When you're thrown into this, you're just trying not to drown. You are just so incompetent on so many levels, you don't even know this is too many cases."

What Carol Dee Huneke was feeling, personally, was in fact a problem that public defenders struggled with all across the nation. Indeed, only ten months before she was assigned to represent Sean Replogle, the U.S. Justice Department had declared a "crisis" in the country's courts. Issuing a scathing report, "Keeping Defender Workloads Manageable," the Justice Department and others drew on reports pouring in from jurisdictions around the country that documented how overworked public defenders were handling anywhere from 200 to 2,225 felony and misdemeanor cases in a single year, compared to private attorneys who would consider 100 clients a crushing workload.[11] The legal community—judges, state bar associations, court administrators, public defenders, and even some prosecutors—were throwing up a red flag; if public defenders can't properly defend their clients, defendants' constitutional rights are being violated on a daily basis. This runs counter to the intent of the U.S. Supreme Court's 1963 decision in a case called *Gideon v. Wainwright*.

Back in 1961, when an itinerant man named Clarence Earl Gideon was accused of breaking into a pool hall in Florida and stealing some liquor and money from a jukebox and a cigarette machine, he asked the judge in his burglary trial for a lawyer to represent him. He was too poor to hire one himself, he said, but he needed one to help him try the case. The judge said the state was under no obligation to provide him with an attorney. So Gideon represented himself—badly—and landed in prison. Gideon fought his conviction, going all the way to the U.S. Supreme Court as he insisted that there was no such thing as a "fair trial" if both sides didn't have attorneys.

Then, in March 1963, the U.S. Supreme Court agreed with him, ruling in the landmark case *Gideon v. Wainwright* that poor people charged with a crime that carries potential jail time have a right to an attorney to represent them in court. Complying with this decision was hugely complicated and expensive for the states, cities, and counties who took on the burden of providing these lawyers for the poor—but it was doable. At the time, the number of indigent folks accused of crimes was smaller and arguably more manageable. On the heels of *Gideon*, cities and counties did one of three things: they established public defender offices with a staff of salaried lawyers who were paid by the city, county, state, or some combination of these; they developed a roster of private attorneys that judges appointed on an as-needed basis, paying them an hourly rate; or they handed over the contract for all local public defense to a single attorney or law firm for an agreed-upon flat fee. It sort of worked. For a while. But today, on the heels of the War on Drugs, the Three Strikes Law, and the lock-'em-up mentality of politicians, indigent clients have flooded the courts. Indeed, the Justice Department reported in 2001 that public defenders represent 80 percent of all criminal cases and "[a]s caseloads have increased, many public defender offices have been unable to obtain corollary increases in staff" and too often "the quality of service suffers," concluding, "[a]t some point, even the most well-intentioned advocates are overwhelmed, jeopardizing their clients' constitutional right to effective counsel."[12]

Since that 2001 report, little has changed on the national scene.

In 2009, the Constitution Project, the National Legal Aid & Defender Association, and the National Right to Counsel Committee investigated the current state of public defense and came to the conclusion that the system of providing counsel for the poor in this country was broken, with defendants' constitutional rights routinely violated. The group drew from news articles, law reviews, and the myriad panicked reports that cities, counties, and states had generated by culling data and creating task forces, blue ribbon commissions, and special councils. They pulled the information together in a comprehensive report titled *Justice Denied: America's Continuing Neglect of Our Constitutional Right to Counsel.*[13]

The report began almost pathetically, arguing on the most basic level for the value of indigent defense. "It helps to define who we are as a free people and distinguishes this country from totalitarian regimes, where lawyers are not always independent of the state and individuals can be imprisoned by an all powerful and repressive state," the authors noted, insisting that "sometimes counsel is not provided at all, and it often is supplied in ways that make a mockery of the great promise of the *Gideon* decision and the Supreme Court's soaring rhetoric."[14] It fails the poor, and underfunding indigent defense in the short run costs society money in the long run, insisted the authors, a group that included policy makers, victim advocates, scholars, judges, public defenders, district attorneys, and law enforcement. "State and local governments are faced with increased jail expenses, retrials of cases, lawsuits, and a lack of public confidence in our justice systems," they wrote. "In the country's current fiscal crisis, indigent defense funding may be further curtailed, and the risk of convicting innocent persons will be greater than ever."[15]

The same month that Sean Replogle's case was slated for trial, in March 2004, another case began quietly making its way through the Washington State courts as a public defender in Grant County made very different decisions about zealously representing his client in court than the ones Carol Dee Huneke was making. His story would serve as a cautionary tale—an inadvertent foil to Huneke's unfolding story with her client Sean Replogle. This incident, though the press did not cover it at all, was destined to alter the definition of "effective counsel" in the state of Washington.

Here, in a town called Moses Lake, less than an hour from Spokane, a public defender named Douglas Anderson decided to keep things moving with his client—one among more than 460 open cases he had on his desk—urged the youngster to plead guilty to a crime, regardless of whether this was a good choice or not.

That February, a five-year-old Moses Lake boy accused his twelve-year-old neighbor of playing "Icky-Poke-U" with him. The five-year-old said that he had climbed up onto the older boy's lap on an easy chair. Then, he said, the twelve-year-old asked if he wanted to play Icky-Poke-U and stuck his hands down the little one's pants. Several days later, the five-year-old told his parents about the game of Icky-Poke-U. Twenty-eight days later cops interviewed the five-year-old about the incident. Then the twelve-year-old was interviewed and, crying, denied the allegations. On July 2, 2004, cops arrested the twelve-year-old and the state charged him with child molestation in the first degree.

While the twelve year old's current attorney agreed to speak with me, his family declined to, so much of the following is drawn from court records and interviews with the boy's present lawyer. Because he is a minor, I'll refer to the boy by his initials, A.N.J., as he is identified in court documents. Both children are white and live in a middle-class neighborhood.

A.N.J. was assigned a Grant County public defender. In addition to A.N.J.'s case, Douglas Anderson had 240 other child criminal defense cases and 200 or more dependency cases—typically abuse or neglect cases—that year. According to court records, Anderson had a staff of one (his wife) to assist him.

A.N.J. was charged in court, without Anderson's presence, on July 19. Because Anderson was not there to advise A.N.J. as to how he should respond, the arraignment was continued until August 2. On September 14, the judge convened a pretrial conference and set a trial date of September 22. But on that day, on the advice of counsel, twelve-year-old A.N.J. pleaded guilty to child molestation.

A.N.J. and his parents barely met with the public defender. "Between the first appearance and the arraignment, Mr. Anderson met with A.N.J. and his father on one occasion," according to a deposition. "According to A.N.J.'s father, this meeting lasted only five minutes. Mr. Anderson did not disagree with this estimate. About the substance of this first meeting, Mr. Anderson testified: 'Initially, he [A.N.J.] was not agreeing with the information in the police reports.'"

Indeed, A.N.J. had told the police that the five-year-old neighbor had initiated the whole thing, that he had climbed onto A.N.J.'s lap and that the younger child had suggested the game of Icky-Poke-U. A.N.J. said he did not want to play, but the younger child took his hands and put them down his pants.

Anderson met with A.N.J. and his parents in court before the arraignment on August 2, 2004, for what his mother describes as a meeting "probably" lasting ten minutes. A.N.J.'s parents were "shocked" by the charges and worried about how they should proceed. Between August 2 and September 14, A.N.J.'s parents called their son's lawyer several times, leaving messages for Anderson. Anderson did not return the calls. Then, on September 15, the prosecutor offered a plea bargain.

According to an appellate brief filed March 5, 2005, the following occurred:

"On September 17, 2004, Mr. Anderson met with A.N.J. and both of his parents. As for the substance of this meeting, Mr. Anderson initially testified that he spent 'well over a half hour' explaining the Statement on the Plea of Guilty. He testified at length about each and every paragraph of the form that he ostensibly explained to A.N.J. and his parents. However, he later admitted that this testimony was false, and that he did not even have the Statement on the Plea of Guilty form at the September 17, 2004, meeting."

In fact, A.N.J.'s parents assert that they saw the guilty plea for the first time on September 22, 2004. In a five-minute conversation, Anderson explained that if the boy pleaded guilty, the charge would be reduced from a class A to a class B felony, and that while he could still serve up to nine months, he could likely agree instead to attend a special sex offender disposition alternative, a series of sex offender counseling workshops. "Then, I just briefly discussed with him the fact that he would be required to register as a sex offender and it was somewhere in that range that the question came up about having this matter removed from his record," Anderson would testify about a year later.

Earlier, A.N.J.'s parents had asked if this would permanently be on their son's record, if he would always be labeled a "sex offender." According to A.N.J.'s parents, the public defender assured them that their son's record would be expunged, though he wasn't sure whether it was at age eighteen or twenty-one. He would check and get back to them.

"I remember asking Mr. Anderson if he found out when it would be off his record, and he said he hadn't had time to look into that," A.N.J.'s parents would state a year later. "And then I said exactly, I remember, I said, 'When does this come off his record?' I didn't say, 'Does it?' I said, 'When?' Because he's a minor and I don't know the law, I'm not a lawyer."

A.N.J's dad recalls the lawyer's response: "Mr. Anderson's reply was, 'I'm not sure. The laws change all the time. I'll have to check into it and get back to you.'"

Anderson never denied this, acknowledging that the charges could be removed between age eighteen and twenty-one, admitting he "did not know exactly what the law stated." He never did get back to them with details. "Honestly, it may have just slipped my mind," he told the court later.

In truth, the child molestation in the first-degree conviction would never come off A.N.J's record.

Instead, Anderson would spend a total of at most an hour and a half with A.N.J. and his parents. "He filed no motions. He made no requests for discovery. In fact, he filed no pleadings or documents at all other than his initial notice of appearance," court documents show. He did not interview any witnesses. He did not hire an investigator. (Money to pay for an investigator would come from the $162,000 flat fee he was paid by Grant County to represent indigent clients. According to a later appellant brief filed by A.N.J.'s new attorneys: "In a moment of candor, Mr. Anderson admitted that this financial reality creates a disincentive for him to hire investigators. The strength of the disincentive is revealed by the fact that Mr. Anderson did not hire a single investigator for any one of his 240 juvenile offense cases in 2004. Reverting to a more defensive posture, Mr. Anderson then denied that there was a need to investigate any of those cases.") Further, "[h]e received the names of two witnesses to contact who would testify that the alleged victim in this case was actually abused by another person rather than A.N.J. Mr. Anderson says that he tried to contact the witnesses by making a telephone call, but he concedes that he 'was unsuccessful.' He does not recall whether he even left a message." And while cases like this, with a five-year-old making the accusation, typically require an expert to carefully conduct interviews without suggestively leading the accuser, ideally recorded for later court use, no expert interviewed the alleged child victim or alleged perpetrator. Anderson declined to consult or hire to testify a single expert. (Again, paying for such a person would come out of his own pocket, according to his flat-fee contract with the county.)

Instead, Anderson simply suggested that A.N.J. plead guilty. Anderson said in a 2005 deposition, "I do not remember many of the details of [A.N.J.'s] case due to the fact that I have a large caseload," and further, "I never independently investigated the claims regarding the alleged victim nor did a background check on the family, I simply reviewed the police reports." He also suggested A.N.J. fudge the truth with the judge. "I told [A.N.J.] that the judge would ask him if he had read [the guilty plea] or if I had explained it to him and to say yes. . . . I spent approximately five minutes with [A.N.J.] going over his statement just before we were called into court." (Later he recanted, saying that he met with A.N.J.'s parents several times and that during one of the meetings the boy "began to admit to me that he had committed the conduct that was alleged in the police report.")

After A.N.J. pleaded guilty before a judge, the boy and his parents learned that his record as a sex offender would never be expunged, that a monitor would likely be assigned to shadow him at school every day from now until he graduated from high school, and he would have to regularly admit his guilt in a therapeutic setting as he attended sex offender group counseling.

A.N.J.'s parents were shocked. Within weeks they sought out a private attorney who advised them to try and withdraw A.N.J.'s guilty plea based on ineffective assistance of counsel.

Meanwhile, A.N.J. was sentenced to fifteen to thirty-six weeks in custody, forced to undergo HIV and DNA testing, and required to register as a sex offender.

The authors of the Constitution Project's 2009 report *Justice Denied: America's Continuing Neglect of Our Constitutional Right to Counsel* back up their assertions about the crushing caseloads public defenders carry with a troubling collection of facts. For example, they noted, in 2008 the U.S. Supreme Court had to step in and order Nevada's Clark County and Washoe County to cut caseloads. Public defenders in the former carried felony and gross misdemeanor caseloads of 364 (more than double the American Bar Association recommended standard of 150), while in the latter caseloads averaged 327. In Knox County, Tennessee, one attorney reported having 240 open cases, while another reported that between January and February of 2008, she had 151 clients (representing approximately 14 people per day). "In 2006, six misdemeanor attorneys [there] handled over 10,000 cases, averaging just less than one hour per case," the authors observed. Miami was another problem region, where public defenders refused to accept more cases when their loads jumped, over the course of three years, from an average of 367 felonies per attorney to 500 and from 1,380 misdemeanors per attorney to 2,225. (See Chapter 2 for a detailed look at Miami's situation.) In Missouri, the authors noted, public defender caseloads were so high that they were required "to dispose of a case every 6.6 hours of every working day." The state's public defender deputy director Dan Gralike said: "The present MASH-style operating procedure requires public defenders to divvy effective legal assistance to a narrowing group of clients," in essence "choosing" which clients will receive effective assistance and which will not.[16]

The legal term for what happens when these overextended lawyers go into court and race through a case doing the bare minimum is "ineffective assistance of counsel." More colloquially, unmanageable workloads mean that all across the country, public defenders cannot properly do their jobs. "Our adversarial system of criminal justice relies upon the effectiveness of counsel for both the prosecution *and* the defense in order to discover the truth concerning the guilt or innocence of the accused," says one of the leading experts on the topic, California Western School of Law professor and managing director of the school's criminal justice programs Laurence A. Benner. "A host of recent exonerations of the wrongfully convicted by innocence projects nationwide . . . have revealed there are serious flaws in our justice system," he wrote in the summer 2011 issue of *Criminal Justice*.[17] He worried that the presumption of innocence—something that was necessarily backed by "a well-prepared and experienced defense counsel supported by investigators, experts, and other resources needed to mount an effective defense"—had been abandoned. Instead, he insisted, "our system has broken faith with that basic premise and forgotten its primary mission, often operating under a presumption of guilt in which processing the 'presumed guilty' as cheaply as possible has been made a higher priority than concern for the possibility of innocence."

Authors of the Justice Department report insisted that "[a]dequately supporting indigent defenders is critical to preserving the constitutional rights of individuals accused of crimes." Others, horrified by the dire situation, eschew the cautious language of the Justice Department and describe the current indigent defense crisis more directly: "All in all, it is just massive lawlessness and indifference by the courts to a Constitutional mandate by the Supreme Court," says Stephen Bright, executive director of the Southern Center for Human Rights in Atlanta, Georgia. "But it's hard to get folks to do the right thing on this."

There are all kinds of problems with the patchwork system of indigent defense in the United States, but by far the most critical is the crushing caseloads that, in essence, violate a defendant's Sixth Amendment right to counsel by providing it, in many cases, in name only.

In Washington State, debates over caseload limits have dominated the reform efforts for more than a decade. The state has made great strides, but it was not there yet. Washington was neither the best nor the worst in the country—but fell somewhere in the middle. And within Washington, Spokane County was neither the best nor the worst. It was merely indicative of what typically transpires in courts around the country on any given day. In Washington State, approximately 250,000 indigent people are prosecuted by the government each year.[18] In 2001, Sean Replogle was poised to become one of them.

As she looked at Sean Replogle, sitting in her office for the first time in the winter of 2001, Carol Dee Huneke, now a seasoned public defender, was struck by the fact that, though he was eighteen and being tried as an adult, "he was basically a kid." He arrived with his father, Chuck Replogle, a gentle man with a long graying ponytail and a careworn face. His dad was at his side that first meeting and every single meeting and court date thereafter, doing his best to understand the case and support his son however he could.

Huneke worried that the facts in the case seemed to be lined up against Sean, but something in her gut told her he was innocent. "The kid had never been in trouble before," she says. "He was super sweet." She asked him about police reports and a witness statement that said he was speeding. Could he have been going as fast as 58 mph in the 30 mph zone, as the prosecutor alleged? (Throughout the investigation and trial, various cops, experts, and witnesses would throw out different estimates of Sean's speed.)

Sean admitted that he was going "maybe a little fast." But he assured her that he was going nowhere near that speed: "I know I wasn't going that fast."

To win its vehicular manslaughter case, the state had to prove that Sean's driving was a "proximate cause" of Lowell Stack's death and, as the prosecutor Clinton Francis put it in an October 2003 memorandum to the Court, "proximate Cause is one which in direct sequence, unbroken by any new, independent cause, produced the death and without which the death would not have occurred." The state could easily present a "prima facie case that the defendant drove recklessly or with disregard for the safety of others" and, he insisted, proving a vehicular homicide occurred meant the state only had to prove that "(1) the defendant drove a motor vehicle, (2) that his driving proximately caused injury to another person, that (3) at the time of driving the defendant operated the motor vehicle either in a reckless manner, or with disregard for the safety of others (intoxication may also support a conviction for Vehicular Homicide but is not an issue in this case) and that (4) death ensued within 3 years of the collision." Francis stated that Sean was exceeding the speed limit by 21 mph in a residential area and insisted this was not "mere oversight or inadvertence, but a conscious act from which a jury may find, after considering all the circumstances, to be a reckless act or at least an act of disregard for the safety of others."

Francis went on to downplay the fact that Sean had the right-of-way when Lowell Stack pulled out in front of him. "One of the reasons for speed limits is to keep speeds at such a level that these foreseeable events are less likely to have the tragic consequences of this case," he wrote in the memorandum, arguing against the motion to dismiss. "The arguably negligent act of the victim should not insulate the defendant from liability under the Vehicular Homicide statute."

For her part, Huneke was skeptical that the "sequence establishing proximate cause" was an unbroken one. For now, in her rush to file a motion to dismiss, she did not investigate Sean's alleged speed or confirm the cause of Mr. Stack's death, but she did argue, in her October 2, 2003, motion to dismiss, that "Mr. Replogle's speed was not the proximate cause of the accident, because Mr. Stack's failure to yield the right-of-way at the stop sign was an intervening cause and thus the proximate cause of the accident." She cited appropriate case law and reiterated in plain language: "It is not reasonable to anticipate that someone with a clear view will fail to yield the right-of-way and pull directly in front of an oncoming car. The law recognizes that Mr. Replogle may assume that other cars will follow traffic rules, and mere speed does not change that assumption." Further, she insisted the undisputed facts failed to show that Sean drove recklessly. "He was sober, and he was not racing or performing dangerous maneuvers. His attention was on the road," she wrote.

A few years back, Huneke stood a good chance of having the case dismissed—or at least, if her client pleaded guilty, getting a good deal for him. (Indeed, at one point, Huneke thought the prosecutor was offering Sean a deal, probation instead of jail time, and Sean was on the verge of accepting this, but it turned out he was offering Sean a year of prison; Sean opted to go to trial even though he could serve up to four years if convicted.) But then, over the course of a few years, prosecutors in Spokane stopped offering reasonable pleas, according to Huneke.

Just about the time Sean arrived in her office as a client, Huneke had simultaneously been investigating why public defenders in her office were now being offered such crummy plea deals for defendants. She did some detective work, crunching numbers, and discovered that in the felonies department, at least, the balance had shifted so that there were thirty-eight prosecuting attorneys and only seventeen public defenders. Admittedly, some clients hired their own private attorneys, but 80 percent of them relied on public defenders, which meant more than twice as many prosecutors as defenders. Indeed, based on 2004 Open Cases reports that she examined, she discovered that prosecuting attorneys carried caseloads ranging from 16 to 36 cases, while public defenders like herself at that time typically had 101 open felonies. "Prosecutors simply stopped making as good offers," she says. In the game of "trial chicken," when prosecutors threaten to go to trial, they actually have the time and resources behind them to do so. For example, a simple drug possession case for a client with no prior convictions typically took a predictable course. "It used to be a no-brainer to reduce that to a misdemeanor," she says. "Say you get caught with some crack in your car but you've never been in trouble before. Most people get a break on their first time. It's reduced to a misdemeanor so the person isn't guilty of a felony [on their record]. Or they do a diversion program or something." A while ago, that would have been an obvious reduction—and the prosecutor would have gone for that. "Then I began to have to fight for a year to get that deal. What would have been two hours of work grew into thirty."

As Huneke was processing Sean's case—and the other one hundred on her plate—she was growing increasingly steamed at what was going on around her in the Spokane courts. Was she alone in feeling overwhelmed? She didn't think so. Many of her colleagues, she says, were similarly distressed. But it was hard to speak out. Sometimes, Huneke says, it was easier, more *efficient* to deal with the huge caseload by persuading more clients to accept bad pleas.

"There is so much subtlety involved in criminal practice," she says. "I can look at a lot of cases and say, 'That's not a good deal.' And it's really easy to sell a bad plea bargain to someone. And maybe you don't even know that's a bad one [because you haven't had time to investigate the case]. You overemphasize the risks a little bit, say, 'This is the best we can get' and you settle a case in two hours instead of in a hundred hours at a trial. And people are afraid. Trials are scary. But if you don't have anything to lose [because the prosecutor is offering such a high sentence in exchange for a guilty plea], there's actually no reason not to do a trial once in a while." Huneke laughs, but it is bitter, devoid of amusement. "The problem is you have to push, and if that isn't valued in your office . . . I think a lot of ills are hidden by bad plea bargains."

In this instance, as she studied Sean's case, she thought about the way she and other attorneys in her office managed their work. "At any one time, you'll be juggling all these cases, some 'trial chicken' and maybe some serious cases, and a thousand phone calls to return," she says. "You end up responding by putting out fires. Whose is the biggest fire today?" But, she says, if you just sell the client a deal and move things along, the situation becomes almost manageable. Judges and bosses are happy because cases get moved along and processed quickly without a lot of time, energy, or money—and "you've got to keep them happy if you want to survive and advance."

She did some soul-searching and wondered if she wanted to be a part of this charade. "It's like due process theater," she began to realize with dismay. "People are dressed up like lawyers and they're standing next to a client, but they are not really zealously advocating."

Who had time to zealously advocate?

Huneke, in the midst of her personal coming-of-age story as a public defender, was trying to honor her ethical obligations to her client, to make the system work. "My client has a right to a trial," she says, explaining the logic. "And the state wants them to give that up. If the state wants my client to give up this thing of value, they have to give up something of value." She shakes her head in disgust, thinking about Sean's plea deal and the hundreds of other lousy crumbs prosecutors have tossed to her clients over the years. "If you are going to give them the same thing they will get from a trial, then why bother with a plea? If they aren't going to significantly reduce things, then why not go to trial?"

But preparing for a trial is time-consuming. And most public defenders triage their cases. Sean's case wasn't a priority because until October 2003, it was pending a motion to dismiss. Then Sean considered what he thought was the state's plea offer of no jail time only to discover in December 2003 that the state did want him to serve time. Suddenly, Sean's case, which had inched along, was on the docket for March 2004.

Meanwhile, since December 15, 2003, Huneke had tried five cases and was prepared to try a sixth before the prosecutor accepted a counteroffer that she had made weeks previously in that particular case.[19] Half of them were fairly straightforward—possession of stolen property, drug possession, taking a car without permission—but the other half were more complex—robbery, burglary, drug distribution. She had been frantically working on those trials, juggling her other cases, and trying to prepare for Sean's trial at the same time. Her conscience was bothering her, nagging her with the slew of follow-up interviews and investigations she still needed to do on Sean's behalf. She woke up in the middle of the night four days before the trial and scrawled out a "To Do List for Replogle's Case." It had fourteen bulleted tasks, including everything from obtaining a history of the intersection to interviewing Stack's family doctor to make sure he had no preexisting conditions to arranging an LCD projector to be available in the courtroom. A few days earlier, she had spoken to the doctor who did the autopsy on Lowell Stack, getting her to translate into plain language the medical jargon on the form. Turns out Stack had died from an infection after surgery. The surgery had been done to fix a hernia, which struck Huneke as curious. Does one get a hernia from the kind of blunt trauma injuries inflicted in a car crash? she wondered. She wanted to know more, to speak to Stack's family doctor and the physician who'd done the surgery. Something seemed amiss here. Also, she needed the standard background for trying a vehicular homicide: Stack's ophthalmology records, his driving history from previous insurance claims, reports from the paramedics, an expert to examine the photos of the skid marks, and so forth. She realized, sitting up in bed in the middle of the night, transcribing her list onto a laptop, that she definitely needed more than three days to prepare properly for this trial.

Sean Replogle was waiting for the trial to begin. It was grueling. He was convinced that everyone was pointing to him as he walked the halls of his high school, calling him a murderer. Everyone knew, he insists today. Everyone despised him for what he'd done to Lowell Stack. "In the office at school, they'd be like, 'Oh, there's the kid that killed him,'" he says. "On the intercom a month and a half after it happened they announced, 'Judy Rodeen has returned from her tragic accident and everyone should say "hi" to her in the office.' And everyone in the class and the school turned and looked at me."

Sean started skipping school. "I didn't want to leave the house," he says, "over fear that anything I did I could go to jail for. I felt like I was in danger of getting arrested for anything, if I was going to prison for speeding." He dropped out of school and got his GED in March. In the fall, at his father's insistence, he took out a student loan and enrolled in Spokane Falls Community College. But he began having panic attacks. "I started breaking down," he says. There were continuances, delays of all sorts, every thirty days or so for two years, he recalls, and each time he had to assume they would actually be going to trial. He couldn't shake his terror; the prospect of prison loomed over everything he did and said and thought. He couldn't focus. Finally, he told his dad, "I can't do it," and his dad relented—"If it's that hard, don't do it," he said—and Sean dropped out of college.

He stayed in the house. "I was really depressed," he says. "I detached from everyone. I didn't do anything for two years." His luck was so bad, he was certain it would continue that way; he'd be found guilty and be sent to prison. "At the time," he says, "I was just this little eighteen-year-old who had been in maybe two fights in my life. I tried to mentally prepare for spending three-and-a-half years in prison. I wasn't mean or anything, but I tried to toughen up." He started lifting weights and watched a lot of HBO's *Oz*. "I tried to picture these tough, crazy people staring at me and wanting to fight all the time," he says. "I stopped playing video games and worked out all the time." He told himself: "This is going to be the most crazy environment, and I have to figure out how to survive it for three years." His family grew worried. He never smiled anymore.

Sean and his father talked about the accident every night. At first, Chuck Replogle wanted his son to admit he was speeding. He didn't know the exact numbers the cops were coming up with, but he suspected Sean was lying, Sean says. "At first, Dad said, 'something bad happened, you have to admit your guilt.'" He, too, was terrified that Sean would go to jail. Maybe if Sean simply admitted he was speeding, if he was sorry, he'd be forgiven and things would go their way. "He didn't 100 percent believe me because police were saying something different [about the speed]," Sean says. "I was an eighteen-year-old boy and I'm sure I had lied to him a couple of times before, so he had his suspicions when he heard what the cops said about the speed. But I was like, 'I'm not lying, I swear. I don't know what else to tell you.'"

Sean says the only person who believed he was not going 58 mph was his public defender, Huneke. (Huneke says she's not sure she *did* believe him about the speed, but she did believe that he should not be sent to prison for this accident; there were so many unanswered questions about the case.) When Sean first met Huneke at her office, she had a stack of papers on her desk and was in the middle of a murder trial. "I have a good feeling about this," she told him when he and his father came in. "You're going to be okay."

This was the first time Sean had some hope. In the midst of what he calls "dark days," Huneke assured him that she believed in him. "If we've got a jury in their right mind, I think it will work out," she told him.

Sean recalls: "She never guaranteed me because she couldn't, but she felt like this was a winnable case."

Still, this glimmer of optimism was regularly overshadowed. "Just because I was innocent, I was starting to realize, didn't mean anything. They could still find me guilty. I didn't trust the system. She was the only person fighting for me."

And she was fighting hard.

When Carol Dee Huneke went into Spokane County Superior Court on Friday, February 27, 2004, the day set for a hearing prior to the onset of Sean's trial, she asked Judge Michael Price for a continuance. The judge, brand new to the bench, denied it. Huneke persisted. She only had the weekend to prepare for the trial, she said, explaining that she had had five back-to-back trials on her calendar. She desperately needed more time, she said, and then played what she thought was her trump card, the magic words that she knew no judge could properly ignore, insisting this would be "ineffective assistance of counsel."

Price, who'd been on the bench fewer than two months, held fast. The trial would not be further delayed, he insisted. It would start on Monday or she'd be held in contempt of court.

Frantic, Huneke spent the weekend agonizing. She knew she was completely unprepared to go to trial—and that to do so now jeopardized Sean's case. She talked to her boss and an attorney at a statewide criminal defense organization, who gave her legal advice about what would happen if she was held in contempt, agreed to show up in court to represent her, and advised her to prepare a written statement about her workload.

Huneke sprang into action. She got co-workers to submit signed affidavits. One colleague, David Carter, explained in writing to the judge that public defenders in Spokane were completely swamped. "The demands on my time during regular Court hours covering arraignments, guilty pleas, case scheduling hearings, and answering docket calls prevent me from being able to do any significant trial preparation during the regular work week. As a result, it must be done in the evenings or weekends," he said. "On nearly every Saturday, Sunday, or holiday that I have been working in the office since November 2003, I have seen Carol Huneke in the office working on preparing a case for trial. Although I am not totally familiar with her trial calendar, I know she has been required to prepare several cases for trial during that time. More often than not, she is still in the office working when I typically leave on Saturday and Sunday afternoon."[20]

Another colleague, John Stine, wrote in Huneke's support that he transferred out of their office in October 2003 "in response to overwhelming caseloads." He said he had more than seventy open felony cases at a time, "which effectively made it impossible to fully prepare cases for trial without significant delays." Worse, he said, "I understand the caseloads have continued to grow since then."[21]

A third public defender, Kathleen Moran, told the court that, after six years in the office and working weekends and nights to stay caught up on the work, she was officially resigning in three days due to "crushing caseloads." Further, she said, "Because the Public Defender's Office is short on funds and staff, much of the work that needs to be done has to be done by the lawyer alone. Approximately 45 lawyers share five investigators and five paralegals. Due to shortages in staffing, it is difficult to schedule witness interviews at times when both the lawyer and the investigator are available."[22] Moran was persuaded that Huneke was similarly overworked. "It has come to my attention that Ms. Huneke has requested a continuance of a vehicular homicide trial because she is not prepared," Moran noted. "From my experiences with Ms. Huneke as a colleague, I believe that she would not request a continuance unless she was truly not prepared to go forward."

Huneke attached a list of how many open cases she had—101—and how many the prosecutor had—28. She also compared other public defender caseloads to prosecutor caseloads, pointing out in her written statement to the judge that "the prosecutor's office has more than twice the attorneys in its felony department, even though the public defender's office handles at least 90 percent of the adult felony cases in Spokane County." She insisted that this disparity created an impossible situation "where the public defender's office is extremely outnumbered, and the prosecutors have little incentive to plea bargain."[23] (The *Spokesman-Review* newspaper also noted that the prosecutor's office was slated "to receive approximately $8 million in funding in 2004 [that same year] compared with $4 million for the public defender's office."[24])

Huneke went on to explain the case's progression: "Up until October 2003, Mr. Replogle's case was pending a motion to dismiss. . . . After the dismissal motion was denied, I decided that my client may want to think about taking what I believed to be the state's plea offer of an exceptional sentence downward of no jail time. However, I discovered in early December that Mr. Francis did not intend to agree to no additional jail time. Thus, in late December, we decided to go to trial and began preparing for trial in earnest."[25] Since December, she'd had five trials and prepared for a sixth before the prosecutor offered an eleventh-hour plea that her client accepted. She estimated that she spent approximately ten hours preparing for a simple trial and a hundred hours for a complicated trial, with two of the previous trials being "complicated."[26] She also kept up with numerous court appearances for her other one hundred clients both in and out of jail, juggling motions, briefs, phone calls, interviews, and pleas. "Despite my best efforts, I am not ready to proceed to trial on Mr. Replogle's case on March 1, 2004," she wrote to the judge. "I cannot provide adequate assistance of counsel. I have a duty to provide effective assistance of counsel, and thus refuse to conduct a trial for which I am unprepared. I take this position not in disrespect for the court, but to the higher calling of adequately, effectively, and zealously representing my client and the constitutional and ethical duty of effective assistance of counsel."

Then, she climbed up on a soapbox to announce the severity of the public defender caseload crisis in Spokane. The local newspaper got wind of the story.

"We were in court with our attorneys, ready to get her out of jail Monday morning," Huneke's boss, John Rodgers, director of the county public defender's office, told the *Spokesman-Review* that week, hoping she wouldn't be sent to jail for being in contempt of court. He also affirmed Huneke's skill as a lawyer. "She's incredibly aggressive and effective," he told the paper.

It was a very risky strategy. One might even argue, a desperate gesture.

How did the crisis in the courts reach this impasse?

31

The last half century of indigent defense in Washington State reflects the experience of states across the nation. Like most states on the heels of the 1963 *Gideon* decision, Washington made a mad dash to meet the broad requirements of the law, leaving the details up to individual counties. The larger cities tended to create public defender offices, hiring full-time staff. The smaller towns and counties were more likely to pay an hourly rate to lawyers typically appointed by judges from a rotating list hired to defend the poor on an as-needed basis. A few jurisdictions in the state—only six in the 1970s—signed a flat-fee contract with an attorney or firm for all indigent defense.[27]

Over the decades, however, the flat-fee system became an expedient way for local governments to control costs. Local politicians and administrators could organize their budgets by agreeing to costs in advance, rather than paying an hourly wage to lawyers for representing clients. Under an hourly system, by contrast, one big murder case with a lawyer zealously representing his client—and chalking up some serious hours in the process—could decimate a small local budget. Thus by 2004, in a development representative of national trends, twenty-six counties in Washington embraced the flat-fee arrangement. But while it may save small local governments money, flat-fee contracts create a disincentive for lawyers to do quality work. Because many flat-fee attorneys also continue in private practice, where they charge paying clients hourly fees, flat-fee defenders are also incentivized to serve their paying clients at the expense of the indigent clients. As long ago as 1984, Washington State officially recognized that clients got wildly disparate defense, depending on which county they happened to live in and how public defense was funded there. The newly formed Washington Defender Association developed a set of professional standards that all public defenders should adhere to (including caseload limits based on the American Bar Association's recommended limits) and began pushing the legislature to mandate compliance with the standards. By 1989, the Defender Association had made only incremental progress with its reform efforts. The state legislature passed a law requiring each county to adopt standards, but declined to specify *what* the standards should be. "The standards endorsed by the Washington

State Bar Association for the provision of public defense services *may* [emphasis added] serve as guidelines," the law read.

Even these vague standards were routinely ignored. In March 2004, the American Civil Liberties Union in Washington State issued a report warning that the "checkered system of legal defense" means there is "no guarantee that a person who is both poor and accused will get a fair trial."

Then a month later, the *Seattle Times* published a three-part investigative series revealing exactly how this "checkered system of legal defense" played out in a solitary county in the state, digging deep into the finances, court records, and history of Grant County, Washington.[28] In April 2004, three intrepid *Times* reporters discovered that about $500,000 was going to a Grant County public defender named Thomas J. Earl, who handled 413 felony cases himself in a single year as compared to the American Bar Association's recommended 150. "At that rate, Earl could devote an average of only four hours per case," the journalists observed. Earl retained about $255,000 himself and farmed out to subcontractors additional cases and the remaining funds. Needless to say, he hired those who would work cheap, and the work they produced for him was below par. Earl's trial acquittal rate between 1999 and 2003 was 6 percent (compared to the state average of 15 percent), while his guilty plea rate was 88 percent (compared to the state average of 76 percent). Reporters discovered that there were two findings of "incompetence" against him, one in a rape case and one in a drug case, and that his license was suspended in February 2004 after the bar "found misconduct in eight cases, including three in which Earl solicited money from indigent clients or their relatives."

The reporters also investigated another Grant County public defender, Guillermo Romero, who had represented more than a thousand clients over the previous seven years but had taken only twenty-three cases to trial, losing all of them. "Twice, reviewing courts ruled that he was so incompetent, the adversarial system had collapsed," reporters noted. "He was supposed to punch holes in weak cases, to intercept police and prosecutors when they ran afoul, to investigate and analyze and advocate," the *Times* noted. "But legal basics eluded him. In a rape case, he once filed a motion seeking

'D and A testing.' What he meant was DNA." In addition to being convicted of assaulting his girlfriend, being sued by creditors, and going into drug rehab, Romero was found by the bar association to have "committed theft and solicited money from relatives of court-appointed clients."

The *Seattle Times* also raised questions about systemic problems. How was there so little oversight that incompetent attorneys could continue landing lucrative contracts? How had they been assigned such staggeringly high caseloads? How common were flat-fee contracts?

In fact, like most states, Washington was plagued by sweeping problems that were jeopardizing equal justice for the poor. Reflecting a national trend, felony filings in the last fourteen years in Grant County had jumped from 278 in 1990 to 1,070 in 2003, the *Seattle Times* reported. Meanwhile, funding for public defense in the same period had gone only from $240,000 to $500,000—meaning the caseload had more than tripled while the spending for defense had only doubled. The impact was measurable. "Grant County leads the state in the percentage of Superior Court cases that are resolved with a guilty plea," the *Times* reported, noting that 85 percent of clients accepted a guilty plea though "[i]ndigent defendants in Grant County have repeatedly complained of court-appointed attorneys failing to investigate their cases or claims of innocence, leaving defendants with little choice but to take whatever deal is offered." Yet, despite the terrible outcomes, county governments continued to opt for the cost-effective flat-fee contracts.

The *Seattle Times* series shined a rare spotlight on indigent defense, and a shocked public—and legal community—finally insisted that something had to be done. On the heels of the exposé, the Washington State Bar Association appointed a Blue Ribbon Panel on Criminal Defense to investigate. The panel reported in May 2004 that the mandate for any kind of standards is "being ignored in many jurisdictions and there is no effective enforcement program." Further, "[t]he lack of enforceable standards, especially caseload standards, jeopardizes the ability of even the most dedicated defenders to provide adequate representation." The panel blamed inadequate funding, poor contracting practices ("especially fixed-rate defense contracts"), and inadequate oversight or accountability.

At the same time, the American Civil Liberties Union in Washington State filed a class action suit, *Best, et al. v. Grant County*. "Despite knowing of the deficiencies in the Grant County public defense system, defendant Grant County has failed to take reasonable steps to protect the constitutional rights of indigent persons," lawyers for the plaintiff stated in the complaint.[29] "Indeed, even after the Washington State Bar Association recommended in June 2003 that Tom Earl be disbarred for misconduct as a public defender, defendant Grant County refused to terminate Earl as the public defender and refused to terminate his exclusive public defense contract with Grant County. Defendant Grant County allowed Earl to remain in this position until finally, in February 2004, the Washington Supreme Court suspended Earl from the practice of law pending the determination of the appeal of his disbarment." According to the ACLU, problems mounted. "Even then, defendant Grant County failed to take reasonable action to protect the rights of indigent persons. Although Earl's suspension had long been a possibility, defendant Grant County failed to make reasonable preparations for the suspension. The Board has, instead, allowed the public defense system to descend into chaos. Things have become so bad that the judges of the Grant County Superior Court recently had to issue a plan that calls for the conscription of attorneys, some with no criminal defense experience, to represent indigent persons charged with felonies."[30]

The need for a serious overhaul of the state's indigent defense practices had long been indisputable; now, for the first time, the public understood the scope of the problem—and the potentially devastating consequences.

All along the way, public defenders make hard choices about how they will represent their clients. Carol Dee Huneke, faced with the possibly dire consequences of taking Sean Replogle's case to trial before she was ready, had set aside her other hundred cases to focus on Sean's. With the judge's refusal to delay Sean's trial hanging over her, Huneke spent the weekend worrying about her fate for publicly refusing to proceed with a trial when she was unprepared and over-worked. Would she be reprimanded? Formally disciplined? Fired? Jailed? She hustled all weekend to collect the facts on the public defender system and the evidence needed to bolster her argument. When it came down to it, this was a fairly straightforward ethical matter: "It was just wrong to proceed," she says.

Sean and his family have nothing but good things to say about Huneke. "She felt so much that I was innocent that she was prepared to go to jail and be held in contempt because she needed more time to prepare right," said Sean. "And she had a three-year-old then. I thought, 'Wow, if the mother of a three-year-old is ready to go to jail for me, if she is fighting that much, I have to fight twice as much.'" Sean recognized that his life was, to some extent, in Huneke's hands, and that bond was powerful and important. "I think she believed in me as a person, too," he said.

That thought sustained him.

When Huneke showed up before the judge on Monday morning and made her case—again—for delaying the start of the trial, she spoke persuasively. Someone had also tipped off a local reporter about the showdown in court; this time the judge granted Huneke a three-week extension. The trial would start in March.

Sean and his family sat through seven days of the trial. Sean wore khakis and a dress shirt and tie that his aunt, a teacher in Michigan, had sent him because the family had no money to buy proper clothes. ("I still have them hanging up in my closet," he would tell me eight years later, "to wear to job interviews.")

The way Sean saw it, the prosecution spent three days painting a picture of him as a "crazy street racer." The prosecutor described his car as a gun, a deadly weapon that Sean kept "firing and missing until [he] hit Mr. Stack."

Huneke really wanted Sean to take the stand and tell his side of the story. She was certain he'd be a good witness. But when his time came, late in the afternoon as the trial was nearing its close, he couldn't do it. "I broke down," Sean says. "I was shaking and crying and I didn't know why." They stood in the hallway of the courthouse. Huneke did her best to calm him, telling him they would wait until tomorrow and begin fresh.

Sean, who'd never seen a trial before in his life—"except for *Judge Judy* or whatever"—had no idea what to expect. Huneke told him to come to her office at 5:30 the next morning to go over things. "She had one of her helpers in the office question me like he was the prosecutor—and he was actually ten times harder, asked more intense questions than the real prosecutor." The preparation helped. When a shaking Sean climbed into the witness box later that same day, he managed to keep his panic attacks at bay and answer the brief questions he was asked. "The prosecutor didn't ask me a single thing about what happened, but only if I was shifting gears really fast," Sean says, explaining that he remembered being in third gear. (Right after the accident, he thought he had been in second, but during the trial, he said he was in third.) Sean says the prosecutor kept insisting that Sean was driving too fast to stop in case a car inadvertently pulled into the intersection in front of him. "But it's not logical to drive like you think every car is going to pull out in front of you," Sean says, still thinking through the accident, still reliving the trial, still evaluating his behavior, still worrying.

Speed became a central issue in the trial, as Huneke knew it would be. The state insisted that Sean had to be going between 51 and 54 mph in a 30 mph zone. This constituted the "conscious disregard of the danger to others" that was necessary to procure a guilty verdict for vehicular homicide. Not only did the state have the witness statement saying that Sean had been speeding, it had photographs of the accident scene and a diagram showing that Sean's skid marks were approximately 175 feet long.[31] Based on 175-foot skid marks and time-distance calculations, the state's accident specialist testified that Sean was going more than 20 mph over the speed limit. (A second accident report would put the skid marks at 114 feet and calculate that Sean had to be exceeding the speed limit quite a bit at impact.)

Fortunately, in the gift of additional time that Huneke had been given by the judge, she hired a retired state trooper to investigate the accident in order to help her re-create it for the jury. He was troubled by the calculations and by the vast gulf between the speed Sean alleged he was going and what the cops alleged. And some of the calculations weren't making sense. Unfortunately, because weeks had elapsed between the accident and the charge and Huneke's assignment to the case, any evidence that existed at the site of the accident had long since been erased. Still, three years after the incident, Huneke's investigator went down to the scene armed with photos the cops had taken of the skid marks that day. As he paced the sidewalk and examined the skid marks, based on cracks in the sidewalk, where the curb was eroded, how the tire marks aligned with other landmarks, he got a firm sense of scale. Shocked, he discovered that the state's accident investigator had doubled the length of the skid marks to do his speed-distance calculations. It was easy to prove this. All he had to do was take a second set of photos, pacing off the actual distance of the tire marks and putting the state's photos next to scale models.

Huneke didn't know whether the state had erred or whether the cops had intentionally lied; either way, the state's case was crumbling. She turned her attention to the coroner next. According to autopsy reports, Stack had died from "acute peritonitis," basically an infection due to surgery—but the medical examiner said the surgery took place to repair a hernia. While Stack seemed okay when emergency room doctors examined him, they had suggested an x-ray to make sure all was well, Huneke discovered. In fact, the x-ray revealed that he had a hiatal hernia. This hernia, often symptom-free, is due to a weakening in the muscle that separates the chest from the abdominal cavity. As the tissue weakens, parts of the stomach creep through. The emergency room doctors operated, Huneke explained to the jury, and Mr. Stack got an infection and died.

When she put Lowell Stack's family doctor on the stand, the case fell to pieces. He testified that, yes, the emergency room doctors had called him, per protocol, when his elderly patient Mr. Stack was admitted but, he said, they did not mention that they were planning emergency surgery. Had the ER doctors mentioned it, he would certainly have objected. After all, he told the jury, Mr. Stack had had that hernia for years. It didn't bother him much and, given his advanced years and fragile state, the doctor thought operating would be too much for Mr. Stack.

"The jury deliberated for twelve minutes," Huneke recalled. They came back with their unanimous decision and delivered it without fanfare. Not guilty.

Several months after Sean Replogle's acquittal, A.N.J.'s parents were struggling to deal with the consequences of their twelve-year-old's guilty plea. They turned to a private local attorney, Garth Dano, for help. He joined forces with a lawyer named George Ahrend—and together they fought to revoke the plea, arguing that the public defender Doug Anderson had not only failed to zealously represent the boy, but he had failed to go through the most basic steps with his client (including never once having an independent interview with A.N.J.).

"When I first met [A.N.J.], he was just over twelve," Ahrend tells me, "and I could totally see one of my own kids facing this same situation—and it frightened me." Ahrend paused. "Goodness, nobody wants to be condoning sex abuse in any form, but it made me worry that maybe we're a little hyper-vigilant, hyper-zealous about this. It did seem pretty innocuous—*if* it even happened."

Among other things, Ahrend was surprised to learn that the five-year-old had reportedly been abused by someone else. That does not mean he wasn't abused a second time, but it could mean he had mixed things up or understood the explosive nature of an accusation. "I won't say I know what the alleged victim has been through," Ahrend says, explaining that the younger boy had exhibited some "sexually precocious behavior that is not common in a five year old," but this is the kind of stuff that A.N.J.'s original attorney should have investigated on his client's behalf. "I don't want to say this kid was not abused," Ahrend says, "but there wasn't a lot that happened here, and [A.N.J.] spent, as a consequence, junior high and high school as a registered sex offender."

Indeed, this hung over A.N.J. for the next six years, essentially his entire adolescence. "One of the things that surfaced was that the public defender had misinformed the family about the consequences of this," Ahrend said. "Not telling them that someone would shadow this kid around school and that he would have this on his record for life." Ahrend and Dano took the case to the Court of Appeals—and lost.

But they persisted. Above and beyond what they saw as the egregious specifics of this particular case, they recognized an opportunity here to make an argument about legal standards. In particular, they hoped to push the state supreme court to play an active role in limiting public defender caseloads, arguing that, indeed, it had a responsibility to do so. If the Washington Supreme Court decided in A.N.J.'s favor here, the ruling would send shock waves through the legal community. It would be a clarion call to local governments that adequately funding indigent defense was no longer optional; thousands of cases could no longer be piled on the backs of overworked public defenders.

First, though, Ahrend had to make the court see the connection between bad lawyering and crushing caseloads. He could not simply state that Douglas Anderson was a crummy lawyer. He had to prove that Douglas Anderson did a crummy job *because* he couldn't possibly do a good job when he was carrying 460 other clients. For his part, Douglas Anderson declined to comment due to a pending lawsuit.

Finally, on Thursday, May 21, 2009, at 10 A.M., Ahrend had a chance to make his case in oral arguments before the Washington Supreme Court. Interestingly, one of the state supreme court judges, Richard Sanders, had been championing indigent defense reform for years and may have been waiting for just such a case to come along.

"I felt like it was a friendly bench," Ahrend said, but he tried not to get too hopeful, reminding himself that they had lost the first round. One of the biggest problems they faced was proving not only that A.N.J.'s original attorney was ineffective, but the requirement—based on a 1984 case called *Stickland v. Washington*—of proving that his unprofessional lawyering had actually swung the outcome of the case and that the bad counsel led to an incorrect verdict. "It's a catch-22," Ahrend says, explaining that if an attorney has not done his job by swiftly interviewing witnesses and others, that means there is no record of interviews with witnesses offering exculpatory evidence, and so forth. It makes a case like this very hard to win, says Ahrend.

But he had been working on this case for years—and hopefully, the Washington Supreme Court was ready to hand down a decision about caseload limits. "Good morning," Ahrend began. "On behalf of [A.N.J.], what we're asking this court to do today is to permit him to withdraw his guilty plea and to proceed to trial with the representation that we believe he is entitled to under the Sixth Amendment of the U.S. Constitution." Ahrend, looking fresh-faced and guileless with his buzzed blond hair, tan jacket, and wire-frame glasses, was, in fact, wily, articulate, and on top of his game. He got right to the point: "Mr. Anderson spent somewhere between thirty minutes and one hour and thirty minutes to defend a twelve-year-old child against class A felony charges of First Degree Child Molestation. . . . Given the kind of caseload he had, it wasn't possible to do what this court has held as required in counseling a defendant on a guilty plea: to render actual and substantial assistance to the accused in deciding whether or not to plead guilty."

"Doesn't your client, the defendant, admit that this incident occurred, even today, but the question is, who was the aggressor?" Justice Charles Johnson, one of Washington's Supreme Court judges, asked. "He said the five-year-old boy, but the fact, my question is, doesn't he admit the incident occurred?"

"No," Ahrend said. "He admits *an* incident occurred. Does he admit that he committed first-degree child molestation? No."

In other filings, Ahrend has pointed out that for first-degree child molestation, there has to be a "desire for sexual gratification on the part of some participant," but that, in this case, neither child appeared to be driven by that—or even too clear on what that was. Before the Washington Supreme Court, with only fifteen minutes to present his argument, Ahrend saves this point for later and drives right toward the guilty plea itself that twelve-year-old A.N.J. had signed. "First point," he said. "Doug Anderson did not read this language to [A.N.J.]. Second point. [A.N.J.] himself did not read this language, and that testimony is undisputed. Instead, what Doug Anderson told [A.N.J.] to do is, he says, 'the judge is going to ask you, did you read this or did I explain it to you? And just tell him that you did' . . . when in fact, he hadn't. [A.N.J.] had five minutes to see this document for the first time before the regularly scheduled trial date, the same date that he pleaded guilty. It wasn't possible. It's nine pages, single-spaced of dense legalese. And this twelve-year-old boy couldn't digest it, and Douglas Anderson did nothing to help him digest it in that five-minute period of time. And so to say that by lying to the judge, a twelve-year-old boy following the instructions of the attorney that's appointed to him by the court represents his interests and to be his voice and his protection against the charges leveled by the state, that, to say that that's an admission by [A.N.J.] of what was in the police reports, when Doug Anderson testifies he never reviewed the police reports with [A.N.J.], is offensive."

"Was there not some suggestion that the children involved, who are the alleged victims, had actually been victimized by other persons?" asked one of the judges, referring to the alleged victim and his sister. "Such that they became sexualized in their behavior and that there might be some reason to credit a viable defense against these charges . . . ?"

"Absolutely," Ahrend agreed.

"And was that ever investigated by the defense attorney? And the reason that I say this is I just think, is there not a duty to give advice to a client in terms of whether or not they have a viable defense before they actually decide to plead guilty?"

"Is there a duty?" Ahrend asked. "Absolutely, yes." He decided to accept this gift the justice was tossing him and run with it. "And this court has repeatedly held the duty of defense counsel is to actually and substantially assist the client in deciding whether to plead guilty. This includes an evaluation of the evidence that the state has against that person. You can't evaluate that evidence unless you, as the defense attorney, have performed an investigation. And here, it is undisputed. Douglas Anderson performed absolutely no investigation whatsoever in that hour and thirty minutes."

Justice Gerry Alexander takes up this question of investigation. "If Mr. Anderson had looked at the police report as I understand it, the young man told the deputy he had never touched this other child," he said. "But the deputy didn't believe him because he was not making eye contact or something like that. Am I right?"

"Correct," Ahrend agrees. "Even Douglas Anderson said when I met with him initially, he was denying what was in the police reports. And again, they didn't review the police reports."

"Says something about the detective—" Justice Alexander continues.

"Correct," Ahrend interrupts. "Detective Matney, he denied it—"

"He didn't just not make eye contact, he turned away and started crying is my recollection of the record here."

"I believe that is correct as well."

"Back to my question," Justice Charles Johnson said. "It seems we've got two paths here in that your argument would be the same based on the facts of this case had this client been the attorney's only client and did the same type of job, and back to the question, to what extent, on review, should the standards in caseload standards play into the equation here? Do we measure competency based on the number of files an attorney currently has when they're representing a person? Or is that just sort of supportive of the factual argument you're presenting?"

All of Washington State's caseload reform efforts hung on this question.

"The answer to your question is, do you need to base your decision here on caseload numbers and caseload number standards? No," Ahrend admitted. But he offered them the possibility—and a way of framing it. "Can you? I think it's permissible to take them into account. And what we're seeing in this case, um, at some point, caseload does impinge upon the attorney's ability to render effective assistance of counsel. And, unless we start getting definitive pronouncements from this court and effective reversals of cases where somebody is clearly wronged like this, they're going to feel free to continue to ignore those caseload standards because it's expensive for the county."

There was some back and forth and then Ahrend reiterated the problem. "What happens is that caseload then gets manifested in all kinds of errors and worse, in this case." Ahrend urged the judges to act decisively. "This court sets the standard for the practice of attorneys around the state and . . . local government entities, judges, and lower courts and attorneys are going to be watching for this decision to see, is this okay? Is it okay what happened here? And I would submit that it can't be okay, because if it is, you're just going to keep seeing cases like this."

As Ahrend returned to his seat, Carole Highland, deputy prosecutor for Grant County, stepped forward. A round woman, she wore her blond hair in a tight ponytail, and approached the podium. She tried to justify the fact that the juvenile court judge had not probed A.N.J. directly to make sure he understood the particulars of his guilty plea. As she began to speak, the justices cut her off. She tried again with another idea. They cut her off again.

"It seems to me," said Justice Alexander, "when you're dealing with a twelve-year-old kid, pardon me, child, that maybe there's a little extra duty there to make sure that they understand what they're doing?"

"Case law says that once an individual has reached the age of twelve, they have the capacity," Highland began.

"Real world, though, a twelve-year-old child? Do you really think they're as able to understand the proceedings as maybe an eighteen-year-old person?"

"Perhaps not," Highland conceded. "But I worked with Mr. Anderson for many, many years. He has been a juvenile defense attorney for many, many years. And he took his job seriously. And he spent time with each and every one of these individuals and each and every one of these youth. And, um, by all estimates, at a minimum, Mr. Anderson spent fifty-five minutes with [A.N.J.'s father]. At the maximum, according to defense counsel, he spent an hour and a half with [A.N.J.'s father]. And I would put it to your honors that, you hear an argument here before you and the total encompassed time is forty minutes. And that's a lot of time. He spent an hour and a half with this youth."

The justices grew prickly here.

"We spend a lot more than forty minutes on the case," Justice Alexander said. "We read the briefs. We confer afterwards. We write opinions. So we don't spend a mere forty minutes on any case."

The justices grilled Highland on whether Anderson ever conferred individually with his client as he is ethically obligated to do (i.e., to determine whether he was simply pleading guilty because his parents wanted him to)—she conceded he did not—and whether the judge was rushed and failed to make sure A.N.J. understood the nature of the plea. And then they circled back to the specifics of

Anderson's investigation. "Did Anderson personally talk to all the witnesses identified in this incident?" Justice Sanders demanded.

"No," Highland said. "I believe he testified in the hearing that he attempted to call the witnesses, that he was unable to reach them, and that after that, subsequent to that attempt, [A.N.J.] confessed to him that he had done this. This was a case—"

"Why didn't he follow up?" Justice Sanders interrupted. "Is it because he had a lot to do? He had 263 clients under contract, that he had an average of thirty to forty active dependency cases at one time and another two hundred cases as well? Would that be the reason?"

"Absolutely not," Highland said.

"He's a busy man," Justice Sanders said.

"I guess my question is, even if the defendant told his attorney, I did this, why would that remove the obligation of counsel to see whether there was a triable case nevertheless?" Justice Madsen wondered. "Guilt certainly doesn't mean you plead guilty, it means the State, whether or not you put the State to its burden to prove that you're guilty, and we have a system that presumes you're innocent. So I guess I'm not understanding why, and particularly when you're dealing with victims who are four and five years old, who are going to be pretty poor witnesses probably—maybe no, but probably—and you have allegations that they were previously sexually molested, so it seems like a pretty good defense case without, I mean, at least [a] good enough case to go and investigate. So I don't understand why you're sort of taking the position that he, you know, what happened was his client confessed, so therefore that's a good excuse for not going further in the investigation?"

"Absolutely not," Highland said, but explained that A.N.J. agreed the event had taken place, but insisted the five-year-old had initiated things. Then, the detective who interviewed A.N.J. said his behavior seemed damning. "[A.N.J.] put his head down. He started crying. He started trembling. Which would certainly be indicative of guilt and consciousness of guilt. . . ."

Highland goes on, but Justice Sanders cut her off, incredulous. "You're confronted, you're a twelve-year-old kid confronted by a police officer? Isn't that a traumatic experience?"

Highland laughed. "I don't know."

"If I get pulled over for speeding, my heart is palpating, you know? And I'm a little more than twelve years old," the justice said.

Highland tried to get around this one, and moved the discussion to A.N.J.'s sex offender record, arguing that it is not always permanent. She pointed out that he could go to court as an adult and make a case to be relieved of the requirement to register as a sex offender wherever he went.

Justice Alexander pointed out that the court did not have to grant him that, however. "It's conceivable that this twelve-year-old child would have to report until, uh, the rest of his life."

"It's conceivable. It's highly unlikely. I've never—"

"But the fact that it's a possibility seems to me that's something that he should have been told."

The justices persisted here, circling around the issue of the permanency of A.N.J.'s sex offender record. Highland tried to wrangle the argument elsewhere. "I would like to say that this plea needs to be upheld for finality, certainty, and closure. Not just for the victim, but for [A.N.J.]," she said.

Closure for Sean Replogle—and indeed, public defender Carol Dee Huneke and car crash victim Judy Rodeen—would prove elusive. On the heels of winning Sean's case, Huneke had a surge of euphoria, before realizing that the victory was just a blip on the screen and she would be headed back to her hundred remaining open cases. She asked to be reassigned to the juvenile division, where she hoped she could make more of a difference. And her boss approved this lateral move.

But Sean's case had made her think about and question authority and the system. Her dawning awareness that the challenges she faced as a public defender with overwhelming caseloads represented vast systemic problems, and that public defenders and legal aid attorneys were facing similar crises all across the country, led to a political awakening. She penned a highly critical article looking at problems in the system and pointing out that reform was unlikely as long as the advocacy organization lacked independence. She thought the Washington Defender Association should be run by the public defenders in the trenches, not department heads and directors who were too eager to please the local bureaucrats and politicians who had a role in their appointment. She titled her paper "WTF WDA?"

When the Washington Defender Association declined to publish it, she self-published the piece on a blog she started called *Public Defender Revolution*. She developed a manifesto and issued a call to arms. "I believe that if we are going to change, we all have to become public defender revolutionaries—every PD, every law professor, every law student, every law dean, every citizen who cares for justice—every one of us has to engage our problem-solving brain and take action," she wrote. "The fact that we underfund our systems, overload idealistic but human lawyers, but allow reform to be someone else's cause is not acceptable. Our current system is unfair to clients, to public defenders themselves, and to a nation that thinks it has a justice system that is fair." She began to get followers. Public defenders from various states began to forward their own stories, news accounts, exposés, abuses. As Huneke published these comments and linked to other stories, her followers grew. She urged them on.

She rabble-roused on the Internet, in her office, in the courthouse, at conferences, on panels—and then, on September 27, 2011, she was fired by the same boss who had weighed in on her lawyering in the *Spokesman Review* a month before Sean Replogle's trial, saying, "She's incredibly aggressive and effective."

It would take six years, and twelve-year-old A.N.J. would be eighteen, before the Washington Supreme Court would rule that his "court-appointed counsel's representation fell below the objective standards guaranteed by the Constitution for effective counsel," and that he would be allowed to withdraw his guilty plea. At that point, Grant County prosecutors dismissed the charges against A.N.J. completely. Douglas Anderson, however, was not censured or even investigated by the state bar. Indeed, news of his role in this case seems to have been completely limited to small legal circles, and he went on to make an unsuccessful bid for a local judgeship.

Six days after the state supreme court's decision, the Washington State Office of Public Defense sent out a memo to everyone involved in the court system announcing, in essence, that the rules of the game had changed thanks to A.N.J.'s case. What had long been considered "recommended" caseload limits were now mandated case limits.[32]

Writing for the Supreme court's majority opinion, Justice Tom Chambers said, "While the vast majority of public defenders do sterling and impressive work, in some times and places, inadequate funding and troublesome limits on indigent counsel have made the promise of effective assistance of counsel more myth than fact, more illusion than substance." He added, "Public funds for appointed counsel are sometimes woefully inadequate, and public contracts have imposed statistically impossible caseloads on public defenders." Further, "[s]uch public contracts for public defenders discourage appropriate investigation, testing of evidence, research, and trial preparation, and literally reward the public defender financially for every guilty plea the defender delivers."

Justice Richard Sanders, in a concurring opinion, went even further in his criticism. "Just because a county attempts to balance its budget on the backs of indigent criminal defendants is no reason for the court to facilitate this constitutional violation," he wrote.

Five months later, in July 2010, the Washington Supreme Court proposed new rules for public defense and finally, in 2012, the Washington Supreme Court approved one of the nation's most comprehensive reform packages. The new rules spell out in laborious detail a list of standards ranging from requirements about an attorney's experience in a particular area of law, to mandates that a physical office space be provided for confidential client meetings (not always the case in rural areas and small courthouses), to proof of continuing legal education, to sworn statements that attorneys are complying with caseload limits.[33]

Washington State is not the first state to recommend or even demand caseload limits, but the Washington Supreme Court is the first to put teeth into its mandate by creating a way to enforce the rules. Here, individual attorneys (not bosses or department heads) will have to certify before a judge, prior to accepting a case, that they meet each of the standards spelled out in court rules; violators are subject to bar association censure.

Meanwhile, as municipalities across the state cut their budgets, the actual need for legal aid attorneys and public defenders is growing. According to Legal Aid for Washington Fund and the Campaign for Equal Justice in Seattle, which drew on census figures, nearly 30 percent of Washington residents live below poverty. Already, the organization reports, only one in five people requesting legal assistance receives it, and requests are skyrocketing. Domestic violence requests have gone up 109 percent, foreclosures 556 percent, unemployment 890 percent.

The Washington State Office of Public Defense noted in its annual 2010 report, "[P]ublic defense in Washington still is not attaining an overall appropriate level of quality, and serious shortcomings persist in many local programs. These deficiencies are only exacerbated by a lingering economic recession that has forced substantial state and local budget cuts, including cuts to public defense." Indeed, the Washington State Office of Public Defense, which funnels money to cities and counties across the state to help them decrease caseloads and improve the quality of services, was hit with a 7.6 percent budget cut in 2010. Spokane County is slated to lose two full-time attorneys and three other staffers.

What that means is that legal representation for the poor in Washington remains very uneven. "You have a situation where you have appalling and almost deliberate mistreatment of people and you have some of the most extraordinary work being done by public defenders that makes the American justice system shine," says Bob Boruchowitz, a professor at Seattle University School of Law. "You can have all of that in the same state. You can have all of that in the same county."

When I meet with Carol Dee Huneke in her second-story Spokane apartment in November of 2011, she wears a gray-and-black striped shirt. She has black hair, black jeans, black fingernails. We sit on white IKEA chairs on opposite sides of her Restoration Hardware dining room table, a long, distressed wood surface full of pock marks, looking down the planked wood at a giant aquarium, where a Russian tortoise named Sheldon occasionally blinks at us, as if listening intently but puzzled by illogical plot twists.

"They fired you?" I ask Huneke, waiting for her to explain.

"Lack of diligence and failure to communicate is their official reason," she says. "And my response?" She takes a sip of her Rockstar energy drink—a dramatic pause. "It was bullshit. I think it all went back to me standing up to them with the trial that I refused to do." She points out that she actually got accolades from them at the time for her stance, and notes that the Washington Association of Criminal Defense Lawyers gave her the President's Award that year for her "distinguished service to the highest traditions of the criminal defense bar." She thinks she was fired out of vengeance. "I think judges complained and [my boss] took their complaints as truth," she says. "And I was trying to exercise my First Amendment rights on my blog—" She pauses a moment, laughs. "Okay, it's hard to say I'm being restrained by advocating 'revolution,' but I wasn't name calling." She thinks for a moment about whether she had considered the consequences of her activism. "I guess I knew what I was doing. I was surprised when I was fired, but I guess I knew I might be. I guess I knew, but I was naively idealistic." She shakes her head. "When people do the wrong thing, it still surprises me."

Now, though, she wonders whether she'll continue the blog, the advocacy, the fight. She has moved outside for a smoke and stands on the covered balcony of her turn-of-the-century brick apartment building—old for these parts—and inhales, a pile of *Better Homes & Gardens* stacked incongruously (she has an apartment, no garden, doesn't seem the type) on a side table. She holds a cigarette in her outstretched arm behind her. The angle is awkward; she is trying to keep the smoke from billowing toward my face in the windy chill.

"It must have been odd," I muse, thinking about the lawyer who went into court with her as she fought to delay Sean's trial a week, "to be a lawyer hiring your own lawyer?"

"Yes," she says. "But I liked it. It was comforting to know someone had your back." She learned things, too. She had a new understanding of how vulnerable someone felt in a courtroom when so much was at stake.

To fill the time, and because she found it therapeutic, she had begun writing a novel. It is the story of a public defender who tries cases that seem an awful lot like the ones Huneke did. The manuscript, which she shares with me, reveals a lot about the public defender's life, her life in particular. She wrote about the disorienting sense that she alone was overwhelmed by her workload and the knowledge that her clients were suffering. And then she had an epiphany. She put her personal story in the larger political context, recognizing that many of the problems she faced with her workload were systemic problems that public defenders across the country were struggling with. "Now I knew it wasn't me—it was the job. I had been given the enormous responsibility of trying to protect people's liberty, and then not given enough time or resources to do the job right," she wrote in this fictional book, as the protagonist prepared for the trial of an innocent nineteen-year-old high school senior in a vehicular homicide case.

As I stand up to leave Huneke's apartment, some five hours later, I ask her what she plans to do next. She pauses, surrounded by the boxes of papers, stacks of folders, files of cases she has emptied in her dining room in a search for some backup document I've asked for and tilts her head to the side slightly, thinking. She's not sure what comes next for her. "Maybe I'll get out of law and do something completely different," she says. She has to act soon. Rent on her apartment is only $500 a month, but she is now divorced, has a twelve-year-old daughter and last week only had $400 left in her account. (No severance package.) "My parents loaned me $5,000," she admits, shaking her head at the sea of papers that surround her, the sea of trouble. "I'm forty-three years old and my parents are supporting me."

When I meet with Sean Replogle ten years after the trial, I am struck by the fact that he is twenty-eight years old but still looks like a skinny eighteen-year-old, retaining a young teen's nervous discomfort in his own skin. We meet at his small apartment in Spokane Valley, where he has moved to be away from his past—"I left because I couldn't walk down the road without knowing that people were looking at me going, 'Oh, there goes that kid who killed someone,'" he explains—but remains close enough to see his extended family regularly.

He sits in a brown recliner facing a flat-screen television mounted on the wall and speaks more comfortably to the TV than to me, sitting on the couch to his left. He has muted the TV's volume, but his pale face is illuminated by its flickers—like flickers of conflicting thoughts—as dusk settles and darkens the room.

It is clear that a decade has done little to diminish the impact of his arrest.

"It made me not trust anyone," he says. He can't help it, he explains, that's just the way he feels. His life's narrative is divided by a coming-of-age story that knocked all his assumptions about the way things worked aside, a pre- and post-accident worldview. "At the time, I trusted everyone," he says. "I was smiley and go-lucky. Now, I'm very reserved. I see any kind of legal case on TV and I feel for the person who's been accused, no matter what the charge, because I know the process." He mentions a local case that has gotten a lot of recent attention—and left him feeling deeply conflicted. The week before, on November 2, 2011, a jury had convicted a police officer, Karl Thompson, for the murder of a mentally disturbed man he beat to death in a convenience store. "I even felt sorry for him," Sean admits. And that's saying something. "After my whole situation, I can't stand police officers—the way they lied about my speed—but I feel bad for anyone involved in a trial like that." He pauses, reconsiders, thinks about his experience with cops. "Once, I thought anyone who said cops would lie were out of their minds," he says. "Then, they fudged all the numbers on my case and now I'm like, wow." He is silent for a moment, trying to pull the right words from the air in some middle ground he stares at between himself and the TV. "I'm still super cautious because I don't want to get screwed over again."

He drifts into reverie and I pull him back, wondering what he felt when the jury came back with its decision. "When I heard the verdict, I was holding my breath," he says. "It was the happiest day of my life." Still, the whole thing confounds him. "And I ended up getting nothing, not even a speeding ticket," he says. He laughs. "And I would have paid that!"

But so much in his life remains linked to that incident. For example, he still cannot get a driver's license due to the money owed to the Stacks' insurance company, so his job prospects are confined to what is available on the limited bus routes. A month after the trial ended, he got a job at KFC and has been working steadily since then. First at KFC, then at Papa Murphy's, a take-and-bake pizza place, then at TacoTime, where he has spent the past four years. Today he works as the Spokane Valley TacoTime closing manager. He is good at it, he says. He locks up the place each night, works a 50-hour week on his feet, and scrapes by financially. Public transportation to and from work on the erratically scheduled buses eats up one to two hours a day and $60 a month. When he closes TacoTime for the night, he misses the last bus and walks the three miles home. Someday, if he can ever get his driver's license back, he plans to go to community college and work a night job—but he can't do both without a car.

Judge Judy is on the TV. Sean picks up the remote and changes the channel to Nickelodeon. *SpongeBob* strides across the screen; a yellow glow floats across Sean's face. Sean tells me that he owes $450,000 to the Stacks' insurance company. He doesn't see how he can pay this. After all, it took him nine years—and his father's help—to pay off a $1,200 student loan for his brief foray into community college, which, with interest, had swelled to $4,000. He ticks off his monthly expenses on his fingers: $550 rent, $100 electricity, $75 cable and phone, and so forth. At the end of the month, he's lucky if he has $100 to work with. "And then I always need something, like shoes for work," he says, explaining that he is trying to save up $1,000. When he gets $1,000, he tells me, he is going to hire an attorney to help him figure out what to do, to determine if he can declare bankruptcy or something, and get the $450,000 he owes the Stacks' insurance company dealt with in some way. (Without car insurance, he was responsible for all the accident-related costs.) If he can get that problem solved, he may be able to finally get his driver's license back.

Meanwhile, he doesn't go out much. "I wouldn't drink a beer and then go walk around outside, because I'd be afraid a cop is going to arrest me," he says. "If they can send me to prison for four years for speeding, they can do anything." He shakes his head. "I don't want to live like that. I've almost gotten over that, where I look at a cop and I'm scared. I tell myself, I'm not a criminal. I'm not a drug user. Why am I scared?"

Last year, he was walking home and a cop pulled up beside him and stopped him and asked for ID. "He said someone had robbed something and looked similar to me. He said, 'You know your license is suspended? You hurt someone?'" Sean answered: "Yes, I know my license is suspended. That's why I'm walking." By the time the cop drove off, Sean was shaking, fighting a panic attack. "This has permanently messed me up," he says.

I wonder if he has ever sought counseling. "No," he says. "I just counseled myself. I don't know—" he drifts off, thinking. "Probably I should have. I've just been trying to keep things cool mentally. I never wanted to get on any anti-anxiety pill or anything, so I just try to be cool with it. I have my little moments. I just calm down and breathe. I can manage my panic attacks."

But there are triggers. "This is a small town, so I still have to see that guy all the time," Sean says, referring to the prosecuting attorney Clint Francis. "He's come into TacoTime." Sean took his order and gave him his food.

I wonder, was he tempted to seek revenge? A little spit in his food?

"No, I didn't do anything to it," Sean says. No spit. No habanero sauce. "I can't do that. I'd have bad fast-food karma, and I eat fast food all the time. But I *was* hoping he would recognize me and worry that I'd done something!" Sean laughs. Then stops. "But he doesn't even recognize me. You tried to put me in prison at eighteen and sat next to me for eight days of a trial and you don't even recognize me?"

Years back, while working at KFC, he also served the cop that "mismeasured" his car's skid marks. He didn't recognize Sean either. Sean realized his case was simply business as usual for these guys.

He tries to be fair. "I've talked to a couple of cops since then, and some were on my side. So I know it's not all of them that are bad," he says. "It's the system. What's wrong with the system that this can happen?"

He throws the question out, where it hangs for a few moments in dusk's silence.

"But I'm not sour about it," Sean says finally. "At least I'm free. And I have a job." He gets up, noticing that the room has grown dark, and turns on the living room light—shaking the mood, dislodging the memory. "I like life and everything."

On an evening in January some ten-plus years after she was in the car wreck on the corner of Garland and Belt, Judy Rodeen still struggles to think or speak coherently about the crash. "I don't remember anything about the accident," she tells me, her voice soft, halting. I strain to hear. "I was in [the] backseat of my parents' car and I, I . . . I don't remember anything. We were coming from Starbucks."

"I'd rather not bring it up at all," she says when I ask about the car wreck, the hospital, the trial. She goes on to bring it up.

"The whole thing . . . it was a terrible experience. My parents died." She tells me that her father was hospitalized, that he lost consciousness. "So I never got to talk to him. . . . Then we had to make a decision to take him off life support." Her mother was "too far into Alzheimer's to be of any help about what to do next." Then ten months later, her mother died. "That's why it was so traumatic to me, because both my parents died that year," she sighs. "It's been a bad few years."

Judy, despite the fact that she appeared to be in the worst shape in the moments after the accident—her face bloodied and cut from going through the window—bore up, and still works as the office manager at the high school. "I had stitches in my head and around my eye and I was black and blue," she says. "But nothing was broken. I've recuperated. No ill effects." She gives a sharp, harsh laugh. "Other than the mental part."

She elaborates: "The young man was at the school that I worked at." She dreaded the prospect of running into him. She didn't know what he looked like and she decided to keep it that way. "I could have looked the student's picture up at school," she says, eschewing the use of his name even in this conversation a decade later. "And I didn't. I was always terrified he would walk into the office and he would know who I was but I wouldn't know him." She pauses. "Still, I never wanted to ever see him, so it was better not to know who he was."

The first she saw of him, she says, was at the trial, where she mostly stared at the back of his head as he sat at the table next to the public defender. And now, all these years later, the very fact of the trial puzzles her. "I was approached by them, by the city," she says, explaining that they told her some days after her father's death that there would be a trial. "Otherwise I would have just accepted it for what it was . . . an accident." She says she was "dumbfounded."

"I just kind of went along with it," she says. "I had no idea what I was supposed to do, what I should do about it." She describes herself as "pretty naive" about the reason. "I think they wanted to charge him with vehicular homicide." She pauses, picks her words carefully. "I never thought he drove with the intent to kill," she says. "It was an accident. And that's just the way I approached it."

"Sometimes people suggest that a trial can bring closure, a sense of—" I say.

She interrupts me. "No, just . . . no, there isn't. I wouldn't say there was any closure."

CHAPTER 2

"All countrys try to give there citizens a fair trial and see to it that they have counsel," a semi-literate Clarence Earl Gideon complained to the U.S. Supreme Court in his 1962 petition, wondering why he was being denied a lawyer simply because he was poor. Photo courtesy of the State Archives of Florida.

"I HAVE NO COUNSEL":

THE MAN BEHIND GIDEON V. WAINWRIGHT

In the summer of 1961, cops in Panama City, Florida, arrested a man named Clarence Earl Gideon for breaking into a pool hall and stealing change from a cigarette machine and jukebox, some bottles of beer and wine, and a couple of sodas. He was fifty-one years old and had been arrested a lot in the past for petty crimes, including theft and gambling.[1] He had done time before—and in the process, took the trouble to educate himself about the law.

He learned one important lesson: the law is pretty complicated.

In fact, Gideon decided, the law is so complicated, he ought to have an attorney to help him navigate his criminal trial. On August 4, 1961, as his trial on the pool hall charges began, he asked the judge if he might have a lawyer. When Judge Robert L. McCrary Jr. of the Circuit Court of the Fourteenth Judicial Circuit asked him if he was ready for trial, Gideon said no.

"Why aren't you ready?" the judge asked.

"I have no counsel," Gideon replied.

The judge asked him a few other questions and then repeated, "Now tell us what you said again, so we can understand you, please."

"Your Honor, I said I request this court to appoint counsel to represent me in this trial."

The judge explained that impoverished defendants were entitled to court-appointed lawyers only in capital cases.

"Let the record show that the defendant has asked the court to appoint counsel to represent him in this trial and the court denied the request," the judge said, inadvertently laying the groundwork for Clarence Earl Gideon's later game-changing plea to the Supreme Court of the United States.[2] For now, though, the trial proceeded with Gideon representing himself. He bumbled through.

This was a small town, with informal small-town justice. Panama City, a Gulf Coast city located on the panhandle between Pensacola and Tallahassee, is the county seat of Bay County. In 1961, the town had a population of approximately 33,000. (Nothing much has changed population-wise in the ensuing fifty years; the 2010 census puts the number at 36,484.[3]) The community of Bay Harbor, where Gideon lived, was located near the International Paper Plant, just outside of the city limits. The place stunk, literally. The stench, and belching smoke from the factory, set the tone for the town. And the area where Gideon lived in a rooming house bore the brunt of this, attracting the down-and-out to its worn buildings and bars, to kick up dust as they ambled down its dirty streets.

Cutting through the settlement was a small strip of commercial establishments: a grocery store, a bar, a hotel, and the Bay Harbor Poolroom. On June 3, 1961, at 8 A.M., the owner of the Bay Harbor Poolroom, Ira Strickland Jr., arrived to open the bar, only to be greeted by a local cop named Duell Pitts. Pitts told Strickland that at some point between midnight the previous night—when Strickland had closed the bar—and that morning, someone had broken into his pool hall. Strickland discovered that a window had been smashed, a cigarette machine and jukebox had been broken into and coins were taken from both machines, and a small amount of beer and wine had been stolen. A police officer by the name of Henry Berryhill Jr. had discovered the break-in during his usual rounds. Berryhill questioned Henry Cook, a young man who happened to be hanging around outside the poolroom at 5:30 that morning. Cook knew Clarence Earl Gideon, and told the cop he had seen Gideon inside the building. Cook claimed that he saw Gideon leave the bar with a bottle of wine in his hand, his pockets bulging with change, as Gideon strode over to a pay phone on the corner to make a call. According to Cook, Gideon then got into a taxi that he had evidently called. On the basis of this eyewitness, along with the account of the taxi driver, Preston Bray—who said that he had driven Gideon downtown and that Gideon had told him, "If anyone asks you where you left me off, you don't know; you haven't seen me"—Pitts questioned Gideon. He discovered that Gideon had $25.28 in quarters, nickels, dimes, and pennies in his pockets. The police arrested Gideon, and charged him with a felony, breaking and entering with intent to commit "petit larceny."

When Gideon went to court on August 4, 1961, he knew the general nature of the charges against him but, having been incarcerated in the local jail awaiting trial, his ability to investigate his own case or even talk to the witnesses he hoped to call was severely curtailed. He'd been in court enough in the past to know that the law was complicated and that trials were difficult for laymen to navigate, thus his demand to the court that he be appointed an attorney to represent him. He insisted he had a constitutional right. The judge gently informed him otherwise. "I'm sorry, Mr. Gideon," he said, explaining that it could not be done. "I'm sorry, but I will have to deny your request to appoint counsel to defend you in this case."

"The United States Supreme Court says I am entitled to be represented by counsel," Gideon insisted.[4]

In fact, the Supreme Court said the opposite. Thanks to a 1942 decision, commonly referred to as the Betts Rule, Gideon could have qualified for free counsel only if there had been "special circumstances" in the case. If a person was mentally disabled, illiterate, or insane he might qualify for a free lawyer due to the "special circumstances" of the case. Also, if the case was particularly complicated, it could count as "special circumstances." But Gideon did not offer up any "special circumstances." From his point of view, the Sixth Amendment was clear: "In all criminal prosecutions, the accused shall . . . have the Assistance of Counsel for his defense." He was, essentially, taking the amendment at its word.

But without any "special circumstances"—or at least any that would be immediately apparent—the judge denied Gideon's request. To his credit, Judge McCrary did attempt to lead Gideon through the process. But during jury selection, he did not give Gideon the option of participating meaningfully in the selection of a jury. Instead, he simply asked the prospective jurors a few questions on Gideon's behalf. After questioning them, the judge turned to Gideon. "Now, Mr. Gideon, look these six gentlemen over and if you don't want them to sit as a jury to try your case, just point out the one, or more, all six of them if you want to, and the Court will excuse them and we will call another, or some others, to try your case," he said. "You don't have to have a reason, just look them over and if you don't like their looks, that's all it takes to get them excused."

Gideon didn't argue. "They suit me alright, Your Honor," he said, making his first—and possibly biggest—tactical mistake.[5]

The trial moved relatively quickly. The opening remarks by Gideon and assistant state attorney William Harris were not recorded. The state called two witnesses, Henry Cook (the eyewitness) and Ira Strickland (the pool hall owner). Gideon called eight witnesses, including two police officers, the cabbie who had picked him up, and his landlady at the rooming house. No particularly new information was brought forward from Gideon's witnesses. Gideon then gave a closing argument of approximately eleven minutes; Harris spoke for nine. These speeches were not taken down by the court recorder. A jury of six men found Gideon guilty. (A jury of six instead of twelve was common here. Also, an all-male jury was the norm across the country. It wasn't until 1975 when the U.S. Supreme Court ruled in *Taylor v. Louisiana* that women could not be excluded that women were regularly seated on juries; in Florida—and many states—the laws vaguely allowed women to serve, if they wanted to, and if they took the trouble to go to the courthouse and file a written request asserting as much, which few did.)

Three weeks later, on August 25, the judge imposed the maximum sentence of five years, and Gideon was sent to the Florida State Prison at Raiford. But Gideon refused to simply sit tight and do time. He decided to fight back, and no one quite knows why or what compelled him so painstakingly to pursue a retrial with an attorney. In any case, two months later, Gideon sent a letter to the Florida Supreme Court, appealing for a writ of habeas corpus, saying he had been unlawfully imprisoned. Handwritten mostly in pencil, and addressed to the "Supreme Court of the State of

Florida," the letter said: "I am a pauper without funds are any possibility of obtaining financiable aid and I Beg of this court to Listen and act upon my plea."[6]

"Gideon's punctuation and spelling were full of surprises," a charitable Anthony Lewis later wrote in his 1964 bestseller, *Gideon's Trumpet*. And indeed, this was the case.

But mixed in with the kind of grammar and spelling problems that you would find in a fourth grader's cahier, were some decent arguments that a first-year law student might make. "I was denied that rights of the 4th, 5th and 14th amendments of the Bill of rights," he wrote, grasping for constitutional backup. "I, Clarence Earl Gideon, will show this court that I did not have a fair trial and was denied my constutional rights that is gurranteed by the constution and the Bill of rights by the United States Government. I was without funds and without a attorney. I asked this court to appoint to me a attorney but they denied me that right."

The Florida Supreme Court denied his appeal. But Gideon was undeterred.

Some years later, on April 30, 1980, CBS aired a Hallmark Hall of Fame TV movie about Clarence Earl Gideon's letter. Jimmy Carter would shortly thereafter lose the presidential election to Ronald Reagan—and the Hollywood fantasy of rugged individualism swept the country. Based on Lewis's book, the movie was also called *Gideon's Trumpet* and was billed as "the true story of a prisoner whose lone voice changed legal history."[7] The movie starred Henry Fonda, who plays Gideon as a hunched, simple, laconic, weather-worn, beaten-down but doggedly determined man on a mission. He is a man who stands alone, a man of few words and few friends. But he is an ethical and moral man—in the movie anyway, which leaves out many inconvenient details of Gideon's actual life—and becomes heroic as he tackles injustice. In a David-and-Goliath plot that we Americans love, the undereducated common man takes on the fancy-pants bigwigs at the Supreme Court. The movie turns on the seminal moment when Gideon (a gaunt and distinguished Fonda in faded prison wear) strides purposefully across the penitentiary yard with his letter to the Supreme Court in his hand. The other prisoners, like a slowly gathering mob of voiceless zombies, drop what they are doing and move as one into Gideon's wake. One man reaches out, asking to touch the letter. Gideon permits this. Then he ceremoniously drops the envelope into the prison mailbox.

In real life, on April 21, 1962, the U.S. Supreme Court received Gideon's four-page letter among the dozens and dozens of letters from prisoners that arrived each day. Once again, it was on prison stationery and written in pencil. He wrote:

> Petitioner cannot make any pretense of being able to answer the learned attorney General of the State of Florida because the petitioner is not a attorney or versed in the law nor does not have the law books to copy down the decisions of this Court. But the petitioner knows there is many of them. . . .
>
> The respondent claims that a citizen can get a equal and fair trial without legal counsel.
>
> That the constitution of the United States does not apply to the state of Florida.
>
> Petitioner will attempt to show this court that a citizen of the state of Florida cannot get a just or fair trial without the aid of counsel. . . .
>
> Respondent claims that I have no right to file petition for a write of Habeas Corpus. Take away this right to a citizen and there is nothing left.

Most poignantly, Gideon added:

> It makes no difference how old I am or what color I am or what church I belong too if any. The question is I did not get a fair trial. The question is very simple. I requested the court to appoint me a attorney and the court refused. All countrys try to give there citizens a fair trial and see to it that they have counsel.[8]

According to Lewis, the *New York Times* reporter who had covered the Supreme Court for years and retraced each step of the case in his wonderful book, the letter was delivered to Michael Rodak Jr., an assistant clerk of the Supreme Court. Lewis writes:

> Mr. Rodak, among other duties, concerns himself with what the Supreme Court calls its Miscellaneous Docket. This is

made up mostly of cases brought by persons who are too poor to have their court papers printed or to pay the usual fee of one hundred dollars for docketing a case in the Supreme Court—bringing it there. A federal statute permits persons to proceed in any federal court *in forma pauperis*, in the manner of a pauper, without following the usual forms or paying the regular costs. The only requirement in the statute is that the litigant "make affidavit" that he is unable to pay such costs or give security therefore. . . . It [also] says that *in forma pauperis* applications should be typewritten "whenever possible," but in fact hand-written papers are accepted.[9]

Gideon's penciled plea had a strange kind of elegance to it. The man was obviously somewhat literate. He had composed his handwritten plea to the Supreme Court. He was not claiming any mental deficiencies or problems. The only outstanding question was race which could sometimes be considered "special circumstances" by the courts. The justices did not know what race Clarence Earl Gideon was—and, since this was not part of the record in any way, this would remain unknown for some time. In any case, the very fact that Gideon was making no effort to declare "special circumstances" made his case a perfect one for the justices to consider.

In the movie, the Supreme Court justices tackled the decision about whether to hear *Gideon v. Cochran* in a heated debate at their weekly meeting. (The original name of the case, *Gideon v. Cochran*, had changed when H.G. Cochran Jr. resigned from his position as head of the Florida Division of Corrections; he was replaced by Louie L. Wainwright.) Tempers flared as they argued about what the far-reaching consequences of the decision would be. They argued at the philosophical level (what did this mean for states' rights?) and the practical level (would every incarcerated prisoner in the nation who had been tried without counsel be freed, or entitled to a new trial, and, if so, what were the financial, administrative, and public safety consequences of such action?). They wondered how narrow or broad to go: Would the right to counsel be limited to only felony cases, or would it include misdemeanor cases? At what point in the process would a person be entitled to counsel—arrest? Arraignment? Bail hearing?

But, of course, this was in the Hollywood version of events. In reality, those conversations took place behind closed doors. They remained private and the screenwriters—and Lewis—mostly speculated about their content. Still, there was enough on the record between oral arguments and formal opinions to know where most of the justices stood. In deciding to hear the case and then making a very conscious decision to appoint the inimitable Abe Fortas (considered one of the finest lawyers in the country at that time) to represent Gideon before the court, they gave Gideon a serious leg up. It was a clear message: change was in the air and they were giving this small-town criminal his day in court. And his day in court had the potential forever to alter the way trials were conducted in this country.

What gives rise to groundbreaking changes in the law? What does it take for a constellation of judges, defendants, lawyers, and cultural forces to align—and for change to happen? For hundreds of years, legal scholars have puzzled over this, trying to find the key that allows them to replicate—or resist—monumental changes in the law.

As long ago as 1881, Oliver Wendell Holmes Jr. was grappling with the issue in the introduction to his book, *The Common Law.* "The life of the law has not been logic; it has been experience," he asserted. "The felt necessities of the time, the prevalent moral and political theories, intuitions of public policy, avowed or unconscious, and even the prejudices which judges share with their fellow men, have had a good deal more to do than syllogism in determining the rules by which men should be governed." He insisted things were uncomfortably complicated. "The law embodies the story of a nation's development through many centuries, and it cannot be dealt with as if it contained only the axioms and corollaries of a book of mathematics."[10]

As he wrote that, he was offering what was then—and still is, to many people—a radical notion of how the law operates. That is, the law does not come from some essential human ethical or moral perspective, or even necessarily from precedent in our country. Instead, he argues, it comes exclusively from judicial decision itself. A judge must decide what is going to be the *best* outcome from present and—especially—future perspectives. In this sense, a judge must be "forward-looking"; the past is not valued for its own sake, but specifically in its relation to present and future circumstances. Also, a decision must make sense within the specific historical circumstances. She or he is not deciding in a vacuum. All of this means that a judge decides a case based on *facts* (but these "facts" may include larger cultural forces at play), and then writes an opinion afterward that offers justification for the decision.

The ramification of this way of thinking about jurisprudence is huge, because it suggests that the law can, and does, shift with historical circumstances. Referring to the "felt necessities of the time," Holmes overtly acknowledged the way cultural and societal shifts, changes in moral values and attitudes, and transformations in thought changed the law. Precedent, though obviously important, is only one ingredient in the mix.

Holmes suggested that there was another way of thinking about the law. And this way of approaching the American judicial system is abhorrent to legal positivists—those folks preoccupied with precedent who are mainly concerned with finding consistency in contemporary cases with prior judgments. Positivists see the law as a series of consistent rules based in thousands of years of ethical and moral human order. To make a decision, the positivist judge must discover previous cases that have relevancy to the one at hand, and by neatly lining the precedents up—and, following this theory, they consistently line up in one direction—the positivist judge can see exactly what the appropriate decision should be. To the positivist, *stare decisis*—the obligation of courts to honor precedent—is key.

Saying that legal decisions are made according to the rather random interpretation of contemporary circumstances—essentially relying on gut reactions and the cultural and political landscape rather than on an expert knowledge of precedent—seems to negate the very authority of the law. It is a little like saying that a judge's decision could be based less on the machinations of the legal system than what he had to eat for breakfast. And it offers an opportunity for radical shifts in the understanding of the law.

As scandalous as it may seem to positivists, there have certainly been circumstances when these kinds of sweeping breaks in precedent have taken place. The Supreme Court's *Gideon v. Wainwright* decision in 1963 is one of those cases. After all, the U.S. Supreme Court had had plenty of opportunity in the preceding years to make a different decision, as similar cases came before them. But in one case after another, the Supreme Court had resisted the kind of changes that these opportunities presented. It's instructive to see what previous decisions had been made that carefully constrained any all-encompassing right to counsel—and how, in 1962, the judges set the stage for their reversal of precedent.

On Friday, June 1, 1962, the U.S. Supreme Court met in formal conference to decide which cases would be considered the following term. The justices announced the list of cases three days later, including among them *890 Misc. Gideon v. Cochran*. The order read:

> The motion for leave to proceed *in forma pauperis* and the petition for writ of certiorari are granted. The case is transferred to the appellate docket. In addition to other questions presented by this case, counsel are requested to discuss the following in their briefs and oral argument:
> "Should this Court's holding in Betts v. Brady, 316 U.S. 455, be reconsidered?"[11]

The court's understatement here should not be misconstrued as insignificant. *Betts v. Brady* was the culmination of ten years of back-and-forth considerations of the portion of the Sixth Amendment to the U.S. Constitution, which reads: "In all criminal prosecutions, the accused shall enjoy the right to . . . have the Assistance of Counsel for his defense." The framers of the Constitution probably didn't envision their 1791 amendment as specifically pertaining to persons too poor to be able to hire lawyers. More likely, it was an effort to make sure that the new country did not adopt a British common-law tenet barring defense counsel altogether in felony cases (even privately paid counsel). Perhaps more importantly, the U.S. Supreme Court historically maintained that the Bill of Rights did not apply to the states; the federal judiciary should not get involved in issues arising out of state laws and actions. This was the logic of the precedent case of *Barron v. Baltimore* (1833) and then, *United States v. Cruikshank* (1875). In *Barron*, Chief Justice John Marshall made it clear that "[t]hese [first ten] amendments contain no expression indicating an intention to apply them to the state governments. This court cannot so apply them."[12]

However, by the twentieth century, a stronger centralized federal government, combined with a more expansive reading of the Fourteenth Amendment ("No state shall make or enforce any law which shall abridge the privileges or immunities of citizens of the U.S.; nor shall any state deprive any person of life, liberty or property, without due process of the law; nor deny to any person within its jurisdiction the equal protection of the laws"[13]) suggested that the Bill of Rights did indeed pertain to state legislation. And by the 1930s the issue of the rights of indigents had become a point of concern around the country—at least for those lawyers working with the poor.

The infamous 1932 "Scottsboro Boys" case, *Powell v. Alabama*, was the first major case dealing with the right to counsel for the poor. The case revolved around a highly charged racial incident that took place on a freight train in rural Alabama, in which a group of nine black youths became embroiled in a dispute with another troop of seven white youths who were traveling with two white females. The altercation resulted in the black group throwing the whites off the train. The white youths informed the local sheriff, who, along with a posse, stopped the train and arrested the African Americans, charging them with rape, a capital offense at that time in Alabama. The trial was a media circus. Local officials called in the militia to "maintain order," but the act incited greater tensions. And although Alabama law maintained that the youths were entitled to counsel, due to the fact that that they were charged with a capital offense and everyone deserved a lawyer in a death penalty case, the judge did not appoint specific lawyers for each defendant during arraignment, instead appointing "all members of the bar" of the county to represent them as a group. For the trial, the teens had a local real estate attorney and a 70-year-old lawyer who had not tried a case in years. The defendants were also not allowed access to the lawyers until just before the trial. As a result, the lawyers' presence was practically insignificant, the trial was a mockery of justice, and a jury quickly pronounced the youths guilty.

Though the Supreme Court of Alabama upheld the convictions, the U.S. Supreme Court reversed and remanded the decisions, holding that due process had been violated. Writing for the court in 1932, Justice George Sutherland described the defendants as "young, ignorant, illiterate, surrounded by hostile sentiment . . . charged with an atrocious crime regarded with especial horror in the community where they were to be tried, [and they] were thus put in peril." And although Justice Sutherland concentrated on the Fourteenth Amendment, he made a specific reference to the Sixth Amendment when he wrote:

> The right to be heard would be, in many cases, of little avail if it did not comprehend the right to be heard by counsel. Even the intelligent and educated layman has small and sometimes no skill in the science of law. . . . He lacks both the skill and knowledge adequately to prepare his defense, even though he [may] have a perfect one. He requires the guiding hand of counsel at every step in the proceedings against him.[14]

The significance of the *Powell* ruling was its suggestion—though technically speaking it offered no hard-and-fast rule to this effect— that in state capital cases there was an obligation to provide a lawyer for defendants, and that a person had a right to counsel, which together set the stage for the rights of indigents.

The next major U.S. Supreme Court decision that took on the right to counsel was *Johnson v. Zerbst*, a 1938 federal case involving a conviction for passing counterfeit money. In a five-to-four decision, the court made it clear that the Sixth Amendment—at least, by the contemporary interpretation—required the appointment of counsel in federal criminal cases. "[T]he average defendant does not have the professional legal skill to protect himself when brought before a tribunal with power to take his life or liberty," Justice Hugo Black wrote. "That which is simple, orderly and necessary to the lawyer," he added, "to the untrained layman may appear intricate, complex and mysterious."[15]

These cases led to a kind of two-layered system for indigent defense: In the state courts, the Fourteenth Amendment required the right to counsel in some cases—though it wasn't entirely specific about which kinds of cases. And in federal cases, the Sixth Amendment required counsel in all criminal trials. This set the stage for the 1942 case *Betts v. Brady*.

Smith Betts was a forty-three-year-old unemployed farm worker from Carroll County, Maryland, who was charged with robbery. During his trial, he asked for a court-appointed lawyer, since he was too poor to afford one on his own. The judge in the case refused, saying that the county was responsible for appointing lawyers only in capital cases. Betts conducted his own defense after electing to be tried without a jury, lost the case, and was sentenced to eight years. Betts then filed a petition for habeas corpus with the Maryland Court of Appeals, which issued a ruling denying his claim, stating, "in this case it must be said there was little for counsel to do on either side."

On June 1, 1942, the U.S. Supreme Court issued a six-to-three ruling upholding the Maryland court's verdict. Justice Owen Roberts delivered the Court's majority decision, stating that the Sixth Amendment did not apply to state cases, and noted that "[t]he due process clause of the Fourteenth Amendment does not incorporate, as such, the specific guarantees found in the Sixth Amendment." Essentially, Roberts and the five other justices took a conservative view of the incorporation of the Bill of Rights through the Fourteenth Amendment. And in very basic terms, Roberts took issue with the idea that a layman could not conduct his own defense in a case such as Betts's. "[T]he accused was not helpless," Roberts wrote, "but a man forty-three years old, of ordinary intelligence and ability to take care of his interest on the trial of that narrow issue. He had once before been in a criminal court, pleaded guilty to larceny and served a sentence and was not wholly unfamiliar with criminal procedure." Roberts did not claim that the right to counsel should never be considered in state cases, but insisted that "[i]ts application is less a matter of rule" than a matter of individual circumstances. Sometimes it's patently clear the defendant needs an attorney, sometimes it's obvious he can handle things just fine on his own, Roberts suggested. "Asserted denial is to be tested by an appraisal of the totality of facts in a given case," he wrote. "That which may, in one setting, constitute a denial of fundamental fairness, shocking to the universal sense of justice, may, in other circumstances, and in the light of other considerations, fall short of such denial."

Not surprisingly, considering his passionate opinion in *Powell*, Justice Black composed the dissenting opinion in *Betts*. He first took on the majority's idea that the Bill of Rights did not apply to the states: "I believe," he wrote, "that the Fourteenth Amendment made the Sixth [Amendment] applicable to the states. But this view, although often urged in dissents, has never been accepted by a majority of this Court." After quoting at length other relevant opinions (including his own in *Powell*), and stating that the right to counsel was "fundamental," Justice Black concluded, "no defendant should be deprived of counsel merely because of his poverty. Any other practice seems to me to defeat the promise of our democratic society to provide equal justice under the law."[16]

The case paved the way for what eventually became known as the Betts Rule, in which state courts could decide to appoint counsel when there were "special circumstances" present. These included the aforementioned overly complex charges, illiteracy, extreme youth, inability to understand English, and feeblemindedness or insanity. Despite its ambiguity and arbitrary nature, the Betts Rule became the litmus test for indigent defense for the next twenty years—until Gideon's petition landed in the U.S. Supreme Court's mailbox.

The players in a major case like *Gideon v. Wainwright* are not incidental, or insignificant. In fact, history and circumstance here clearly favored one side over the other. The savvy and experienced Abe Fortas represented Gideon. On the other side was Bruce Jacob, a twenty-six-year-old graduate of Stetson University College of Law in Gulfport, Florida, who was chosen to represent the state's case. At the time that Gideon's writ was received by the Supreme Court, Jacob was working in the attorney general's office in Tallahassee in the criminal appeals section. The U.S. Supreme Court, in selecting Fortas, purposely stacked the deck.

At the time of the case, Abraham Fortas was a fifty-two-year-old high-powered Washington lawyer, a partner in the D.C. firm Arnold, Fortas and Porter. After graduating from Yale Law School, Fortas worked with a number of New Deal legal luminaries, and in 1942 he became undersecretary of the interior. He served in that position for four years before going into private practice. At the time of *Gideon*, Fortas was one of the top corporate lawyers in the country. As Anthony Lewis put it:

> Fortas's most important activities as a lawyer take place not in courtrooms but in the offices of corporations. He advises business executives on how to enlarge their market power and their profits while staying within the myriad rules laid down by government. . . . One acquaintance says his business is "corporate wheeling and dealing. . . ."[17]

It would have been difficult to find a representative who was more different than his client. Fortas was erudite and intellectual (as Lewis puts it, "with a touch of Mephistopheles"[18]); he was an art connoisseur, a violin virtuoso, and very wealthy. His wife, Carolyn Agger, was a highly successful corporate tax lawyer. In 1960, she was at the center of an insurgence that rocked the legal world when she led a revolt of partners from the firm Paul, Weiss, Rifkind, Wharton and Garrison. She defected to Fortas's firm, and took the other firm's entire Washington office with her.[19] The couple drove a Rolls-Royce and had a large collection of antique furniture and contemporary art in their Georgetown home.[20]

Fortas had a tremendous amount of resources from his law firm at his disposal with which to work on his *Gideon* brief. He hand-picked a selection of young and shrewd legal minds to help, including a young partner in the firm, Abe Krash; an associate, James F. Fitzpatrick; and a twenty-four-year-old Yale law student who was clerking at the firm for the summer, John Hart Ely. Ely's contribution to the main thrust of Fortas's argument before the court was incredibly important—during his summer post at Fortas's law firm, he wrote a set of memoranda discussing everything from the weakness of the *Betts* special circumstances rule to the question of whether the Fourteenth Amendment was intended to incorporate the Bill of Rights intact. Ely's research and analysis became the centerpiece of Fortas's argument before the court. (Ely went on to become the youngest member of the Warren Commission, and eventually became one of the most widely cited legal scholars in U.S. history before his death from cancer in 2003.)[21]

Meanwhile, back in Florida, in early March 1962, assistant Florida attorney general Reeves Bowen called Bruce Jacob into his office. He informed him that they had received a request from the Supreme Court, and asked Jacob to prepare a response. Over the next few months, the twenty-six-year-old lawyer worked with Bowen and other members of the attorney general's staff on the case.[22]

However, in between the time that he prepared the response to Gideon's writ and his actual appearance before the Supreme Court, a lot of changes had taken place in Jacob's life. After returning from a stint in the National Guard in June, Jacob had been interviewed for a position at the firm of Holland, Bevis and Smith in Bartow, Florida. Jacob was offered the position and took it. He was slated to work on the case in October. However, because of a delay in the filing of the Florida brief—mostly because of a disagreement between Fortas and Jacob as to whether the transcripts of Gideon's original trial could be included in the printed record—Jacob had switched jobs and was no longer on the attorney general's staff when he wrote the brief or argued the *Gideon* case.

In September, Jacob married Ann Wear, who ended up being a key partner in Jacob's work on the case. (Wear had been the personal secretary of the secretary of state of Florida.) Because Jacob had just started a new job, he decided that work on the *Gideon* case had to be done on his off hours. As a result, most weekends during the fall of 1962, Jacob and Wear drove two hundred and fifty miles to Tallahassee to the Florida Supreme Court Library or to the Stetson Law Library in Gulfport to do research. Jacob and his wife would also use the weekends to visit Judge Bowen regularly for consultation on the case. Jacob wrote the brief in longhand in the evenings in November and December; in the morning, his wife would type up what he had written. Though Jacob has argued otherwise—he claims that he "consulted with some members" of the Holland firm on the case—it is clear that the preparation of Florida's side of the case was considerably different from what was happening simultaneously in Washington, D.C., on Gideon's side of the case.

Regardless of the resources involved, there is no doubt that pitting Jacob against Fortas was an unequal pairing. There has been a tremendous amount of speculation about why a lawyer as inexperienced as Jacob was tapped for the case. Jacob claims that other members of the attorney general's office had already argued cases before the Supreme Court, and that it was essentially his turn. Despite this, even Jacob acknowledges, "Bowen could have kept the case for himself, on the ground that it required an older, more experienced lawyer."[23]

It's also quite possible that the state attorney general's office already saw the writing on the wall—that Betts was in trouble, since it had been roundly criticized by legal scholars for the past two decades. "The cases decided by the Court under the Betts formula are distinguished neither by the consistency of their results or the cogency of their argument," complained University of Michigan law professor Francis Allen in 1959 in the DePaul Law Review.[24] It was a criticism typical of the times. Perhaps because of these critiques, clear shifts were occurring in the Supreme Court itself; it had decided in favor of every state prisoner whose right-to-counsel claim it heard since 1950.

Jacob also inadvertently found out that few states backed Florida's position of refusing to provide legal counsel to the indigent. In the summer of 1962, he composed a letter that was sent out to all of the other state attorneys general in the country, asking them to submit amicus briefs on behalf of the state of Florida. The letter had the opposite effect. It alerted state attorney generals everywhere that Florida's fight was going all the way to the U.S. Supreme Court, and that this may well be an opportunity to secure Supreme Court backing for the indigent defense they understood as desperately needed. (Even today, the fact that the U.S. Supreme Court mandates free legal counsel for the indigent is a helpful tool to hold over state and local governments who routinely underfund public defender programs.) Meanwhile, back in 1962, only half the states responded to Jacob's call for amicus briefs—and most of them responded only by disagreeing, asserting instead that they thought providing free criminal defense for those who couldn't afford it was a good idea. In fact, many states were already doing just that. Walter F. Mondale, then attorney general of Minnesota (and eventual vice president of the United States), went even further. He wrote Jacob back, telling him that the courts were wrong on *Betts* anyway. "I believe in federalism and states rights," he said. "But I also believe in the Bill of Rights."[25] Then, he got up on his soapbox and sent a copy of his letter (and Jacob's) to a slew of folks, including the attorney general of Massachusetts, Edward McCormack Jr., and his assistant attorney general, Gerald Berlin. They took things a step further. Not only did they decline to file an amicus brief on Florida's behalf, McCormack and Berlin decided to file an amicus brief on Gideon's behalf. They distributed the brief to all the other attorneys general around the country—and twenty-two states signed on, urging the court to reconsider *Betts*.

On August 28 of that year, U.S. Supreme Court Justice Felix Frankfurter retired, another development tipping the scales in Gideon's favor as the case crept forward. Throughout his career, Frankfurter was a huge proponent of judicial restraint and the importance of precedent, and he was also a firm believer in the importance of states' rights. Frankfurter's conservative, positivist views seemed antiquated during a time of a more liberal, activist-leaning court. "There is now almost a universal consensus that Frankfurter, the justice, was a failure, a judge who . . . became 'uncoupled from the locomotive of history' during the Second World War, and who thereafter left little in the way of an enduring jurisprudential legacy," legal scholar Michael E. Parrish once said of the judge.[26] And indeed, this made his retirement particularly fortuitous as Frankfurter had been a proponent of *Betts*. This stance had put him squarely at odds with Justice Hugo Black, which was not the only source of tension between the men but was indicative of how ideologically opposed they were and how fractious their relationship had become. If Frankfurter represented the idea of conservative restraint, Black was the epitome of liberal activism. The stories of their disputes are the stuff of Supreme Court lore: Frankfurter once wrote to Justice John M. Harlan that a Black opinion "makes me puke!" and after a heated conversation in closed chambers, Black told his son, "I thought Felix was going to hit me today, he got so mad."[27] If anyone was going to rally the conservative block to uphold *Betts*, it was Frankfurter. With him gone, *Betts* was clearly in jeopardy. Gideon stood a good chance of winning.

Finally, on January 15, 1963, the Supreme Court heard oral arguments in *Gideon v. Wainwright*. Everyone in the legal community understood the huge ramifications of this decision—and all eyes were on the court.

The morning before, Bruce Jacob had to arrange for his admission to the Supreme Court Bar—a prerequisite to arguing before the court. A lawyer is eligible only after three years practicing in a state's highest court. Jacob barely made the requirement.

Meanwhile Fortas, who had argued before the U.S. Supreme Court on numerous occasions, used his casual Tennessee twang to soften his sharp arguments. He began by assuring the judges that they were deciding an easy, "narrow" issue.

"The question, of course, is the right of accused in State criminal proceedings to the appointment of counsel. . . . In the present case which you have before you, the question is an exceedingly narrow one," he began. "The question in the present case is whether . . . the accused being concededly indigent, it is the duty of the State to accede to that request and to appoint counsel."[28] He went on to build his case by explaining why the Betts Rule did not apply, and yet had, in any case, become completely obsolete. "This record . . . does not indicate that Clarence Earl Gideon is a man of inferior natural talents," he said. "This record does not indicate that Clarence Earl Gideon is a moron or a person of low intelligence. This record does not indicate that the judge of the trial court in the state of Florida, or that the prosecuting attorney in the state of Florida, was derelict in his duty. On the contrary, it indicates that they tried to help Gideon. But to me, if the Court please, this record indicates the basic difficulty with Betts against Brady. And the basic difficulty with Betts against Brady is that no man, certainly no layman, can conduct a trial in his own defense so that the trial is a fair trial."

"Betts and Brady did not proceed on that basis," corrected Justice Harlan. "It did not deny the obvious. Obviously, a man . . . who is not represented . . . hasn't had as good a shake in Court as the man who is represented. Betts and Brady didn't go on any such basis as that."

Fortas didn't miss a beat. "[A]re you suggesting, Mr. Justice Harlan . . . that the real basis for Betts against Brady is the following: That a man does not get a fair trial if he . . . is not represented by a lawyer, but that the demands of federalism overweigh the absence of a fair trial?"

"That's what I understood the basis of Betts and Brady to be, yes," said Justice Harlan.

Fortas circled around to state the obvious, but got his simple argument on the record. "I believe that the right way to look at this, if I may put it that way, is that a court, a criminal court is not properly constituted, and this has been said in some of your own opinions under our adversary system of law, unless there is a judge, and unless there is a counsel for the prosecution, and unless there is a counsel for the defense," he says. "Without that, how can a civilized nation pretend that it is having a fair trial under our adversary system, which means that counsel for the State will do his best within the limits of fairness and honor and decency to present the case for the State and counsel for the defense will do his best similarly to present the best case possible for the defendant and from that clash there will emerge the truth? That is our concept."

Very quickly, the topic moved into the general concept of federalism and states' rights, that oldest of arguments among American thinkers and politicians since the country's founding: What is the right balance of power between the federal government and the state governments? "Well, that isn't quite so simple as that," said Justice Harlan, "because under our concepts in the federal system, apart from the Sixth Amendment, we would consider that a man in a felony case hadn't had a fair shake if he wasn't tried before a jury. I suppose the State could do away with the jury trial and yet you wouldn't say this trial was inherently unfair, would you?"

"That's right," Fortas agreed.

"I think you've got to argue this on the basis of federalism," Justice Harlan said.

"I appreciate that and I am happy if we can clear the debris, if I may say so," Fortas went on. "And I just want to say and to nail this, if I may, that we are not, and we cannot, as I think this colloquy has disclosed, Mr. Justice Harlan, proceed on the assumption that there is any such thing as a fair criminal trial where the defendant is not represented by counsel."

"Well, this federalism that Justice Harlan mentions is implicit," said Justice William O. Douglas. "I don't know if . . . any member of this Court has come out and said in so many terms, it's the constitutional right of the State to provide a system whereby people get a fair trial."

"Well, Mr. Justice Douglas—" Fortas began.

"I don't believe I suggested that, I don't suppose—" Justice Harlan interrupted.

"I thought that's what we were talking about, isn't it?" Justice Douglas asked. "You mean, if a person can't have a fair trial without a lawyer and this is the problem of federalism, you come down to . . . how a State has a constitutional right to provide a system that perpetuates unfair trials?"

"I do believe that it is a proposition that proves itself," Fortas said. "We start with the proposition that the Fourteenth Amendment requires a fair trial and we say that the defendant in a criminal proceeding cannot get a fair trial unless he has counsel. . . . I think I may be wrong about this, but I do believe that in some of this Court's decisions, there has been a tendency from time to time because of the pull of federalism to forget . . . the realities of what happens downstairs, of what happens . . . to these poor, miserable, indigent people when they are arrested and they are brought into the jail, and they are questioned. And later on, they are brought in these strange and awesome circumstances before a magistrate, and then later on they are brought before a court. And there, Clarence Earl Gideon, defend yourself. . . . Construe the Statute of the State of Florida which says that breaking and entering with intent to commit a misdemeanor is a felony. You should know, Clarence Earl Gideon, that the State of Florida, the Supreme Court of the State of Florida, has construed this statute and it has made available to you various defenses. Well, then, how can Clarence Earl Gideon do it?

"I was reminded the other day as I was pondering this case about Clarence Darrow's trial," Fortas continued. "Irving Stone's book says that the first thing that Clarence Darrow realized was that he had to have a lawyer. He was a man who, by our folklore anyway . . . was our greatest criminal lawyer. *He* needed a lawyer. He *got* a lawyer. He was eventually acquitted. But I think that in some of the Court's opinions, if I may say so, Mr. Justice Harlan, this element, this failure to remember what happens downstairs, has crept in not because of an insensitivity of the judges, but because of the understandable pull of the sensitivity about the State's own jurisdiction . . ."

Justice Harlan interrupted to correct him. "*Understandable sensitivity* to describe a basic principle of our Government doesn't seem to me to be a very happy expression."

"Well, I'm—uh—I'm sorry, sir," Fortas apologized.

According to Anthony Lewis, who was present in the courtroom, this last exchange angered Justice Harlan. "This usually gentle man visibly reddened," he noted.

Approximately fifty minutes into the argument, the justices acknowledged the elephant in the room. What about the financial costs and problem of caseloads? If federal law mandated a right to counsel for *all* indigent defendants, wouldn't that put an unfair burden upon the states? Justice Potter Stewart questioned Fortas on one hypothetical. "How about the traffic violation?" he demanded. "A person who can afford a lawyer is entitled, as far as I know in every state, to hire a lawyer for [a] traffic violation."

"I see no real difficulty," Fortas replied, "in saying to . . . people . . . when they're arrested for [a] traffic violation, 'If you want to see the public defender, he's in Room 102,' and to assign [one]." Fortas was insistent that the logistical and financial problems here were surmountable. "It really works," he said. "It will work. It sounds crazy, perhaps, but it [will] work. It will work. I'm sure it will."

"Suppose you don't have [a public defender]?" Justice Tom C. Clark asked.

"More and more states, Mr. Justice Clark, are building orderly systems and, of course, one of the great functions that this Court performs by announcing the law and clarifying the principles of law is to provide an impetus to the States to erect such systems," Fortas said. "But there are many systems that are now available—"

"I just wonder if the legal aid would want to take on a traffic [violation]?" Clark continued. "They have so many felons already. . . ."

"Again, Mr. Justice Clark, I think that . . . if I may use a vulgarism, the 'oddball' who's involved in a minor traffic offense who will say that he wants a lawyer," Fortas said. "But . . . if a person involved in [a] traffic offense has a real problem and a real defense and . . . thinks he should have a lawyer, why not?"

With this problem of scope hanging in the air, the justices called a lunch break. Fortas ate at a table across from Jacob in a room set aside for lawyers, and the two, according to their respective accounts, chatted amicably, Fortas apologizing because he had mailed a letter to Jacob inviting him to a dinner party at his house the night before, but he had sent it to Jacob's old address—and so Jacob had not received it in time. After lunch, the two men filed back into the formal chambers and Fortas continued his argument. Toward the last five minutes of Fortas's time, Justice Stewart brought up the Fourteenth Amendment clause ("No State shall . . . deny to any person within its jurisdiction the equal protection of the laws").[29] Fortas had avoided that clause, and instead focused on the Due Process Clause ("No State shall make or enforce any law which shall abridge the privileges or immunities of citizens of the United States; nor shall any State deprive any person of life, liberty, or property, without due process of law"[30]). Justice Stewart wondered about this.

"Could you—in telling us your thoughts as to the scope of this right, are you—just as a matter of technique, are you relying now on [the] Equal Protection Clause?" Justice Stewart followed up.

"I think that the Equal Protection Clause teaches us something here," Fortas explained. "That is to say, you can say that equal protection means that the indigents in a situation where the State is an adversary, a criminal procedure, that [the] Equal Protection Clause requires that the poor shall not be subject to a disability to which the rich are not subject."

"You are arguing equal protection rather than the Due Process Clause?" Justice Stewart asked.

"That is equal protection. So far as I'm concerned, Your Honor, I reached the result—"

"Either one?" Steward interjected.

"—through the Due Process Clause standing alone and I can— and I also get comfort from the Equal Protection Clause," Fortas said. "But I believe the Equal Protection Clause reaches only a phase of this problem, and the Due Process Clause reaches it in its entirety and is self-sufficient."

Fortas had tried to concentrate on the Due Process Clause rather than the Equal Protection Clause because bringing up the latter opened the Pandora's box of whether or not the Fourteenth Amendment mandated states to incorporate the Bill of Rights or not. He had skirted the delicate issue a bit by not concentrating on the thorny and complicated question of what constituted "equal protection."

But Justice Black, who had argued continuously throughout his career that the Fourteenth Amendment incorporated the Bill of Rights, grew irritated. "Am I to understand that you think the Fifth Amendment's guarantee or the Constitution's guarantee of the right to counsel has nothing to do with this?" he demanded. "It solely deals with due process?"

"I didn't say that," Fortas corrected.

"Do I understand that you lay aside the federal guarantee of the right to counsel?" Black asked.

"No sir, I certainly do not lay it aside," Fortas said. "And you'll see in our brief that we argue it[, but] not, Mr. Justice Black, in terms of the argument that the Fourteenth Amendment incorporates with respect to the States the provision of the Bill of Rights."

"Well, with reference to . . . what, then?" Justice Black inquired. "Sir?"

"How does the Fourteenth Amendment do it?"

"Fourteenth Amendment? Mr. Justice Black, I like that argument that you have so eloquently made time and time again—" There is laughter on the bench and in the audience at this. "I can't make it to this Court as an advocate because this Court's turned it down so many times." More laughter. "I hope and pray that you will never cease contending for it."

As Fortas's time wound down, J. Lee Rankin, one-time solicitor general in the Eisenhower administration, then came up as a friend of the court on behalf of the American Civil Liberties Union. The ACLU's argument focused less on Gideon and his particular case, and more on the general state of indigent representation in the country. Rankin was brief but pointed and ended his remarks by saying that he believed that the reconsideration of *Betts* could not simply be prospective—that is, only apply to cases from that point forward. "I do think that there is a problem if you determine something is unconstitutional, in my own thinking, to not apply it back to where the error occurred. I know," he continued, "there are those who have advocated to the contrary, but for myself, I do not accept that and I would ask that you go back to the point where the error occurred and correct it."

Then, Jacob stood up to argue his side. Later, he'd describe feeling like he was "in a pit" as he stood before the justices who he recognized were predisposed to argue against him. The questioning was absolutely brutal, and even when I speak to Jacob forty-nine years later on the phone, he vividly recalls the "nerve-racking" moment in tremendous detail. "The court bombarded me with questions," he tells me. "There were ninety-two interruptions and almost all came during the first thirty minutes. That's three times a minute." (The court had allowed for hour-long—as opposed to the usual half-hour long—arguments in the case.) Because he had never argued before the Supreme Court before, he neglected to even bring a pencil or paper to the lectern with him so that he might jot down the justice's overlapping questions and make sure he addressed each. "Questions came so fast, I would be trying to answer one and another justice would interrupt with another question. And before I could get to that second one, a third justice would butt in—and I'd try to remember who had asked what."[31]

Jacob began by giving some general background on Gideon. He brought up Fortas's demand, made several months earlier, that the original trial transcript be included in the official record. It was a bad tactic.

An irritated Justice Harlan immediately attacked him. "Why do you have to waste time on that?"

"Okay, Your Honor, I was—I wanted to be sure that the Court did not rule upon the transcript as it appears in this—" Jacob said.

"His position is that we are faced in this case really with either affirming, adhering to Betts against Brady, or overruling it," Justice Harlan corrected. "And that's the only premise he's argued his case on."

"Okay, Your Honor, I'll proceed with our argument—"

"Well, I take it you're not raising any questions at all about this being, the judgment that's here for review, being a final judgment—" Justice Byron R. White interrupted.

"No, Your Honor."

"—of the highest court in the State of Florida, on the merits. . . . And there's no question of our appellate jurisdiction here?" Justice White continued.

"No, Your Honor."

This examination set the tone for Bruce Jacob's entire appearance. Six years after the appearance, in a letter to the *Harvard Law Review*, Jacob described his dawning realization of what he was up against. "It became obvious, during the argument, how deeply the Court was committed to the overthrow of *Betts v. Brady* and its progeny," he wrote. "Never in the eighteen cases which I had previously argued in the Florida Supreme Court and other appellate courts had I encountered anything like the zeal and emotion that emerged in the questioning. Anger seemed to characterize my most relentless questioner. [Jacob was referring specifically to Justice Hugo Black.] A constant rain of hostile questions came from most of the justices. Concessions made in a spirit of candor that I thought to be the State's duty seemed only to excite fresh attack. Florida's position was obviously hopeless; my ten months of work devoted to the case were of little avail."[32]

Jacob admits the barrage of questions flustered him. And there was a certain condescending attitude exhibited at moments, such as when Jacob suggested that states should have the freedom to experiment with various low-level criminal proceedings, even possibly doing away with counsel on either side and letting a judge handle the case by himself. This evoked a response from Justice John M. Harlan: "Careful now. Don't go too far."

Jacob's nadir came when he suggested a non-lawyer could defend another person. "And of course, I think [a defendant] can have adequate representation even though he represents himself in some instances," he said. "It would be absurd—"

"But I suppose I am right in my assumption that I made earlier that Florida wouldn't permit Gideon or any other layman to defend anyone else in the State on trial, would it?" Justice Potter Stewart asked.

"No, it wouldn't, Your Honor," Jacob said. "Gideon could—if a man came into court and said, I want to be defended by Gideon, then certainly the court would not object."

"It wouldn't?" Justice Black demanded.

"Wouldn't Gideon maybe get in trouble for practicing law without a license?" Justice Stewart said.

"With the local bar association?" Justice Black pursed.

"I'm sorry, Your Honor," Jacob conceded. "That was a stupid answer."

After Jacob concluded, George Mentz, assistant attorney general of Alabama, one of only two states (North Carolina was the other one) that had offered an amicus brief on Florida's behalf, came forward. Mentz basically reiterated the states' rights position, and then at one point tried to suggest that some indigents might be *better off* without a lawyer. "[A]t the last meeting of the bar association, when I talked to a group of the state solicitors and they were of the widespread agreement that an indigent appearing without aid of counsel really stood a better chance of getting a lighter sentence or even an outright acquittal than one who does have an attorney," Mentz said. "And I think one reason for that is that the prosecuting attorney feels free to pull out all the stops if he's got an opponent and the average opponent, at least in Alabama, the average lawyer there is just not sufficiently versed in criminal practice to cope with most of your career prosecutors." He continued: "Another thing, I think that since *Betts v. Brady* there's been a progression in the education of most groups and I believe that if the average man who has got a real valid defense is sufficiently articulate enough to get it across to the jury—he may not do it in the nice legal niceties, but he gets the story across."

"That's not very complimentary to our profession, is it?" Justice Black observed dryly.

"Well, not completely, no, sir."

At the end of Mentz's argument, Justice Harlan asked a pointed question about the efficacy of *Betts* in contemporary legal terms. "Supposing you had the choice . . . of maintaining Betts and Brady on the books, and then having a succession of cases in this Court where in every instance where a state did not appoint counsel, the case is brought up here and you have it automatically reversed, finding special circumstances, so that while Betts and Brady is being obeyed in form—paid lip service to—any discerning person would know that unless the State does that, the case is coming up here and getting reversed?" he asked. "Do you think that between maintaining that kind of a situation and just getting Betts and Brady off the books, which would you think was the better?"

"I'd rather see each case decided individually," Mentz said.

"Even though you know they're all going to be decided the one way?"

"Well," Mentz quipped, "hope springs eternal."

As onlookers chuckled, Fortas returned to the lectern for a short, five-minute rebuttal. It was at the end of his five minutes that Justice Harlan—the last positivist holdout after Justice Felix Frankfurter's departure and a firm advocate of *stare decisis*—expressed his concern about what the ramifications of this case really were: "[W]hat one is left with is to get his hands on something that has happened between 1942 and 1963 that has made what the Court then regarded as constitutional suddenly become unconstitutional."

His comment was a fairly overt signal as to which way the justices were leaning. And indeed, the court announced its unanimous decision in favor of Gideon on March 18, 1963. *Gideon* overruled *Betts*, making the Sixth Amendment's right-to-counsel provision applicable to all felony cases. Not surprisingly, Justice Hugo Black penned the decision. Interestingly, despite the concerns of Justice Harlan, Black made no attempt to suggest that the overruling was necessary due to legal and social shifts in the two decades since *Betts*. Instead, he claimed that the court had "made an abrupt break with its own well-considered precedents."

"We think *Betts* was wrong . . . in concluding that the Sixth Amendment's guarantee of counsel is not one of these fundamental rights," he wrote. And referring to *Powell v. Alabama*, he said, "Ten years before *Betts v. Brady*, this Court . . . had unequivocally declared that 'the right to the aid of counsel is of this fundamental character. . . .' [I]ts conclusions about the fundamental nature of the right to counsel are unmistakable." And he continued:

> In returning to these old precedents, sounder, we believe, than the new, we but restore constitutional principles established to achieve a fair system of justice. Not only these precedents, but also reason and reflection, require us to recognize that, in our adversary system of criminal justice, any person haled into court, who is too poor to hire a lawyer, cannot be assured a fair trial unless counsel is provided for him. This seems to us to be an obvious truth. Governments, both state and federal, quite properly spend vast sums of money to establish machinery to try defendants accused of crime. Lawyers to prosecute are everywhere deemed essential to protect the public's interest in an orderly society. Similarly, there are few defendants charged with crime, few indeed, who fail to hire the best lawyers they can get to prepare and present their defenses. That government hires lawyers to prosecute and defendants who have the money hire lawyers to defend are the strongest indications of the widespread belief that lawyers in criminal courts are necessities, not luxuries. . . . The Court in *Betts v. Brady* departed from the sound wisdom upon which the Court's holding in *Powell v. Alabama* rested. Florida, supported by two other States, has asked that *Betts v. Brady* be left intact. Twenty-two states, as friends of the Court, argue that *Betts* was "an anachronism when handed down," and that it should now be overruled. We agree.[33]

Though the decision was unanimous, three other opinions were also entered into the record—a separate opinion from Justice Douglas, and two concurrences, one each by Justices Clark and Harlan. For his part, Harlan agreed that *Betts* should be overturned, but he considered it "entitled to a more respectful burial than has been accorded." Harlan's main point was that *Betts* had actually not broken precedent as Black suggested. According to Harlan, *Powell* rested on its own set of "special circumstances" and *Betts* had actually expanded indigent defense by suggesting that it could be applied in noncapital cases. "At the same time, there have been not a few cases in which special circumstances were found in little or nothing more than the 'complexity' of the legal questions presented, although those questions were often of only routine difficulty," he wrote. "The Court has come to recognize, in other words, that the mere existence of a serious criminal charge constituted, in itself, special circumstances requiring the services of counsel at trial. In truth, the *Betts v. Brady* rule is no longer a reality."[34]

And while some states have made strides in acknowledging this reality, others have failed to do so. "This evolution, however, appears not to have been fully recognized by many state courts, in this instance charged with the front-line responsibility for the enforcement of constitutional rights," he added. "To continue a rule which is honored by this Court only with lip service is not a healthy thing, and, in the long run, will do disservice to the federal system."[35]

As a result of the Supreme Court's decision, Clarence Earl Gideon was now eligible for a new trial—this time with counsel. The Florida ACLU stepped forward with an attorney, but Gideon was oddly uncooperative about the appointment of his new lawyer. After Gideon wrote a letter to the Florida ACLU asking for support, an attorney from the organization, Tobias Simon, went to meet with him at Raiford in April of 1963. Gideon was highly agitated; he believed that he could not get a fair trial—it was scheduled to take place in the same district, before the same judge—and that the new trial would constitute "double jeopardy." (It wouldn't.) The new court date was July 5. Simon went to Panama City with Irwin J. Block, a criminal lawyer who had offered to assist him on the case. Gideon refused to meet with them, and the next day, when Gideon, Simon, Block, and the prosecutors met in Judge McCrary's chambers, a distressed Gideon told the judge that he did not want the two lawyers to represent him, that he wanted a change of venue, and that *he wanted to plead his own case.* "I don't want them to represent me. I DO NOT WANT THEM," he said.[36]

McCrary excused Simon and Block (Simon later wrote an article about the experience, which was subtitled, "How the Florida Civil Liberties Union Wasted $300, and How Two Attorneys

Each Traveled over 120 Miles and Killed an Otherwise Perfectly Enjoyable July Fourth Weekend"[37]), but the judge made it clear that on no account would he allow Gideon once again to conduct his own defense. He asked Gideon if there was *anyone* who he felt would be acceptable counsel. Gideon responded, yes, there was: W. Fred Turner, a local criminal lawyer.

Why Gideon chose Turner is unclear. It may have been because Turner had represented Gideon's wife at one point in an attempt to get child support, so Turner was on Gideon's radar. Also, Gideon would know that Turner was a local—Turner knew the lay of the land quite literally, where the pool hall was in relation to the phone booth and rooming house. He knew the local folks who would be in the jury pool—and they knew him.

In any case, Turner's work on Gideon's behalf essentially proved the point of right-to-counsel supporters—that having a lawyer can make all the difference in the world. He began by laying down the law. He sharply reprimanded Gideon for meddling in the case, telling him, "I'll only represent you if you will stop trying to be the lawyer."[38] On August 5, when the trial began, Turner paid particular attention to the jury selection process. In contrast to Gideon's approach ("They suit me alright, Your Honor"), Turner made sure he personally knew four out of the six of them. He quickly struck two prospective jurors, one because he was a "teetotaler" and the other because it was clear that he generally favored conviction. Three of the jurors were admitted gamblers, a point that Turner believed would work in Gideon's favor.

The key way that Turner was useful to Gideon, however, was in planting seeds of doubt in the minds of the jurors. For example, Turner was very familiar with the prosecution's key witness, Henry Cook—he had, in fact, represented him in a different case and knew about his previous run-ins with the law. Casting doubt on his credibility as a witness, Turner asked Cook, "Have you ever been convicted of a felony?"[39]

"I stoled a car one time and got put on probation for it," Cook answered.

During the previous trial, Gideon had asked whether Cook had ever been convicted of a felony, and he responded, "No, sir, never have." Turner jumped on this. "The last time you testified in this case you denied that, didn't you?"

"Now, if the Court please, that is not proper cross-examination by Mr. Turner and the State objects to it," the prosecutor quickly countered.

"Rephrase your question, Mr. Turner," the judge said.

There was some back-and-forth as Turner rephrased and the prosecutor interrupted him with objections.

"I can point out his prior inconsistent testimony any time, Mr. Harris," Turner said, deftly explaining to the jury just why this is not a credible witness.

"You can ask the question, Mr. Turner," the judge said, "if you will do it properly, lay the proper predicate for the question, then ask the question, if you will do it properly, you may proceed."

"Well, Your Honor, I'm trying to do it that way," Turner said.

"If you are going to argue about it, let's not do [that] in the presence of the jury," the judge said. "Mr. Sheriff, will you take the jury out, please."

After about ten minutes of lawyerly wrangling at the bench, the judge called the jury back in. Despite more objections from the prosecution, Turner managed to continue his line of questioning. "Mr. Cook," he said. "Have you ever denied, under oath, that you had been convicted of a felony? Prior to today, I'm speaking of."

"Yes, I did—" Cook said.

"When and where did you deny your criminal record, Mr. Cook?"

"Right here, the last time [Gideon] was tried, two years ago."

Later, the prosecutor tried to restore Cook's credibility. ("What did you mean when you said you had not been convicted of a felony and yet, you say you pled guilty to stealing an automobile?" "Well, I didn't quite understand what a felony was.") However, the damage was done.

By the time he gave his closing argument, Turner had masterly planted an idea in the jury's collective head—via small, specific details about what was stolen and how much money was taken—to suggest that Cook should actually have been the one on trial. "The probationer has been out at a dance drinking beer," he said. "He does a peculiar thing [when he sees Gideon in the poolroom]. He doesn't call the police, he doesn't notify the owner, he just walks to the corner and walks back. . . . Why was Cook walking back and forth? I'll give you the explanation: He was the lookout." Significantly, Turner had also pointed out that the owners of the pool hall ran a gambling ring—and that Gideon was often hired to run one of the games. This explained why Gideon was apprehended with so much change in his pockets. He took a cut from the winnings each night, that's how he was paid.

After final arguments were completed, Judge McCrary reminded jurors that they must believe Gideon was guilty "beyond a reasonable doubt." After an hour and five minutes of deliberation, the jury returned with the verdict: not guilty.

After two years in prison, Gideon was a free man. Lewis mentions an anecdote at the end of *Gideon's Trumpet* in which, after the trial, a reporter sidled up to Gideon and asked him if he felt like he "accomplished something."

"Well, I did," Gideon replied.

Indeed, Gideon forever altered the criminal justice system for the poor in this country. There were seismic shifts in the way local governments provided indigent defense and in the various ways in which city, county, and state officials found funding for public defense programs or cobbled together alternatives. The progress was genuine and significant. But in the years since the court ruled in *Gideon*, the legal landscape has shifted dramatically. Between 1963 and 2013, massive changes have taken place in the culture and the courts: politicians have passed mandatory drug laws, cops have arrested folks in increasingly larger numbers, district attorneys have prosecuted more and more cases, the courts have jammed, incarceration rates have soared.

Ironically, one of the areas hardest hit by these changes—and the subsequent failure of the indigent defense system to keep pace with the demand for representation—is in Gideon's home state of Florida. There, the crisis in the overburdened courts reached epic proportions in the last decade. The chief public defender in Miami, struggling with massive caseloads, fell on his sword a few years back, sacrificing his job and reputation by refusing to accept more cases.

A visit to the Miami-Dade County public defender's office—or PD-11, as the program calls itself, referring to the county's status as the Eleventh Judicial Circuit—is instructive. Walking in the door to the office, the first thing visitors see is the program's "Commitment to Clients" printed on cream paper and showcased in a black frame in the waiting area. The sign mentions the usual commitments: the public defender's office will treat clients fairly, consult with clients on their cases, maintain attorney/client privilege, be loyal to clients, and handle cases competently and diligently. But three commitments stand out:

"Advocate for more access to mental health and substance abuse treatment services."

"Work to make our legal system more accessible and responsive to our clients and their families."

"Advocate for rehabilitation laws, including removing barriers to educational and employment opportunities."

These commitments focus on reform and a necessarily more holistic approach to the legal problems clients are encountering—a trend that is increasingly evident in large-city public defender systems—and the advocacy on behalf of this population is not all that surprising given PD-11's history. Starting with Bennett Brummer, the county's chief public defender for thirty-two years until 2009, and now continuing with Carlos Martinez, chief public defender since then, PD-11 has fought to reduce its excessive caseloads, which since 2004 began steadily climbing and by 2008 crept as high as seven-hundred-plus cases a year for some assistant public defenders.

"We were always overloaded," Brummer says, reflecting back on his long career as a public defender in Miami. "I've been overloaded for thirty years there. One more case doesn't make too much difference." But something happened in 2004—and things did get dramatically worse for public defenders in his office. To explain why, Brummer has to go back to 1978, one year after he was elected to his first four-year term as chief public defender and the year he filed the first of many "motion[s] for relief from excessive caseloads." Since then, he had been complaining to anyone who would listen that public defenders in Miami could not provide effective assistance of counsel when they had the high number of clients they were commonly assigned to cover. He filed a formal complaint, and by 1980 the case had moved up to the Third District Court of Appeal, which denied the motion. So he appealed the decision to the Supreme Court of Florida, which ruled in favor of PD-11, saying that the public defenders there should not be responsible for taking every case assigned to them, and, furthermore, if the state was not providing enough funding for indigent defense, the Miami-Dade county government would need to make up the difference.

Obviously, the county didn't care for this shift in responsibility. The Florida Supreme Court's decision meant Dade County would have to dedicate millions of dollars to indigent defense. And this would hold true for counties across the state that would suddenly be responsible for making up funding shortfalls. Banding together, the counties fought this decision. With their combined power, they were able to get a motion on the ballot at the next state election, giving residents an opportunity to vote on whether state governments should be the legislative body responsible for the state court system. The motion passed and, in 2004, the state began fully funding indigent defense again.

However, in the meantime, there were tremendous casualties and, in the protracted battle, as the state and counties battled over who would assume the burden of paying for public defense, public defender's offices across the state suffered. The Miami-Dade County public defender's office lost thirty-two attorney positions in the process.

Without these lawyers, PD-11's caseload grew worse. The American Bar Association, the National Advisory Commission on Criminal Justice System Standards and Goals, and the National Legal Aid & Defender Association all publish recommended caseload limits; the organizations advise a maximum of 150 noncapital felony cases per public defender, per year. Meanwhile, a Florida governor's commission on public defense set a maximum standard of 100 felony cases per lawyer per year while the Florida Public Defenders' Association recommends 200 cases.

No one says seven hundred cases per attorney is okay. And that, Brummer says, is the insane level at which public defenders in his office were expected to work. (In 2008, the *New York Times* reported that each lawyer handled five hundred cases a year; specific numbers from the era are hard to verify.) Attorneys who worked the misdemeanor circuit had twice as many cases: 2,225 in 2008 compared with 1,380 cases in 2005, the *Times* reports.

PD-11 also faced a slew of other challenges, including an 8.5 percent budget cut between 2007 and 2009 (losing a total of $2.4 million); high turnover among assistant public defenders due to low salaries ($42,000 starting salary); crippling time constraints caused by the also overburdened interpreters who were needed for so many cases in Miami—both for interviewing clients and witnesses in advance and for translating in court—and whose unavailability created delays; traffic in the Miami area, which had attorneys wasting endless hours traveling to and from the jail for interviews with their clients (significantly, this was a huge issue for them and recent technological upgrades have allowed some time-saving video conferences); and the Florida legislature's recent decision to give prosecutors several statutory resolution avenues to increase jail time, thereby increasing the time it takes for lawyers to complete these cases.

"You do your best to cope," Brummer says today, reflecting back on his days at PD-11 and his decision to bring his fight for reasonable caseloads to the courts themselves. "You don't want to be complaining. You want to make sure that by the time you go to court the numbers are so clear that the court can't in legitimacy deny your motion." With that in mind, and after four years of suffering the consequences that came with losing dozens of lawyers, Brummer filed a motion for relief in the Trial Court of Florida in 2008, asking that his office have the right to turn down future noncapital felony cases until the lawyers had caught up on their current workload. The Office of Criminal Conflict and Civil Regional Council, one of five offices in the state created in 2007 to represent the indigent in court when public defenders have a conflict, would be enlisted to pick up the slack and the remaining unassigned indigent clients.

PD-11 won, and on June 26, 2008, Chief Judge Joseph P. Farina of the Eleventh Judicial Circuit Court of Florida found that PD-11 could sometimes appoint other counsel to noncapital felony cases that had yet to be assigned to attorneys. New cases, Judge Farina ruled, would affect the office's ability to respond diligently to its current caseload, thus creating a conflict of interest.

But relief did not come. In July 2008, the state attorney's office for the Eleventh District Circuit Court of Florida, who requested and was given permission to participate in this case as an "amicus curiae," or friend of the court, filed a response to Judge Farina's decision, saying that the Office of Criminal Conflict and Civil Regional Council, which would handle PD-11's excessive noncapital felony cases, was not adequately staffed or funded to do so. The state attorney's office said that the trial court's decision to give PD-11 relief could set a precedent in which the Office of Criminal Conflict and Civil Regional Council could also file for relief if their caseloads become excessive. The state attorney's office also took issue with the fact that PD-11 was seeking relief from the 40,651 indigent defendants it represented in noncapital felony cases, which involve more violent and dangerous crimes, instead of the 46,888 misdemeanor cases. Furthermore, the office said that PD-11's motion for relief was not in the interest of the general public.

"I don't know how [the state attorney's office] can justify their positions that you can handle 700 or 800 cases a year if the lawyer is saying they can't do it," Brummer says, still sore about this response. The Third District Court of Appeal hasn't helped either, according to Brummer. "The nature of the judges there, they're like the most conservative you can imagine and the most irresponsible. . . . They put every obstacle they could in our way. They said that the office couldn't do anything about this and the chief defender couldn't do anything about this."

Carlos Martinez, Brummer's chief assistant public defender for twelve years and, since 2009, the chief public defender for PD-11, is equally baffled by the state attorney's office's response, pointing out that this is an ethical decision for the public defender. "I have never been able to figure out what their interest is," he says. "Their attorneys are just as overworked as our attorneys, so it makes no sense for them to jump in and say, 'You don't really have a workload issue.' . . . If the attorney can't investigate your case or talk to you, then how on earth is that the right to an attorney?"

The case was batted around the courts for several years until the state supreme court accepted jurisdiction in May 2010. It has been sitting there ever since; public defender caseloads remain largely unchanged.

Sadly, Florida's situation is not aberrant. It is the norm. Back in 1963, as the justices debated *Gideon*, one of the major concerns regarded the complexities and caseload ramifications of all the incarcerated folks asking for their cases to be retried, with attorneys to represent them. The worry (which turned out to be somewhat valid) was that states would be overburdened with old cases; after *Gideon*, no fewer than four thousand Florida convicts demanded new trials. But it has turned out that the bigger problem is the actual, current caseload that has exploded; in a sense, Justice Stewart's concern about traffic violations has come true—though instead of needing a lawyer for running a red light, Florida indigent defendants need them for carrying twenty grams or fewer of marijuana.

As a result, it's hard not to question Abe Fortas's response to Stewart's fears: "I see no real difficulty, Mr. Justice, in saying to . . . [someone] when they're arrested for [a] traffic violation, 'If you want to see the public defender, he's in Room 102,' and to assign a public [defender]." Fortas, unable to anticipate the changes coming with mandatory sentencing and drug laws, was blissfully ignorant and optimistic. "It really works," he said. "It will work. It sounds crazy, perhaps, but it [will] work. It will work. I'm sure it will."

Important legal decisions often come out of mundane circumstances and commonplace characters. Nine-year-old Linda Brown, who was denied admission to her elementary school in Topeka, Kansas, because of the color of her skin, led to *Brown v. Board of Education*. Ernesto Arturo Miranda, a laborer with a ninth-grade education who confessed to charges of rape and kidnapping without being informed of his right to counsel and against self-incrimination led to *Miranda v. Arizona* and the institution of "Miranda" rights. Fifteen-year-old John Tinker, who was suspended from his Des Moines, Iowa, high school for wearing a black armband to protest the Vietnam War, led to *Tinker v. Des Moines Independent Community*

School District and an extension of First Amendment rights to public school children. Similarly, there is nothing extraordinary about Clarence Earl Gideon, or the circumstances of his arrest and conviction. Indeed, one of the ACLU attorneys who eventually represented him referred to Gideon as "a nut."[40]

How do we have a conversation about indigent defense that allows human complexities to exist right alongside the fundamental notion that all poor are "deserving poor" and thus entitled to due process? From the very beginning—despite Henry Fonda's heroic portrayal of him in the movie—Clarence Earl Gideon has demanded that we address this fundamental problem of perception.

When he wrote his letter to the U.S. Supreme Court in 1962, Gideon was a fifty-one-year-old petty criminal and drifter. In October of that same year, Gideon mapped out his life story for his lawyer Abe Fortas, who had sent him a letter two weeks earlier requesting "a careful and detailed biographical description," emphasizing that he should be "absolutely accurate in any information that you send along." Gideon promptly complied, sending Fortas a meticulously detailed twenty-two-page letter detailing a circuitous and checkered past, a life, as he put it, of "utter folly and hopelessness." Gideon explained that he was born in Hannibal, Missouri, on August 30, 1910. His father died when he was three years old and his mother remarried two years later. Unhappy at home, Gideon "accepted the life of a hobo and tramp" at age fourteen, and ran away from home. His mother eventually tracked him down in California and brought him back to Hannibal, and had him put in jail. Gideon escaped, burgled a store for some clothes, was caught and put back into jail. This became the leitmotif for the next forty years of Gideon's life—a small petty crime, incarceration, another petty crime, another incarceration, and so on. ("I suppose," he wrote, "I am what is called individualist a person who will not conform.") He said in his letter:

> When I was arrested for stealing government property to wit an armory. [Gideon and his companions stole guns from an armory, but their getaway car got stuck in the mud and they were arrested when a deputy sheriff stopped by to help them.]

I was tried in Federal Court and on a plea of guilty was sentenced to Ft. Leavenworth Kansas prison for a term of three years with a concurant sentence of three years for conspiracy. I worked in shoe factory again. During this time I saved a little money that I was paid by the prison my parents had lost their home during the depersion. So I sent them my money to make a down payment on another place. I done a little over two years and was released on contional release January 1937. There still where not an jobs all though the government was helping the people by this time I was not entitled to any of this because by this time I am a outcast.[41]

Gideon's life more or less continues on this kind of trajectory. By the time he married his fourth wife, Ruthada Babineaux, in October 1955, Gideon had spent more than half of his life behind bars. He was also gambling heavily. After serving time on what he claimed were trumped-up charges in Panama City, Florida, Gideon served enough time in detention that his wife had "started to drink" and his children were placed in foster care. When Gideon was released, he found that his wife "was to far gone and I could get no help from the social workers." Gideon, "out of desperation," placed his children in the care of a Baptist church, a move that he eventually regretted. "Now I class that organization in the same class as I do the K.K.K. Because they hate to many persons and things. . . ."[42] He eventually lost contact with his wife and children, and was again picked up on various charges, including burglary and vagrancy (he maintained his innocence on these charges). By June 1961, Gideon was making what money he could from gambling, running poker games in the Bay Harbor Poolroom, and living in a rooming house across the street. He concluded his letter to Fortas thus:

> I am not proud of this biography. I hope that it may help you in preparing this case, I am sorry I could not write better I have done the best I could.
> I have no illusions about law and courts or people who are involved in them. I have read the complete history of law ever since the Romans first started writing them down and before of the laws of religions. I believe that each era finds a improvement in law each year brings something new for the benefit

of mankind. Maybe this will be one of those small steps forward, in the past thirty-five years I have seen great advancement in Courts in penal servitude. Thank you for reading all of this. . . .

Sincerely yours
Clarence Earl Gideon[43]

So the question remains, was he in fact guilty of breaking and entering, robbing the poolroom? Or was he innocent? Bruce Jacob, who represented the State of Florida in the case, tells me, when I talk to him on the phone one afternoon in the fall of 2011, that people ask him that question all the time. Instead, he says, they should be asking a different question: Did Clarence Earl Gideon really take on the U.S. Supreme Court all by himself? Or did he need a lawyer to do it?

As noted earlier, in Anthony Lewis's book about the case, and certainly in the movie, *Gideon's Trumpet*, Clarence Earl Gideon is portrayed as a down-and-out heroic everyman figure—a contradictory character. Contradictory because he simultaneously stated the obvious—the American legal system had become far too complex for the average person to navigate—and undercut it, figuring out a way to not only navigate the system but to successfully petition the highest court in the land. Gideon's petition is full of grammatical and spelling mistakes, as noted earlier and witnessed above. He had dropped out of school in eighth grade and even before then, his education was clearly spotty. Nevertheless, he invoked the formal language of the law with his *habeas corpuses* and *writ of certioraris* and references, in his letter to the U.S. Supreme Court, to the Bill of Rights and his Fourth, Fifth, and Fourteenth Amendment rights.

This is a man who spent his life in and out of prison and made what little money he had from small-stakes gambling. But he is also a person who wrote to his lawyers that he had "read the complete history of the law ever since the Romans started writing them down," who assisted other inmates with their legal needs, and who made a reference at one point to "Milton's essay on liberty" (though it is possible he was actually referring to John Stuart Mill's "On Liberty"). Fonda, in the movie *Gideon's Trumpet*, reinforces the image of David meeting Goliath, Gideon taking on American juris-prudence. The movie delivered a sanitized-for-public-consumption version of Gideon's story to the broader public. But since the book's publication and the movie's airing, what we know about Clarence Earl Gideon has changed—and the story's looping complexities pile up, throwing into question the received wisdom about the landmark case—and casting a shadow of doubt on the official story line of Clarence Earl Gideon's singular triumph.

In fact, the plot takes an odd twist.

"Fred Turner told me about [Joseph] Peel," Jacob tells me on the phone one afternoon—and, I admit, I am puzzled. What Jacob is trying to tell me is that Gideon in fact had a jailhouse lawyer while in prison. Literally. His cellmate was a notorious local attorney who had been convicted of murder. The story is long and convoluted but does, in fact, shed new light on Gideon's petition to the U.S. Supreme Court.

Gideon's cellmate in the Raiford prison was a man named Joseph A. Peel Jr. Peel, who came from a respectable Florida family, had been a West Palm Beach lawyer for many years. Then, during a 1952 divorce case, he instructed a client to lie. The Florida Circuit Court judge presiding over the case, Curtis E. Chillingworth, discovered the perjury and read Peel the riot act, publicly. The judge's rebuke destroyed Peel's reputation, killed his practice, and forced his resignation from the Florida Bar Association. Inexplicably, given his reputation, Peel was soon thereafter appointed to serve as a municipal judge in West Palm Beach. Very quickly, he created a lucrative side business issuing warrants for the investigation of gambling dens, while simultaneously tipping off the operators—for a cool $500. He also took kickbacks from moonshiners and the sellers of illegal lottery tickets. Peel's weekly take? Approximately $3,000, according to contemporaneous news accounts that would later surface.

Judge Chillingworth (a name and nemesis worthy of Hawthorne) discovered Peel's nefarious schemes, and confronted him in 1955, threatening to expose his crimes. On June 15, 1955, Chillingworth and his wife Marjorie disappeared from their oceanfront home. No one knew what happened to the couple and no bodies were ever found; this was a mystery locals puzzled over for five years. Then in 1959 a man named Floyd "Lucky" Holzapfel confessed to killing the Chillingworths, after being hired by Peel. Holzapfel and his accomplice had broken into the Chillingworths' home, he confessed. They beat the couple, bound and gagged them, and deposited them in a motorboat. Holzapfel and his accomplice took the boat four miles offshore, and after drifting for approximately an hour, tied lead weights to the couple's legs, and threw them overboard. Marjorie Chillingworth was unconscious after being pistol-whipped; however, her fifty-eight-year-old husband, despite being weighed down by lead weights, attempted to swim ashore. In order to stop him, one of the killers hit him over the head with an oar. He sank from sight.[44]

In 1959, Holzapfel was lured into confessing to the murders through an elaborate sting operation, and eventually turned state's witness against Peel in return for having his death sentence commuted to life behind bars. Holzapfel testified that Peel hired him and his accomplice because Chillingworth intended to go public with Peel's misdeeds, not only forcing Peel from the bench, but dashing his hopes for higher office. On March 30, 1961, a jury convicted Peel and sentenced him to life in prison; he spent eighteen years at Raiford, where Gideon was incarcerated, before the state paroled him in 1979 in order for him to begin another eighteen-year federal sentence for mail fraud. In 1983, the parole board freed Peel after he was diagnosed with terminal cancer. Nine days after his release, he died. Not long before, Peel admitted his guilt—though barely. "I'm guilty of not using my influence to stop what was going to happen," Peel told the *Miami Herald* just days before his death, adding, "and I could."[45]

And here's where it gets interesting; the plotlines intersect. In 1963, Peel was placed in a maximum security cell at Raiford because, against prison rules, he'd been caught preparing writs for other prisoners' new trials under Florida's then-new public defender law. After *Gideon*, no fewer than four thousand Florida convicts demanded new trials. Peel himself prepared so many of these kinds of writs that he was called the "jailhouse attorney," and one prison official was quoted at the time as saying, "we just had to crack down on him for trying to practice law in prison."[46] Jacob, who went on to befriend Fred Turner, the lawyer who represented Gideon in his second criminal trial, says he and Turner had many conversations about Gideon. "Fred Turner told me that Gideon told him that Peel helped him out," Jacob recalls. "He said they were cell mates. Since then I've tried to figure out if they were actually in the same cell." The record shows they were in prison together. "I'm not 100 percent sure they were actual cell mates," Jacob tells me, "but Turner told me that. And according to Turner, they were writing that petition in their cell—and Joe Peel would stand over Gideon's shoulders, looking down and telling him what to say."[47] Jacob went on to suggest that Peel not only helped prepare Gideon's writ, but masterminded the idea of not including any "special circumstances" in it, so that the Supreme Court would be more inclined to use the case as an excuse to reexamine *Betts*. He also cynically suggests that Peel may have retained Gideon's misspellings and grammatical errors to impress the court with this determined but unlettered man. In any case, there is little doubt that the colorful Joseph Peel was an unrecognized character in the drama of *Gideon*—in a way that both challenges and affirms the reasoning behind the Supreme Court's decision. While Americans tend to espouse the notion of an uneducated underdog taking on the unfair laws of the land, the truth may be that even Clarence Earl Gideon needed a lawyer to prove his point, that all men need lawyers in the court of law.

CHAPTER 3

Greg Bright sits on his porch in May 2012, reflecting on the twenty-seven years he spent wrongly imprisoned. "It feels like a minute since I been out here," he says, musing over the notion of time—time past, time lost, time wasted. Photo by Karen Houppert.

A PERFECT STORM:

LOOKING FOR JUSTICE IN NEW ORLEANS

The coroner's report is a yawn—just another dead black boy, in a city where 183 died that year. He wrote:

> The body is that of a thin, small, young black male, appearing his stated age of 15 years, weighing 113 lbs. and measuring 4' 10" in height. The head is covered with black hair, which is braided and bloody. There are two recent bullet entry wounds of the left temple . . . There are tattooes [sic] over the left forearm, the letter "W." and a figure resembling an asterisk, over the right upper arm, "W." There is a transverse 3.5 x 0.1 cm. scar on the left antecubital skin. No needle tracts or recent punctures can be seen anywhere. The chest and abdomen are symmetrical. The genitalia are well developed.

The coroner, pathologist, and morgue attendant viewing the body of teenager Elliot Porter at the New Orleans City Morgue at 9 A.M. on October 31, 1975, agreed that rigor mortis was not yet present. Based on this, the boy could not have died more than three hours earlier. They estimated the time of death as between 5 A.M. and 8 A.M. that same morning.

This seemingly inconsequential detail would prove important to Greg Bright, one of the men accused of murdering the boy.

But getting to it would take twenty-seven years.

New Orleans has its own peculiar notions of time. This is true on a day-to-day level where folks may turn up for a scheduled appointment at the agreed-upon hour, but are just as likely to turn up an hour later. It is also true on a month-to-month level, where citizens—largely poor, black male ones—can be legally held in jail for up to two, three, or four months while the district attorney takes his time deciding whether or not he will prosecute them for a crime. (Locals call it "doing DA time," and it shocks the sensibilities of most in the legal community where seventy-two hours is the national norm.) It is also true on an epochal level where most of the world divides time between B.C. and A.D. but New Orleans residents organize history into the sweeping categories "pre-Katrina" and "post-Katrina."

Time is a relative thing in Louisiana. Justice, too. Talk to almost anyone in the New Orleans criminal justice system and they will laud the "post-Katrina" reforms. But this is a little like celebrating the move from caves to shacks. (This is not an abstract metaphor; the Orleans Parish Prison still houses hundreds of its residents in oversize tents in the heart of this often sweltering city, visible from a nearby highway overpass as drivers glance beyond the coils of razor wire.) When Hurricane Katrina hit in August of 2005, it laid bare the hoards of problems that besieged the poor in this city. Fixing these problems is taking time, New Orleans's time—leisurely, friendly, wink-and-nod, hot, humid, old-world, slow-moving, don't-kick-up-a-sweat time.

Like a stop-action film, criminal justice in the city flickers slowly enough to be studied frame by frame. This makes the city a good place to see how the various pieces fit—or fail to fit—together into a workable system that protects the constitutional rights of the accused, addresses the restorative needs of victims, and ensures public safety. After all, Louisiana is the largest "consumer" of the justice system. It sends more people to prison per capita than any other state in the country. It executes more people than forty-one other states do.[1]

In 2012, state inmates numbered more than forty thousand. As New Orleans's *Times-Picayune* newspaper observed in a meticulously reported and deeply troubling eight-part exposé called "Louisiana Incarcerated: How We Built the World's Prison Capital" in May 2012, "one in 86 adult citizens is behind bars"—and many of them will live out their lives there due to the state's especially harsh mandatory sentencing laws. It is one of only six states that completely exclude the possibility of parole for lifers[2]—and leads the nation in the percentage of those behind bars who are serving life without the possibility of parole.[3] In 2012, that translated to 4,500 "lifers" and approximately $1 million per prisoner if he enters in his twenties, as most do, and lives to his seventies.

Despite decades of these tough-on-crime, zero-tolerance, three-strikes, lock-'em-up-and-throw-away-the-key policies, Louisiana's murder rate was the highest in the country last year, according to the FBI's Uniform Crime Report.[4] And Louisiana's largest city, New Orleans, consistently has the highest homicide rate in the nation with 58 murders per 100,000 residents in 2011 (compared to the national average of 5 per 100,000).[5] It also has more miscarriages of justice than almost every other state, exonerating more people on death row or serving life sentences per capita than everyone but Illinois, according to the National Exoneration Registry.[6]

So what's going on with the cops and the jails and the prisons and the courts and, indeed, the whole criminal justice system there that it so profoundly fails its citizens? This is a question that has plagued a small but persistent group of reformers in New Orleans who, in the aftermath of Katrina, saw an opportunity to step into the vacuum left in the storm's wake and reinvent the way that justice is perceived and delivered in the city.

They seized the moment. Against the tremendous obstacles of entrenched corruption, cronyism, patronage, and a history of racist practices, they made real progress. But this is not a success story. This is a miles-to-go-before-we-sleep narrative in which, in order to understand the strides the city and state have made, it's important to set the recent past up against the present, Greg Bright's pre-Katrina story against Clarence Jones's post-Katrina experience in 2012. These two indigent African American men—accused of murder and burglary, respectively—span the range of crimes and years that saw reformers battling a deeply flawed criminal justice system in New Orleans.

On the night of October 30, 1975, fifteen-year-old Elliot Porter clumped down the stairs of his home in New Orleans's Central

City Calliope Project. "It was about something to eleven when I asked him not to go outside," his mother Myrtle Porter recalled at the time. She heard him clambering down the steps from where she lay on her bed and called out, telling him to stay put. It was a Thursday night. "You've got to go to school tomorrow," she told the eighth grader. "And, he say, 'I'm not going anywhere. I'm going right downstairs.'"[7]

But he did not just go downstairs. He went outside. He took a walk with some friends and never came back. The next morning, a paperboy delivering the *Times-Picayune* discovered his body in a crawl space beneath another building in the projects. There were two bullet holes in his head.

Police began looking for leads, interviewing family members, people in the projects, a friend of Elliot's. Their investigation produced a series of suspects. Several public housing residents suggested Elliot Porter was smoking a lot of weed—and dealing a little on the side. Several witnesses came forward alleging that the boy had accepted $300 for a bag of marijuana that he promised to deliver, but then skipped out on the pair of buyers. They fingered a woman and a man from Thibodaux, Louisiana, as the thwarted buyers who sought revenge. They had threatened to go after him. Chances are, they had. Chances are, they shot him. That was the word, anyway, from folks in the project.

But before cops could follow up on this, they got a tip from a local resident named Sheila Robertson, who pointed them in a completely new direction. Robertson, twenty-three, announced eleven days after the shooting that she had actually witnessed what went down the night Elliot Porter was killed.[8] She happened to be sitting at her window smoking a cigarette and waiting for her boyfriend around 1 A.M. on the night of the shooting, she told police. She saw two guys walk along the sidewalk with Porter between them. "Then I saw Elliot Porter broke out and run, he a little ways and ran between the two buildings," she told a detective on November 10. "I saw him crawl through a hole in the fence and that's when I heard two shots."[9] The next day, she learned that Elliot Porter was dead.

On November 15, a few days after this witness came forward, cops banged on Greg Bright's door at 2 A.M. Greg was a tall, slim

African American man who lived a few blocks from the scene of the crime. Sheila Robertson, who knew him from the neighborhood, told cops where they could find him, and asserted he was one of the men she saw with Elliot Porter. The police cuffed Greg, put him into the back of a cruiser, and took him to the city jail.

Locals refer to the jail by its street address. "While I'm at Tulane and Broad, I discover there is another guy on the tier arrested and charged with the same offense. Earl and I were thrown together on a crime that neither of us had anything to do with," Greg says, referring to his co-defendant, a seventeen-year-old African American kid named Earl Truvia who was an eleventh grader at Booker T. Washington High School and whom Greg first met at "Tulane and Broad" when he learned they were charged together with murdering Elliot Porter. Greg knew Earl's brother, but didn't know him. "Now how do you take two innocent people and frame 'em up? Haul them into a courthouse? Don't give them an opportunity or chance to say nothin'?"

Greg asks me this and shakes his head, recalling the series of events for me as I sit on his front porch in New Orleans's 7th Ward one hot day in April 2012. Thirty-seven years after his arrest, Greg Bright conjures up this moment as vividly as if it were yesterday. "At the time, I had never been in the back of a police car," he says. "You could imagine the horror that would come after two police officers knock on your door at two in the morning and say that they have a warrant for your arrest. For murder." He shakes his head. For nearly four decades he has been worrying this moment, reliving it, arguing it, insisting he knew nothing about the crime.

Today, at fifty-six, he is a lanky, bone-thin man dressed in khaki shorts, a grey Saints T-shirt, leather sandals with socks, and a black do-rag. He has a scruff of grey hair on his chin and has a gap between his front teeth. He perches on a wooden captain's chair that he has dragged outside from the dining room and leans forward, then back. He removes his glasses, then puts them back on. He gestures with his hands, then stills them. Both hesitant and compelled to talk, he drifts back in time to remember the twenty-seven years he spent imprisoned at Louisiana's notorious Angola prison for a crime he didn't commit, offering up his story as a cautionary tale, and backing it up with reams of dog-eared court documents, the coffee spills and curled edges and underlined passages testament to the hours—decades, really—that he spent poring over these same papers.

His story, which should be ancient history, is not.

Reforms have radically improved the quality of representation in the public defender's office in the last six years, but the problems are entrenched.

Many of the city's systemic issues that kept him locked away for so long persist today. Greg fought a host of them: inadequate funding for public defense; a casual disregard for the letter of the law when it comes to sharing exculpatory information; unchecked prosecutorial misconduct; regular refusals to provide the poor with legal help for appeals; misaligned financial incentives for public defenders, prosecutors, and the sheriff; an insular judicial culture and old-boy network of cops, lawyers, and judges; and maybe even a racist presumption of guilt.

As Greg Bright sat in jail at Tulane and Broad that first day in November of 1975, he knew he faced a lot of trouble. "The way things was going, I knew nothing good was going to come out of this," he said. He is prone to understatement.

When Greg had his day in court in 1976—and indeed all the way up until 2007, despite the U.S. Supreme Court's 1963 ruling in *Gideon v. Wainwright*—legal representation for the poor in New Orleans was a shaky prospect. In the years before Katrina hit, there was no statewide public defender system in Louisiana. The sixty-four parishes were divided into forty-one judicial districts, and in each of these districts the local judges appointed an indigent defense board to operate an indigent defense system. In systems cobbled together ad hoc over the years, some districts had an assigned counsel, where judges appointed local attorneys as needed (as say, Atticus Finch was in *To Kill a Mockingbird*), some had a contract system where the local board would contract with individual lawyers or firms to handle all their indigent defense cases, and some had a public defender's office. The quality of defense clients received was wildly divergent across the state. The districts had only one thing in common: the local judges were ultimately in charge of public defenders, even if it was at the narrow one-step remove of appointing the public defender board, typically their chums.

In the case of Orleans Parish, the local bar association was supposed to recommend lawyers for the indigent defense board. "But mostly judges appointed private criminal defense lawyers who were prominent and good friends with the judges," says Steve Singer, assistant clinical professor at Loyola University New Orleans School of Law and supervisor of the criminal law clinic there. Further complicating this patronage was a system in which public defenders were assigned to a particular judge and courtroom. Judges casually referred to these lawyers possessively as "my public defender" and the linguistic lapse was telling: public defenders knew who their boss really was and knew they had to keep the judge happy. Sometimes, this led to horse trading. If a cranky judge was likely to grant only one or two favors a day, which client would the public defenders appeal for? Who would get sold down the river? Because these same public defenders were also representing private, paying clients for half the day, those clients were often the recipients of the lawyers' extra efforts.

For poor clients, the public defender was paid the same whether he or she spent two hours or two days on a case. Obviously, this was not true with the hourly-billed paying clients. The financial incentives, then, pushed the lawyer to spend as little time as possible on the public defense cases and as much as possible on private cases. (Also, private clients accrue via word-of-mouth, so a client's sense that she or he was well-served mattered tremendously; indigent clients were randomly assigned and, given the seemingly endless supply of arrests in the city, new cases cropped up as quickly as old ones were disposed of.) Public defenders were paid in the low to mid-$30,000s in 2004 to 2006. The less time spent on public defender cases, the fewer motions filed, the more guilty pleas encouraged, the fewer cases taken to trial, the more time a public defender saved to spend on paying clients. "You don't have to be a bad person or a bad lawyer [to operate this way]," says Singer, insisting that the pre-Katrina public defender's office contained both good and bad attorneys. "But either way, the system they were stuck in made it bad."

Those who loved the setup were the judges. Having your very own public defender in your courtroom all the time meant she or he was always at your disposal. It was an efficient system, because judges could move briskly through the business of the day, processing pleas and clearing their dockets. They never had to wait or rearrange or reschedule things because the public defender on the case was dealing with a different client in someone else's courtroom. The conflict of interest here was obvious, but the judges, who controlled the courts, were disinclined to change things. "Who it didn't work for were the clients," Singer says.

Even on the most mundane, practical level it was a mess. The thirty to thirty-five part-time public defenders didn't have their own office space but used a basement room in the courthouse at the pleasure of the judges. They had cubbies but no rooms with doors for confidential meetings with clients. They had one copy machine and one phone line. They had no voice mail. They had no case management system more sophisticated than index cards in a recipe box. They had four computers, two with dial-up Internet access. Together they averaged twenty-eight thousand clients annually.[10]

All this was problematic, but by far the most troubling aspect of the criminal justice system here was the fact that, after being arrested, a poor person could sit in jail for up to 45 days on a misdemeanor, 60 days on a felony, or 120 days on a murder without any contact with an attorney while the Orleans Parish district attorney decided whether or not to prosecute the case. Pamela Metzger, an associate professor at Tulane University School of Law, describes this Kafkaesque scenario most eloquently in a 2007 *Tulane Law Review* article: "If one takes the Miranda warnings literally, one expects that upon arrest a poor person can request the appointment of counsel and that an appointed lawyer will thereafter be provided," Metzger writes. "True, after hearing the police intone 'you have the right to an attorney, if you cannot afford one, one will be appointed to represent you,' an arrestee might rightly invoke his right to counsel and then look wonderingly about the jail as the police explain, 'you have to see a judge to get an attorney appointed.'" Metzger then goes on to describe how our hypothetical arrestee experiences justice, Louisiana-style:

The arrestee asks: "When will I see the judge?" "Tomorrow." The arrestee heaves a sigh of relief: "So, I'll get my lawyer tomorrow." "Not exactly," is the police officer's reply. "There will be a lawyer in the courtroom when the judge sets bail, but that lawyer's in that courtroom every day for every new arrest. That won't be your real lawyer. You'll get one of those later."

"When might that be?" the suspect wonders. The officer explains: "The DA has to decide if he wants to prosecute you. He's got 60 days to decide about you, that's a rush job because you're in custody; if you bond out, they get 120 days to decide."

"So once the district attorney decides, I'll get a lawyer?" asks the suspect. "Not exactly, is the officer's reply. "Once charges are filed, you're arraigned. That's where you say 'not guilty.' You get your lawyer at that proceeding."

"When will the arraignment be?" asks the increasingly alarmed prisoner. "Within 30 days of the DA's decision—all told, you're guaranteed to have your own lawyer within 90 days."

Desperate, the suspect asks: "Can I just go ahead and agree that the district attorney should charge me?" "Nope," says the officer. "They make that decision on their own."

"But I'm not guilty," wails the prisoner. "In 90 days it will be too late. There won't be any way to find all the witnesses who saw what happened. And I'll have lost my job. My wife won't be able to make the rent. Can't this go any faster?" The officer smiles. "Perhaps you'd like to make a statement to us after all? We could try to clear this whole thing up and send you on home."[11]

Metzger contends that the "extraordinary length of the Louisiana screen period converts an otherwise appropriate administrative charging function into an illicit system of plea extortions and punishment without trial." Even if the person is never charged, the damage is often done. "Louisiana's mind-boggling sixty-day screening period means that the old criminal justice maxim, 'you can beat the rap, but you can't beat the ride,' is truer in Louisiana than elsewhere," she says.[12]

Norris Henderson, founder and director of Voice of the Ex-Offender (VOTE) and a board member of the reentry program Resurrection After Exoneration, both New Orleans–based advocacy and service organizations for ex-offenders, elaborates on the impact this has. "What's happening to that person sitting in jail for sixty days before, say, the prosecutor drops the charge?" he asks, then answers: "The damage is done." The accused person may not have a record, but by the time he is released on day fifty-nine, he likely lost his job, lost his apartment because he couldn't make rent, lost his slot in a drug-rehab program, lost his car when it was repossessed, and had his kids taken by child welfare if he had custody or, if not, would quickly find himself back before a judge for lapsed child support payments.

If the DA *does* decide to pursue prosecution and files a Bill of Information, basically an official charging document, the defendant has now lost several months languishing in jail without an attorney to investigate his case. Alibi witnesses have forgotten whether or not they were with the defendant that Wednesday night three months ago when the crime took place. Tread marks on the road have disappeared. Blood fades from the carpet. Glasses with potentially useful DNA get washed. Receipts—proof of purchase—get tossed. Time frames and markers—"I distinctly remember I was watching *The Colbert Report*, so it had to be around 11:30 P.M."—fade from memory.

And in Orleans Parish, when the defendant is finally appointed a lawyer after 45, 60, or 120 days in jail, the lawyer is likely to be handling that case along with six hundred other cases.

Things came to a head in 1993, when a public defender named Richard Teissier was struggling with a crushing caseload in Section E of Criminal District Court.[13] In addition to his slew of other clients, Teissier was readying a serious case for trial, representing an indigent client named Leonard Peart. Peart was charged with armed robbery, aggravated rape, aggravated burglary, attempted armed robbery, and first-degree murder. Teissier didn't see how he could provide effective representation for Peart in addition to his other clients. He filed a Motion for Relief to Provide Constitutionally Mandated Protection and Resources and Section E's Judge Calvin Johnson held several hearings. He discovered that Teissier, a part-time employee, had seventy active felony cases, had clients who were typically in jail one to two months before he met with them, had little access to an investigator, had a trial on every available trial date, and had, for an eight-month period the year before, 418 clients, 130 of whom entered guilty pleas at arraignment.

Change was in the air in the country. Many state legislatures were hearing about the crisis in indigent defense and beginning to look at restructuring services and refunding programs. New Mexico, Missouri, and Kentucky radically boosted funding in 1989, while Georgia and Tennessee created statewide public defender boards. Public defenders had begun clamoring for reforms. Sometimes, people listened. In New Orleans, Judge Johnson was one of them. He agreed that this was unconstitutional and ordered Teissier's caseload—which by then had swelled to 785—reduced. In the short term, he did this by appointing members of the local bar to represent indigent clients in his courtroom. Long term, he ordered—or tried to order—the legislature to fund the city's public defender office adequately. The state appealed the ruling. While the defendant Peart was tried and acquitted of armed robbery and murder, Judge Johnson's ruling that the legislature adequately fund public defense traveled to the Louisiana Supreme Court. Not surprisingly, the court found that indeed the kind of lawyering going on in Section E— assembly-line style—was not up to constitutional snuff.

This was a victory. Sort of. But the judges also side-stepped the issue, saying: "We decline at this time to undertake these more intrusive and specific measures because this Court should not lightly tread in the affairs of other branches of government and because the legislature ought to assess such measures in the first instance." In essence, the court said whether or not individual clients appearing in the future in Section E are getting adequate counsel should be decided on a case-by-case basis. One dissenting judge thought the decision, narrowly applying to only one out of twelve courtrooms in Louisiana's Criminal District Court, was absurd given the system-wide problems, insisting this was like "saying that a person in early term is 'only a little bit pregnant.'" The remedy did not begin to address the "systemic constitutional deficiencies" in the state realistically. He blasted his colleagues for offering up Section E as a "lamb for burnt offering," and insisted they were delusional, "hoping that an all-knowing, benevolent deity will miraculously cure the ills of the indigent defense system in that section and elsewhere."

The benevolent deity passed them by, but a malevolent one intervened. "How do you break up that kind of system?" Singer asks, shaking his head as he maps out the long, troubled history of indigent defense in New Orleans. Then he answers his own question: "You have a hurricane."

What did indigent defense in the city look like in those pre-Katrina days? Greg Bright was learning, firsthand, the answer to that question.

On December 4, 1975, approximately a month after he and Earl Truvia were arrested, an Orleans Parish grand jury heard ten minutes of testimony from a single witness, Sheila Robertson.

"Would you tell the ladies and gentleman just what exactly you saw and where you were and what took place?" assistant district attorney Kurt Sins asked her.

"Well, one night I was in the bedroom. It was the night before Halloween, and I was in the bedroom looking out the window, which I always do," Robertson said. "I always be looking out the window most every night . . . and there be three guys. Two of them . . . one of them was on one side of [Elliot Porter] and the other one was on the other side. He was in the front, and it looked like they was arguing. So, when they saw me in the window, they started hugging, and they were hugging, you know, like they were laughing, you know, as if they were . . ."

"Did they all three go to laughing?" Sins asked.

"No, just the two, not him."

"Where were they?" Sins asked. "Was one on one side and one on the other?"

"Right," Robertson agreed. "And when Elliot saw me in the window, he was trying to beg me to help him if he thought I had a phone or anything, or maybe he thought I could get in touch with the police or something, but I didn't. So, I didn't understand what he was trying to tell me then."

"What do you mean, 'he was trying to tell' you? Did he actually speak to you?"

"No, he was looking at me like if, you know, something was going on, and he was trying to get somebody to help him."

"Did he have a frightened look on his face?"

"Yes, but I didn't know, see, I didn't know what really was going on at the time, so I didn't know what to think. I looked at him and, you know, and uh . . ."

"What happened?"

"O.K. Then they walked, they walked, he got like about two steps, two steps, and then he broke out and ran. The other two boys broke out and ran behind him. They broke out and ran behind him on the side of the building, and the next thing I knew they were shooting. The other two boys ran back, and one stopped and glanced at me. You know, he looked at me real hard. The other one told him to 'come on,' and he started running, and they went back to around the Miro [Street] side. The other side which was Miro, and, uh, then about a couple of night later the same two guys came in on me. I was laying on the bed. I thought I heard somebody, but I wasn't sure. I didn't get up. I said, 'Nobody can't get in because the door is locked.' But they took the window out on the top porch, and they came in. When they came in, they was coming up the steps, and I thought somebody, you know, I saw his head, but he reared back so I couldn't see it. I said, 'Well, that's just my imagination.' So, uh, then before I knowed anything both of them had ran in. One jumped over the bed, you know, like crossing it, and he held me like that. He said, 'We just come to remind you not to go to the police.' I said, 'Well, I'm not going to the . . .' I didn't tell him that. I was telling him like this here. I was nodding my head telling him I wasn't going to go to the police. I wasn't going to tell or nothing. The other one looked at me and said, 'Cause if you tell anything, we're going to come back for you. We're coming back for you. We'll be back.' And they were doing like this here, and I told them I wasn't going to tell."

"Did you get a good look at them?" Sins asked.

"Yes."

"Were they the same two people you saw out in the courtyard?"

"Yes, the same two."

Sins asked some questions about the lighting outside, which Robertson assured him was good. Then he moved on to the light inside. "That night when they came in your apartment, did you have any lights on in your apartment?"

"Uh-huh," Robertson said. "I keep my kitchen light on. I keep the bathroom light on, and the hall light. I always keep that on."

"O.K. And that gave you plenty enough light to see the two people?"

"Right. The light . . . my bedroom [is] right here, and the bathroom was right there, and we were facing each other."

"Do you recall what clothing they were wearing the night when they killed Elliot?"

"No, not really," Robertson said. "I know one had on a pair of jeans. I know that for a fact because I seen his jeans. I couldn't see the shirt."

"How about that night when they came in your house a couple of nights later?"

"They didn't have that on. He had something different on."

"How long have you known Elliot?"

"I didn't really know him."

"Did he live around you?"

"Yeah, he . . . I stayed like in this driveway, and he stayed across the street in the next driveway."

"What floor do you live on?"

"I was living on the second and third floor."

"And the bedroom window that you were looking out of, was that on the second or third floor?"

"That was on the third floor."

"Had you seen these two guys before, prior to this time?"

"I seen them around. I seen them, like, they be's on the corner, standing on the corner where I go to the grocery at, the corner grocery store. All of them be's on the corner and stuff, you know, sitting around sometimes. They be laughing and talking sometimes. Sometimes they be boxing, you know, different things."

"Are these the same two people whose picture you picked out when the detective showed you the pictures?"

"Uh-huh, same two."

Robertson said she saw the two men pass by beneath her window and then go around the corner.

"Did you actually see the shot fired?" Sins asked.

"No, I didn't actually see him shot. I'm not going to say that."

118

"That was around the corner?"

"Yeah, that was on the side [of the building]. I don't know which one shot him."

Sins tried to get a sense of the timing, but Robertson couldn't recall how much time passed between the time they went around the corner and she heard shots fired. "After the shots were fired, about how much time went by before you saw them running back?"

"They ran right off," Robertson said.

"Right away?"

"Uh-huh."

"O.K. Sheila, now, think. When Elliot ran and the two guys were chasing him, did you notice any one of the two guys chasing him with a gun, or pull a gun out of his hand, while they were chasing him?"

"No."

Sins asked if any of the grand jurors had any questions. Several did. "After you saw this, you didn't go to the police right away?" one asked.

"No," Robertson admitted.

"And then they came in and threatened you, and that's when you decided to tell the police?"

"I told my mama what happened," Robertson corrected. "So, mama told me to get in touch with the housing authority and see if they couldn't, you know, get me out of that apartment so it would be safer for me. After I called the housing authority, and I talked to the lady, the secretary at the housing authority, that's when she called the police and she told them that I called in and said that I knew what had happened."

"Thank you very much for coming down here," Sins said.

It was damning testimony.

The grand jury indicted Greg Bright and Earl Truvia with one count each on the second-degree murder of Elliot Porter. The trial would take place on July 29, 1976, seven months later.

At the time of his arrest in 1975, Greg Bright worked a series of odd jobs, sometimes in restaurants, mostly on the riverfront where he had a regular gig cleaning oil and other debris from the holds of barges. He could barely read, having dropped out of school in sixth grade to take care of his ailing father, and his knowledge of the law was nonexistent. He had no money to speak of. His mother worked at General Diaper Services, where she folded diapers and sheets for twenty-nine years. Greg sat in jail for months hoping he would get a lawyer, hoping the lawyer would come visit him, hoping the lawyer would ask what had happened, hoping he'd get a chance to explain to the attorney that he had gone to a bonfire at a local community college that night with a girl, that he'd gotten a ride with a friend, that the girl at the bonfire, the friend driving the car, and his mother at home would all attest to his whereabouts that evening. He tried not to worry; he had an alibi.

The court appointed a public defender named Robert Zibilich to represent Greg, a private attorney who worked part-time as a public defender while juggling his paying clients. All the public defenders in the city worked this way. According to Greg, his attorney never visited him in jail. An investigator visited him there once to ask some questions about where he was that night and that was it. Another lawyer, Greg says, stood up for him in court to enter his not-guilty plea. "I met with [my lawyer] once before the trial at a motion hearing," Greg says, explaining that this first conversation with his attorney took place after he sat in jail for approximately three months. (Greg's attorney later disputed this, agreeing that he never visited him in jail but insisting that he talked to him several times at the courthouse when Zibilich was there to file motions.)

To his credit, Zibilich did file discovery motions promptly in January 1976, asking for any documents or information about the case. But the assistant district attorney's response is essentially rejection after rejection of each request. For example, Zibilich asked for a list of witnesses that the state intended to call during trial. "Defense is not entitled to this information," prosecutors responded. The defense asked for "any and all items of physical evidence or tangible property obtained from any person" whether via search warrant or otherwise that it intended to introduce during trial. "Defense is not entitled to this information," prosecutors responded. The defense asked for "any and all medical reports of examinations conducted by the Coroner's office for the Parish of Orleans reflecting the medical condition of the victim named in this indictment." "Defense is not entitled to this information," prosecutors answered. The defense asked for the rap sheet on the defendants "and that of any witness the State intends to call." This information, critical in the case of the state's sole eyewitness, Sheila Robertson, would be denied in the usual fashion: "Defense is not entitled to this information." Finally, the defense requested all Brady material be shared. The 1963 Supreme Court decision *Brady vs. Maryland* requires that all exculpatory evidence be shared with the defense. That means any conflicting statements offered by witnesses, any information about a witness that impeaches their credibility, any police reports indicating alternative scenarios to the one presented by the district attorney, anything that could influence a jury's assessment of guilt or punishment must be provided to the defense. Here, Bright's attorney spelled it out to properly cover all the bases, requesting, "Evidence materially favorable to the defendant either as direct or impeaching evidence." In particular, Zibilich asked for "[w]ritten statements or interviews reduced to writing obtained by the State through police investigative procedures from any co-defendant, accomplice, accessory, suspect or any other person having knowledge or information regarding the charge contained in this Indictment," and so forth. This time the prosecution asserted: "State is not in possession of any."

On July 29, 1976, Greg and Earl were tried for second-degree murder in Section B of the Criminal District Court for the Parish of Orleans. The assistant district attorneys, Henry Julien and Patrick Quinlan, laid the groundwork for their case in opening arguments. "The meat of this case," Julien told the jury, "will get down to the testimony of one individual." The prosecution identified this witness as Sheila Robertson and said she would tell the jury how "on the night of October 31, the early morning hours at least on October 31, she was sitting at her window." There, she saw three young men walk by. "She will identify those young men to you today, two of them being the defendants here, and the third being Elliot Porter. And as they walked in front of her house, something seemed amiss, something seemed wrong. . . . A struggle ensued. She could see the struggle. And it appeared that the two people were attacking Elliot Porter, a fifteen-year-old." Julien went on to explain that she would further testify that those two men—Greg and Earl, whom she didn't know—broke into her house two nights after the murder and threatened to kill her and her eighteen-month-old baby if she told the police what she'd seen. "And that, ladies and gentlemen, is basically the case the state will present to you," Julien said.

"You won't see any weapons introduced here today," he admitted. "But, I believe, from the facts that you will see, and from the testimony you will hear, and the circumstances surrounding those facts—now, I'm not saying circumstantial evidence. I'm saying the circumstances surrounding those facts, which is the only way you can really determine those questions . . . you will determine, or will be able to determine, that the two defendants before the bar murdered fifteen-year-old Elliot Porter. Which one actually pulled the trigger, I don't know. But they are principals, acting in consort. . . . Thank you."

Greg Bright's attorney, Zibilich stood up. "If Your Honor please, Mr. Bright relies on his presumption of innocence," he said. He sat down, his opening argument complete in this single sentence.

Very little about the way justice was delivered to the poor in New Orleans changed between 1975 when Greg Bright's case went to trial and 2005 when disaster struck—and shook things up.

Hurricane Katrina swept through New Orleans on August 29, 2005, and within days, the ensuing storm surge and levee breaks flooded the streets, leaving 80 percent of the city underwater. This included the courthouse and adjacent jail. As the water levels rose, 6,700 Orleans Parish Prison inmates, as well as several thousand others who had been evacuated *to* this jail from surrounding parishes as the storm approached, were trapped. Some were trapped in cells as the water levels rose in the building, according to Human Rights Watch, which interviewed 1,000 prisoners in the weeks after the storm, and, as deputies fled to safety with their families or in the course of evacuating inmates to other jails in the state, hundreds of prisoners were left without food, medicine, or even air (as the windows were sealed and all electricity, including air-conditioning, failed) for four days.[14] Meanwhile, most of the prisoners were evacuated, scattered to the wind in dozens of jails across Louisiana and bordering states, while several hundred others were contained for days in the open, in a pasture where food and water were simply tossed by deputies to the masses who fought for supplies, the strong prevailing over the weak. The sheriff, ostensibly, had a list of who was where, but it was unreliable; prisoners had traded around their ID bracelets, switching up identities and thus, crimes committed and times served.

Adjacent to the jail itself, the courthouse had also flooded, water gushing into basement evidence rooms and scattering and destroying years of evidence. Photographs stuck together, guns rusted, mold ate through fabrics, confiscated marijuana rotted, new DNA evidence went unrefrigerated for weeks, and, according to the *New York Times*, a non-English-speaking cleanup crew hired to try and salvage evidence relied on guesswork to figure out which collections of evidence belonged to which cardboard box of crime investigations.[15] Meanwhile, with the city emptied of residents, witnesses to crimes had fled the storm—some never to return. Juries, of course, were nonexistent. Even the public defenders were AWOL, only seven of them remaining to try and sort through the chaos.

Criminal justice in New Orleans ground to a complete stop.

Judge Calvin Johnson, who was *trying* to run a court out of a spare classroom at a college in Baton Rouge, knew those inmates' constitutional rights were likely being violated. Folks picked up for misdemeanors like DUIs or shoplifting were lost in the system, still in jail somewhere in the state where they were languishing for longer than any sentence that would have been meted out. Those charged with felonies, 90 percent of whom relied on public defenders, had no lawyers to press their cases. Some, picked up by cops in the hectic days before Katrina hit, had no official paperwork affirming their existence in custody.

Judge Johnson, then chief judge of the Orleans Parish Criminal District Court, appointed Steve Singer's Loyola University School of Law clinic and Pamela Metzger's Tulane Law School's clinic to represent the interests of all of the city's indigent defendants, which amounted to just about everyone in jail at the time (some 6,500 to 8,000 people), excluding the small fraction of folks who had private lawyers. The two of them, on the ground immediately in the days after Katrina hit, helped spearhead the myriad reforms to indigent defense that were subsequently put in place over the years since the storm. Today, Metzger serves on the Louisiana Public Defender Board, and remains immersed in the struggles indigent defendants face in the city. Metzger says New Orleans has made "extraordinary strides" since Katrina. But understanding what happened during the storm is essential to understanding why the city is having such a difficult time maintaining its progress.

As she sits in her office one bright, sunny day in April 2012, in a vintage-style dress, cherry-red pumps, and a cardigan, Metzger explains she is dressed up because she is heading over to the court-house later; she was tapped to be an expert witness in a lawsuit against the jail in which public defenders were demanding proper, timely access to their imprisoned clients. It is hard to imagine the legal and administrative chaos she describes in the aftermath of Katrina, but her office hints at it. The room is piled high with boxes and papers and books in stacks that have swelled beyond the con-fines of the floor-to-ceiling, wall-to-wall bookshelves to spew out into columns on the floor—many of the file boxes containing in-mate files from the days after Katrina. She is still holding on to these files, hoping they can be archived someday, testament to a level of disorder, disarray, and tumult that the criminal justice sys-tem was plunged into on the heels of the storm.

"Katrina laid bare just how bad the public defender system was in New Orleans," she says. After the hurricane hit and the levees broke and everyone who could fled, the city was deserted. No peo-ple, no functioning traffic lights, no functioning parking meters, no meter maids, no courthouse, no traffic court, nothing. "It wiped out all the money," says Singer, explaining that for three, four, five months, this income stream that had been used to pay for public de-fenders was completely decimated. The forty-two part-time public defenders couldn't be paid and stopped working.[16] The office was reduced to five part-time attorneys, a chief public defender, and one administrator.

At the same time, Singer's and Metzger's own lives were chaotic. Metzger had evacuated to Atlanta, where her parents lived, with her two kids and her dog, was in the midst of separating from her husband, and had a set of clients from Tulane's law clinic whose cases she was supervising. She began commuting, leaving Atlanta on a 6 A.M. flight Monday mornings, catching a flight back on Thursday nights. As she and Singer began to assess the situation, they realized that the troubles with indigent defense were even deeper than they had anticipated. Metzger got on the phone with Singer. "Do we have a list of clients?" she wanted to know. There was no list. They couldn't find a list of these 6,500 to 8,000 prisoners they were supposed to represent. No one seemed to know who the public defenders' clients were. This was shocking. Could it be that *no one* in the public defender's office kept such a list? Singer and Metzger discovered that not only had individual public defenders routinely failed to keep a list of who they represented, but that no office-wide list existed either. There wasn't even a record of which clients were in jail or to which jails inmates spread out across the state had been moved.

Eventually, the sheriff provided a list of who was in each of the jails scattered around the South. "We began to try and systematize who was in jail that shouldn't be. Who was in jail and needed a lawyer right away," Metzger says. They divided the court sections, Metzger's law clinic taking two sections, Singer's law clinic taking another two, and another attorney, Meghan Garvey, taking one. They quickly discovered, however, that not all of the clients on the sheriff's list were showing up with any kind of case record in the courts. "There were eight thousand clients, three lawyers, and twenty students," Metzger says. "It couldn't be done. It was very surreal."

The federal government gave a grant of $2.8 million, which helped, but it was a drop in the bucket compared to the $10 million estimated by a federal Justice Department study to be necessary for getting the public defender system up and running properly. The Louisiana State Bar Association commissioned a study and kicked in for the salaries of three lawyers for a year, but clearly many more were needed.

Metzger says lawyers around the country offered to volunteer and help represent clients, but they had so many strings. They were available only during a certain two-week stretch one month from now and they did this particular kind of case. Metzger says no one realized the level they were working on. "When all these law firms said, 'What can we do?' I said, 'I need file folders. If you could have someone type up labels and put them on folders, etc.' Or, if you could go into the computers and have someone print the criminal history and put it in the folders for us, that would be miraculous—because we had eight thousand of them and could not do the physical labor. But they don't want to do that, they want to be heroes in court."

Metzger and Singer and their law school students were reduced to traveling personally to jails around the state to interview inmates, asking for basic information: Did they have an attorney? How long had they been incarcerated? What was bail set at? What had they been charged with (although some had not even been formally charged)? Did their family know where they were? Did they know where their family was? "Steve and I used to have these conversations during those first months," Metzger recalls, bemoaning the fact that they were so completely overwhelmed with the scope of the problem, so desperately in need of more hands and yet "nobody is coming." Then, in the winter of 2006–2007, help came from an unexpected place: young people.

The Student Hurricane Network, an outreach effort run by college students to facilitate bringing volunteers to New Orleans, put out word about the dire state of indigent defense. Calling their effort Project Gideon, Metzger and Singer sought students to help them with all the unglamorous but essential grunt work. They were still trying to collect information on five hundred of the most difficult cases, cases that were confusing in terms of where these inmates actually were, what their record was, what had been done on their behalf thus far. They needed someone to physically travel to each of the prisons, talk to the prisoners, get statements from them, get police reports, create a file. When their plea went up on the Student Hurricane Network, they asked other law clinics to send a supervisor for every eight students and the plan was for student volunteers to spend their winter break helping. "We have seventeen students and fifteen supervisors," a professor from the University of the Pacific McGeorge School of Law in California told Metzger over the phone one day. "I said, 'That's great, maybe we should find something for those other supervisors to do,'" Metzger said. But she had misunderstood. "'No,' they said, 'We have *seventy* students and fifteen supervisors.' And I sat down on the floor of my office and I cried." Her eyes fill with tears as she recounts this moment, some six years ago. On the scheduled date of December 14, three hundred student volunteers showed up to help for three weeks. "We never anticipated the response we received," she says. Some arrived having driven for a day and a night to get here and then happily jumped in their cars for another seven-hour drive to a remote jail to interview one person. They were spread out, crashing and working in every available space at the school, with paperwork and files everywhere as they handwrote all their notes and collected information in files (there were not enough working computers, and those that existed were used to search the criminal justice databases). "We cleared the backlog and it was incredible. Here we had been all this time, with these major organizations saying they would send someone as a fellow or for a trial the second week in November and we kept waiting for all these lawyers to come, but we were asking the wrong people. We should have been asking the students. We got more work done with student volunteers and supervisors than we did from any single law firm or public interest firm. Period."

"We started filing habeas cases," Metzger says, explaining that this was a collective strategy where she petitioned the court saying the prisoners had been wrongly held. She went into Judge Arthur Hunter's courtroom, listed a group of people by name, pointed out they had not seen a lawyer, there were no lawyers in sight, there were no juries, and they ought to be released. "Suddenly, all these fabulous plea bargains were made available [by the DA]," Metzger says. That was troubling, Metzger says, because she often had no idea whether that was a good deal for them or not, having no idea of the history, their criminal history, the facts of the case. "This was triage," she says. "There was no individual representation, this was mass representation. So we had hearings. And the testimony was heartbreaking."

Metzger wrote about one man, Pedro Parra-Sanchez, one of the eight thousand detainees hurled into the post-Katrina chaos, in her *Tulane Law Review* article:

A man went to the Gulf Coast in October of 2005, just days after the storm. He went with his construction buddies and their boss; they have come to rebuild New Orleans.

The man is named Pedro Parra-Sanchez. He is a Mexican citizen and a lawful resident alien residing in the United States with a valid green card. He lives in Bakersfield, California, with his wife and four children. He has lived in the United States for twenty years.

On October 13, 2005, New Orleans police arrested Mr. Parra-Sanchez and charged him with battery. He is forty-four years old and has never before been charged with a crime. None of the courts are open and the local jail is flooded.

The police handcuffed Mr. Parra-Sanchez and took him to an old Greyhound Bus Station that has been converted to a makeshift jail. A piece of plywood hangs crookedly over the door; across it someone has scrawled: WELCOME TO ANGOLA SOUTH.

Mr. Parra-Sanchez waited. Court proceeded in a blur of activity he cannot understand. No Spanish interpreter is available, so everyone in the courtroom manages as best they can: Spanish is made to suffice. The public defender in the courtroom that day neither met Mr. Parra-Sanchez nor interviewed him about his bail prospects.

Louisiana's Code of Criminal Procedure entitled Mr. Parra-Sanchez to have counsel appointed to represent him from the day of his initial appearance through the resolution of his case.

The judge tells Mr. Parra-Sanchez that the public defender is his lawyer for that day only. He will get his own lawyer if and when the prosecution decides to accept the charges against him. Thus, the public defender who meets Mr. Parra-Sanchez is not his lawyer at all. The lawyer is just constitutional and statutory window dressing, allowing the system to place a check mark in the counsel column. The lawyer is not a true check on the power of the prosecution or the court.

Because Mr. Parra-Sanchez is unrepresented, no one gathers information about Mr. Parra-Sanchez and his family. No one contacts his wife and children to tell them where he is. No one argues for his release. The judge knows only that Mr. Parra-Sanchez is a Mexican citizen who is charged with aggravated battery.

The judge sets the bond at $20,000. To secure his release, Mr. Parra-Sanchez will have to get the unthinkable sum of $2400, in cash, to a local bail bond company. He has no way to reach his family, and no attorney has offered to contact them.

The Code of Criminal Procedure gives the state an unprecedented period of sixty days in which to charge or release Mr. Parra-Sanchez. Accordingly, the court sets the case for a status hearing sixty days later; if the district attorney has not filed a bill of information, the court will order Mr. Parra-Sanchez released without any bond obligation.

The clerk is indifferent to Mr. Parra-Sanchez's plight. He does not enter Mr. Parra-Sanchez's case into the court's docketing system: neither Mr. Parra-Sanchez's case, nor his potential release date appear on any judicial calendar. Because the public defender is appointed for initial appearance only, that lawyer makes no record of Mr. Parra-Sanchez's existence. The public defender has no case file for Mr. Parra-Sanchez, no notes about his circumstances, not even a calendar notation of Mr. Parra-Sanchez's [legally required charge or] release date.

Sixty days come and go, then ninety, then one hundred and twenty. No charges are filed. No release is ordered. No lawyer petitions the court for Mr. Parra-Sanchez's release. Mr. Parra-Sanchez is lost.

More days go by. More weeks. Months. Guards move Mr. Parra-Sanchez to a small jail in rural St. Charles Parish. No lawyer comes to visit. Days drag on. Other prisoners leave for court appearances. Others return and then leave again for court—for hearings and conferences, and even for trials. Others never return; they have been released and sent home or sentenced and remanded to a state penitentiary in the north. Mr. Parra-Sanchez never leaves the jail. Not once.

In early January 2006, someone in the district attorney's office accepts the charges and files a bill of information against him. Perhaps the district attorney's office believes Mr. Parra-Sanchez is not in jail; under those circumstances the Code of Criminal Procedure gives the district attorney ninety days to file charges against him. No one seems quite sure.

The bond in the case is suddenly reduced to $15,000, although nothing in the record suggests that anyone has taken any action on the case. No one tells Mr. Parra-Sanchez that his bond has been reduced. Of course, the bond reduction is of little use to him now. His family has sold his tools to pay for food and clothing. After several months without his income, the family is behind in the rent and will soon be evicted from their home. . . .

So, as January turns into February, February into March, and March into April, Mr. Parra-Sanchez continues to sit in the St. Charles Parish jail. He sees the jail psychiatrist, implores her for help; she cannot help him unless his case goes to court. He begs the guards. "Will I have a court date? When? When can I go home?" They are kind, but they cannot help him. Thousands of Orleans Parish prisoners are scattered across the state asking the same questions to similar guards in similar prisons. The answer is always the same. A shrug and a brief explanation that they cannot do anything until the court sends for him. Mr. Parra-Sanchez makes a few friends in jail. They share with him the little they know about Louisiana criminal procedure. Those who speak English help him file two pro se motions for a speedy trial.

In May 2006, the Parra-Sanchez case appeared on the docket in a criminal district court. The case is set for arraignment: the appointment of counsel and the entry of a preliminary plea of "guilty" or "not guilty." No one calls St. Charles Parish jail and tells Mr. Parra-Sanchez to get ready for a trip to court. No one tells the public defender's office about a new case on the calendar. The arraignment date arrives. Mr. Parra-Sanchez is in the St. Charles Parish jail. The judge orders his deputy to call Mr. Parra-Sanchez's name three times in the hall. No response. The judge issues an arrest warrant based on Mr. Parra-Sanchez's willful failure to appear in court. This warrant for failure to appear will appear on any future court records or criminal history records. Mr. Parra-Sanchez knows none of this. He is still in jail. No new court date is set.

May, June, July, August, September, and October pass in the same way for Mr. Parra-Sanchez. He is in a small jail, in a small town in southern Louisiana. He misses his children and his wife. He has already missed Thanksgiving, Christmas, New Years, and Easter. His family has moved into an RV park. His eldest daughter has run away from home to live with her boyfriend; her struggling mother could not support all four children. Mr. Parra-Sanchez can do nothing. He has no lawyer. He has never been to court. Independence Day comes and goes. Columbus Day, Halloween, and Veterans Day. More than one year has passed.

In November 2006, someone calls the Tulane Law Clinic asking about Pedro Parra-Sanchez. My students and I file a habeas petition for his release and move to dismiss the charges filed against him for violation of his constitutional right to a speedy trial. He is released in mid-November, 2006.[17]

It became increasingly apparent that the slew of problems around record keeping and timeliness of trials and sharing of necessary information across court constituents and effective representation for the indigent had long existed in New Orleans. Katrina had simply exposed the terrible, preexisting fault lines in the system, the short shrift that poor clients had been getting for decades.

Greg Bright and Earl Truvia's joint murder trial lasted one day. In fact, the transcripts run ninety-three pages, which means, given approximately one minute per typed page, the trial was likely completed in under two hours. (For comparison, consider that the transcripts of Rodney Young's murder trial discussed in the following chapter ran more than four thousand pages.) The state called four witnesses. The defense called none.

First, the state called James McCraney, the fourteen-year-old newspaper boy who found Elliot Porter's dead body around 7:30 A.M. on the morning of October 31. He explained how he found the body, how he knocked on a few doors to rouse an adult, how someone called the police. Greg Bright's attorney asked McCraney seven questions, all pertaining to clarifying the address where the body was found—a fact not in dispute.

Next, the state called Myrtle Porter, the mother of the victim. She testified that her son went out the night of the murder at "something to eleven" and confirmed, after viewing some photos tendered into evidence, that these were indeed photographs of her deceased son. She said she didn't know Greg Bright but she knew Earl Truvia, who was friends with her son. "Now as far as you know, was he one of your son's close friends?"[18] asked assistant DA Henry Julien.

"No, he wasn't. He was an associate. You know, he used to be around where they stay. But I don't think he was a close friend of his."

When Greg's public defender stood up, he had four questions for Porter. "Was your son going to school at the time?"

"Yes, he was."

"And was Friday due to be a school day?"

"Yes, it was."

"You had indicated that you didn't see him again after he went out that night. Did you know whether he was at home, or not, during the night?"

"Yes, I know he wasn't at home."

"You know he was not?"

"Because my daughters came in. They had went to a social around 12 or 1 o'clock."

"Thank you. I have no further questions," Zibilich said and sat down.

Earl Truvia's lawyer, who had asked some questions of residents in the Calliope Project about Elliot Porter's activities, heard he had been peddling drugs. When it was his turn to question Mrs. Porter, he asked about some new outfits the boy had been wearing, questions the boy's mother had also admitted raising with him. "Now, you were about to explain to me about an extra job or something, or work that your son did when he was in the eighth grade," Edward Haggerty said. "What type of work did he do?"

"I said, he worked over at the Superdome. He used to sell cokes. That's all. He didn't work there that long. He was laid off."

"To your knowledge, did he ever make enough money to buy himself a new outfit?"

"No, I don't think so."

"Well, if he got the money to buy him a new outfit, where would he get the money from, Mrs. Porter?"

"Well, that's what I would like to know. He was out there doing something. You know, somebody had him out there because I know he didn't bum with nothing but the big boys, you know."

Several minutes later, the prosecutor, Julien, followed up on this line of questioning: "Now, Mrs. Porter, you said, in answer to a question from Mr. Haggerty, that you thought your son was involved in some kind of drugs. Is that correct?"

"Yes."

"What was it that made you believe that?"

"Well, when I used to go to school, his teacher used to tell me, you know, keep a close watch on him because he have plenty—she asked me, did I give him plenty of money. I told her no, I couldn't afford to. So, I said, maybe a dollar or sometime two dollars. She said, no, I mean five or ten. I said, well, no, I say, I don't know no ways he would be getting it from. So, she told me, well, you better keep a close watch on him because he's following big boys. She say, they might have him out here selling, you know, like marijuana or something like that."

"I have no further questions."

"I would like to ask another question," Haggerty said.

"Very well," the judge agreed.

"In other words, prior to this October 31st, you had had a previous conversation with some of the teachers where they saw your son having [an] excess amount of money such as five or ten dollar bills, and they know if he didn't get it from you, there was a suspicion he was getting it from selling marijuana or other dope?"

"Yes, that's what it was."

"Is that the reason why you told someone that you thought your son was killed because this was related to some drug?"

"Yes."[19]

Bright's lawyer, Zibilich, said nothing.

On redirect, the prosecutor tried to undercut the possibility that Elliot Porter may have been shot because of a drug-related incident, pointing out that Mrs. Porter lives in a New Orleans neighborhood called Central City—and, of course, her kid was mixed up in drugs, but that doesn't mean dealers from Thibodaux killed him. He asked her: "To your knowledge, do you know a lot of young people who've been caught up, more or less, in drugs, one way or the other? In that area?"

"I don't know," Porter said. "There's so much happening around up in that area, you know."

"Would you say that your fear that perhaps your son might have been involved in something illicit or illegal was a normal fear for a mother living in that area?"

She conceded that it was.

The judge put in his two cents: "I think that's true all over the city."

In the months following Katrina, as surviving residents slowly crept home to rebuild their homes and lives, folks in the criminal justice system were similarly weighing rebuilding—from the ground up. Is there a better way of doing business than the way it had historically been done in the city? reformers began to ask. And, with the flooding having cleared the decks at the public defender's office, might change actually be possible?

"After Katrina, there was a void because suddenly you didn't have all these employees vested in the existing system and fighting to keep it," Loyola Law School's Steve Singer says, seeing this as the thin silver lining to New Orleans's decimated indigent defense system. "And because there was no money, there was no money to control, so the judges didn't care as much. Nobody cared because there was nothing there. So it created a vacuum at the top and the bottom." This was an opportunity, a kind of blank slate, to allow reformers to step in and re-create the system.

So they did.

One of the models considered, in rethinking the Orleans Parish public defender's office was the Bronx Defenders. The Bronx Defenders are nationally recognized for their unique, holistic approach to legal representation. For example, if a client is out on bail, and they are hoping to improve his situation, they might find out that the person is a drug addict and needs counseling and maybe needs to get his GED so that he can access a better job. With social workers on staff, the Bronx Defenders try hard to address some of the root problems their clients are struggling with. In pre-Katrina New Orleans, this was a hard sell. Norris Henderson, director of Voice of the Ex-Offender, describes the reaction reformers got in the days before the hurricane: "We don't do it that way in New Orleans, so take your hare-brained scheme somewhere else."

But slowly, after the storm and after some skirmishes on the local public defender board, a new slate of board members endorsed the changes. The board agreed to hire full-time public defenders and give them a decent—though still skimpy—starting salary and bumped them from the pre-Katrina rate of $29,000 to $42,000 (which is what it remains today).[20] Steve Singer was temporarily appointed to head up the new office and transition team, and he moved to a system of "vertical representation." This means the lawyer hired to represent someone stayed with the client the whole time, from arraignment to trial. Vertical representation builds rapport between client and attorney, and the defendant begins to trust the lawyer. "If you're an attorney coming to talk to me and I don't know you, I don't know if you're vested in my case; I'd be reluctant to share information," says Henderson, who was himself exonerated after spending "twenty-seven years, ten months, and eighteen days" in prison. "You may have to come and talk to me four or five times before I feel comfortable saying the first thing about my case. In the past, a lot of attorneys would see that as resistance and try to get off the case."

After the storm, backed by a new, reform-minded Public Defenders Board in New Orleans, interim director Singer was able to push ahead with changes. He moved the public defender's office out of its basement room at the courthouse into a nearby office building where there was room for confidential conversations with clients and witnesses, along with working phone lines, computers, a case management system, copy machines, investigators, and administrative help. For the first time, there were performance standards, discussions about limiting caseloads, training and mentoring for new hires, and a system of record keeping and data collection.

Sounds simple, basic. But these were things that had eluded the public defender's office for a long time. When an outside agency, the Bureau of Justice Assistance, stepped in to assess the situation and offer the above recommendations, it concluded its April 2006 report with one caveat: "It is imperative that a stable and adequate funding source be established for the Orleans Parish public defender program and without that commitment, it will remain impossible to provide defendants with the representation to which they are constitutionally entitled."

On July 29, 1976, the state of Louisiana put its fourth and final witness, Sheila Robertson, on the stand—and sealed Gregory Bright's fate. Julien, the prosecutor, led her through her testimony, reminding her when she forgot essential aspects.

"Why were you up at that particular hour of night?" he asked.

"Waiting on a friend," Robertson said.

"And why were you in the window particularly?"

"Looking for a friend."

"And you were looking out the window, looking for him?"

"Right."

"Now, when these three people walked by you, the two defendants and the victim, you say that they were arguing?"

"Yeah."

"Did you notice the victim do anything unusual at that point?"

"I don't understand."

"Did the victim make any kind of motion to you, gestures or anything?"

"I don't understand you."

"The boy who was killed."

"Did he say anything to me?"

"Yeah."

"No. He just only did, you know, like if you would ask for help. You know, he did like this here. You know, like he was asking for help."

"Did he appear to be afraid, upset?"

"Right."

"And he broke out and ran. Is that right?"

"Right."

"And the two defendants are the people you saw run after him?"

"Yeah. They got him as far as to where I marked on there," she said, pointing to a map of the projects that Julien had introduced.

"Where you made the circle?"

"Right."

"And that's where you saw them fight?"

"They started fighting before. I circled that, the last I saw is where I circled at." They disappeared behind a bush, she continued, and then she heard shots.

"Now, what happened after you heard the shots? Did you see anybody after you heard the shots come from that direction?"

"Did I seen anyone come back from that direction?"

"Yes."

"Yes, I did."

"Who did you see?"

"I saw those two guys."

"Now, the two guys that you're referring to, do you know them from the area? From the neighborhood?"

"Yeah. Matter of fact I spoke to both of them."

Julien asked a few more questions, then circled back. "When was the next time you saw them?"

"About two nights later, they came into my apartment," she said.

This didn't jibe with a statement she originally made to police, but no one batted an eye here. Although Robertson had reported to the police ten days after the murder that the two men had broken into her apartment that very night, no one remarks on her inconsistent testimony here. This is the first the defense has heard about a break-in; Greg's and Earl's attorneys have never seen the original police report. As for the assistant DA, it is not in his interest to point out this inconsistency in his star witness's testimony. Instead, Julien simply asked: "What happened? Would you tell the ladies and gentlemen of the jury what happened? What were you doing? What time of night was it?"

"I couldn't really say, Mr. Henry Julien, but it was late," Robertson said. She described hearing some noise, "but then, I said, no, well, that's just my imagination." She laid back down, dozing, she said. "So, the next I seen some flashes of, you know, some heads. I said, no, that's just my imagination. And the next thing, about a second maybe, before I can really say, you know, this guy jumped over the bed, and was over my child, and he held a pistol to his head, and told me, you know, they were only coming to remind me not to go to the policemen, and the next time they come back, I would know what they coming for."

Out of the blue, Robertson had thrown Julien a bone. In her previous statements to police and to the grand jury, she had described being choked. No gun was mentioned. (Once again, the defense did not know this, having never seen previous statements.) Julien, however, would run with it; it upped the ante so nicely. "And your child was sleeping in the bed with you?"

"Yeah, he was sleeping in bed."

"And he pulled a gun on you?" Julien said, referring to the defendants.

"Right."

"Which one, who was it?"

"He didn't pull one on me. It was my kid."

"He held a gun to your kid's head?"

"Right."

"How old is your child?"

"Well, at the time he was a year and four months, maybe five or six. Really I couldn't say, but he was a year and something like that."

"Did you get a look at that person?"

"I beg your pardon?"

"Did you see who that person was?"

"Yes, I did."

"Who was that person?"

"It was that dude right there," she said, pointing to Earl.

"Who else was in the room?"

"The other guy next to him."

"Now, Miss Robertson, did you call the police after this happened?"

"Did I call the police immediately after that?"

"Right, immediately after."

"No, I didn't."

"What did you do?"

"Really, okay, I took—I talked to Housing Authorities. My intentions wasn't to call the police period because of my protection, and also my child's. So—"

"Why did you call the Housing Authorities?"

"To get out of the apartment. I wanted to move out the apartment." The Housing Authority called the police for her.

Julien returned to the question of what she saw the night of the murder. "Did you have any trouble seeing who walks by your window?"

"No trouble at all," Robertson assured him.

Zibilich and Haggerty cross-examine her for thirteen minutes, asking her again what she saw that night, why she did not immediately report what she saw to the police, whether she knew the defendants, and so on.

The state entered a few items into evidence—some photos, the autopsy report—and rested its case.

"Very well," the judge said.

"If Your Honor please, on behalf of Mr. Bright, the defense rests," said Zibilich.

Without calling a single witness on behalf of his client, Zibilich concluded the murder trial in fewer than two hours. Though Greg's eight subpoenaed witnesses sat in the courthouse hallway waiting to be called into the courtroom, several of them alibi witnesses ready to explain where Greg had been that night, Zibilich did not avail himself of them. The judge called a brief recess.

Greg recalls conferring with his attorney: "He said he wasn't going to use the alibi witnesses because he thought it would aggravate the jury, who he said were tired and aggravated that the trial was taking so long." (Later, Zibilich would argue that he didn't think Greg's witnesses were credible.)

Meanwhile, Earl Truvia was having a similar conversation with his attorney, who advised against calling witnesses or letting Truvia himself testify. "He said the jurors were under the impression that we was guilty and the jurors wanted to leave and he said only—if we were to testify, it would only aggravate our situation."[21]

Back in the courtroom, both Zibilich and Haggerty failed to put forward any alternate scenario for the murder, and indeed declined to deliver a closing argument altogether. The jury quickly returned a verdict: Guilty of murder in the second degree. Both Greg and Earl were sentenced to "serve the balance of their natural lives at hard labor in the custody of the department of corrections." It was Earl's eighteenth birthday.

Louisiana, as noted before, leads the country in imprisoning more of its residents per capita than any other state, standing at the forefront of what is really a national trend of over-incarceration. Fueled by the War on Drugs (which has many citizens arrested for possession of small amounts), an increasing tendency to hold more people pretrial with higher bonds, and a tough-on-crime policy reflected in mandatory minimum sentencing laws, the number of people incarcerated in the United States has shot up from 300,000 thirty years ago to more than 2 million today.[22]

Convinced by law enforcement and prosecutors that judges were doling out uneven penalties based on race and socioeconomic status, Congress and state legislatures adopted mandatory minimum penalties, primarily in drug cases. What sounded like good policy at the time essentially shifted the power to adjust a sentence based on factors such as age or family circumstances from judges to prosecutors. So, for instance, the sale of a small amount of drugs prior to the adoption of mandatory minimums might have merited a sentence ranging from probation to ten years. Mandatory minimums, however, would prevent the judge from imposing a sentence any lower than five years. The prosecutor, on the other hand, has the ability to charge the defendant under a different statute that doesn't carry a mandatory minimum (conspiracy, possession, use of a telephone to facilitate a drug crime), but the defendant must plead guilty and pay whatever other price the prosecutor exacts in negotiations. "Cooperation," or becoming an informant, is often required by the prosecutor as the cost of freeing the judge up to consider a lower sentence.

In federal prisons, the numbers of inmates who had received a mandatory sentence rose by 155 percent between 1995 and 2010, from 29,603 to 75,579, according to a 2011 report by the United States Sentencing Commission.[23] Because the number of offenses carrying mandatory minimums has increased so rapidly, inmates serving time in federal prison under such penalties make up almost 40 percent of the prison population. Once again, Louisiana leads the way, with some of the harshest sentencing laws in the country. Three drug convictions can land a person in jail for life, without parole. And the legislature is micromanaging the kinds of sentences meted out, for example, passing a law in 2005 to mandate punishment for thieves stealing sacks of crawfish from ponds, a crime that can send a person away for ten years "depending on the value of the crustaceans," the *Times-Picayune* reported in May 2012.[24]

As a result of these trends, Louisiana has seen an explosion in its prison population, with one out of every eighty-six residents doing time in 2012. In the aforementioned series on incarceration in the state, "Louisiana Incarcerated: How We Built the World's Prison Capital," *Times-Picayune* reporters follow the money to reveal who is profiting from the prison boom that swept the state in the '90s. In the debut article in the series on May 13, 2012, reporter Cindy Chang reports that 53 percent of the state's inmates are housed in "local prisons run by sheriffs or private companies like LaSalle Corrections for the express purpose of making a buck." Chang explains that sheriffs or private companies such as LaSalle Corrections pay small parishes for the privilege of operating the prisons. For example, Jackson Parish, with a population of sixteen thousand residents, gets $100,000 from LaSalle for the privilege of running a 1,147-bed prison there—and the added advantage of one-hundred-plus new jobs for locals working to run the place. Jackson's local sheriff, Andy Brown, who gets a brand-new workforce of deputies at the prison, proudly told the *Times-Picayune* that it was a win-win situation for his small community: "There's a lot of patronage here by hiring all these people. . . . We employ X number of people and don't spend any money, plus the $100,000-a-year sponsor fee. I get the patronage." These local, privately run prisons also house lots of overflow prisoners from the crowded city jails in New Orleans and Baton Rouge—and then try to squeeze a profit from the $24.39 a day they get for each prisoner. (Louisiana spends less than any other place in the country on its inmates.) The privately run local prisons make Angola, a state-run prison, look like the Ritz. Clay McConnell, who inherited the LaSalle prison empire from his father, doesn't dispute that he's after the bottom line. "We realized that prisons are like nursing homes," he told the *Times-Picayune*, referring to the family's prior experience in the nursing home business. "You need occupancy to be high. You have to treat people fairly and run a good ship, but run it like a business, watch food costs, employee costs." This "incarceration on the cheap," Chang reports, typically means no rehab services, no GED programs, no classes to learn a trade. "If you are sentenced to state time in Louisiana, odds are you will be placed in a local prison—a low-budget, for-profit enterprise where you are likely to languish in your bunk, day after day, year after year, bored out of your skull with little chance to learn a trade or otherwise improve yourself."

Later, writing about the 4,500 aging prisoners who are in Angola serving life without the possibility of parole, Chang notes, "while most have committed violent crimes, nearly one in 10 are locked up forever on drug or other nonviolent offenses." Further, "[t]hree out of four are African-American men." Here, in the state-run prison, the Department of Corrections gets slightly more per prisoner ($55 a day, though this is still less than any other state) and they at least offer classes. "The dormitories at Angola sleep about 80 men and have heating in the winter but no air conditioning," one caption in the series read. "Even under the spartan living conditions, a lifer who enters prison in his early 20s will cost taxpayers more than $1 million if he lives past 70. The prisoners have the opportunity to learn a trade, including air-conditioning repair."

Meanwhile, in the city of New Orleans, conditions at the Orleans Parish Prison are notoriously bad. Still, the numbers of incarcerated swell. On the surface, the numbers of incarcerated—and the overcrowding and understaffing in the prisons—appear to have little to do with the problems at the city's public defender's office. But studying the "perfect storm" of problems in the criminal justice system here makes apparent the monetary disincentives and the power imbalances that fuel troubles in the public defender's program here, and in similarly strapped cities nationwide. Prisons, and who controls and fills them, shape policy and reform efforts.

Historically, New Orleans marches lockstep with the nation in this regard. In the 1970s, when New Orleans's population was larger than it is now, the jail had 800 beds. By the time Katrina hit the city in 2005, that number had grown to 8,000 beds. "We have 300,000 [residents] in New Orleans now, which, based on the national average, means we should have 800 or 850 beds in the jail," insists Henderson, of VOTE and Resurrection After Exoneration. "One in fourteen black men from New Orleans is behind bars, compared with one in 141 white men," the *Times-Picayune* reported, and "[o]ne in seven men from the city is either in prison, on probation or on parole."[25]

In the aftermath of Katrina, which destroyed huge swathes of the massive Orleans Parish Prison, multiple circus-style tents were erected to "temporarily" house inmates; seven years later, the tents are still housing prisoners.

In March 2012, the U.S. Marshals Service pulled all its prisoners from the facility due to concerns about safety, the rampant violence, inadequate medical care, and the many deaths that occurred in the facility in the previous five years.

Then, a week later, on April 4, 2012, the Southern Poverty Law Center filed a class-action suit against Orleans Parish Sheriff Marlin Gusman, who runs the New Orleans jail—or Orleans Parish Prison, as it is called—in United States District Court, Eastern District of Louisiana.[26] The suit is one of two hundred lawsuits filed against the jail in the preceding three years. The 3,400-bed jail, which holds mostly people awaiting trial, is a massive complex stretching several blocks behind the courthouse, and more than 35,000 people each year are processed through intake. The Law Center alleges, "Violence is rampant." (To back this up, Southern Poverty Law Center lawyers spoke to dozens of current and past prisoners and studied ambulance records, noting that for the month of February 2012 alone, deputies called for ambulances twenty-three times to transport prisoners to the hospital for "fractures, puncture wounds, lacerations, trauma and the like" and this did not include medical emergencies handled on site.) The facility is understaffed, the lawsuit alleges, leaving prisoners in huge dormitories to police themselves for most of the day while a single guard watches hundreds from an enclosed booth. "The people imprisoned at OPP live in unconstitutional and inhumane conditions and endure great risks to their safety and security. . . . Because OPP is dangerously understaffed and because existing staff lack the training and supervision necessary to care for the people in their custody, corruption and violence are rampant." In the tents, there is one deputy per eighty-eight prisoners; in the House of Detention, a multistory building, one deputy supervises sixty prisoners. "The classification system is inadequate, and fails to screen for prisoners with enemies, as well as fails to sort prisoners into dorms according to propensity for violence or risk of harm. Prisoners face threats to their lives and safety on an almost daily basis, and struggle to secure even the most basic services at OPP. Mental health care is dangerously deficient, exacerbating—and in some instances causing—the violent crises within the facility."[27]

Although national statistics indicate that 64 percent of inmates in local jails suffer from mental illness, the lawsuit notes that in the Orleans Parish Prison there is a policy of suspending all medication for a minimum of thirty days upon admission. "This makes people living with mental illness particularly susceptible to abuse because symptoms of their mental illness begin to manifest acutely when they are denied medication," lawyers assert in the complaint. The one full-time psychiatrist in the 3,400-bed facility, the complaint alleges, "does not conduct minimally adequate assessments or review necessary information before diagnosing (or dismissing) patients and making determinations about whether to prescribe medication. They elaborate:

> All suicidal prisoners are forced to strip naked and change into a suicide smock, and are housed in a large holding tank, together. They are forced to stay in this holding tank for 24 hours a day. In the direct observation tank, there is nowhere to lie down or go to the bathroom. They are denied access to telephones, families and lawyers. People are housed in this tank until they sign a contract stating that they will not harm themselves or others. . . . The psychiatric floor reeks of urine and is extremely hot and loud. Most cells are two-man cells, but many have three men in them, with people sleeping on the floor. Each of the psychiatric tiers also has a six-man cell, which routinely house between 10 and 15 prisoners, with men sleeping on the floor, sometimes without mats.[28]

Sheriff Gusman shut down the House of Detention, one of the most dilapidated buildings, on April 10, 2012.[29] Then, three weeks after the Southern Poverty Law Center filed its class-action suit, the Department of Justice sent a letter to the New Orleans sheriff on April 23, citing the "alarming conditions" at the prison.[30] The inspection uncovered "shockingly high rates of prisoner-on-prisoner violence and officer misconduct," including reports of "widespread sexual assaults, including gang rapes," a "pervasive atmosphere of fear" due to understaffing and reliance on appointed prisoners "to provide security supervision through 'Tier Reps.'" The detailed list of "largely uncontestable" constitutional violations runs twenty-one pages.

Then on May 1, the Southern Poverty Law Center asserted that things were growing even worse in the jail and filed for a preliminary injunction, asking a federal judge to intervene immediately.

All of these troubles make it more difficult for prisoners to receive adequate defense. The sheriff, who in many ways is all-powerful in the city, makes it hard for public defenders to protect their jailed clients. Indeed, he can even make it difficult for them to talk to their clients. Consider: At the same time as the Southern Poverty Law Center was decrying conditions at the jail, the public defender's office, which had also filed a suit against the jail—this one in an effort to force the sheriff to allow the public defenders better access to their clients—reached a tentative agreement with the sheriff mapping out new rules. Public defenders had long complained that it regularly took two hours or more for deputies to produce their clients when the attorneys visited the jails. The sheriff's deputies also commonly failed to produce prisoners in court when they were scheduled to appear. (This ties the public defender's hands and slows the progress of the case when delays pile up.) Further, the hours were very restricted as to when lawyers were even allowed to meet with their clients in jail; many of the buildings had no place for lawyers to have a private conversation with clients and, in the lawsuit, public defenders alleged that their conversations were being monitored and recorded. The new agreement mandated a minimum of seven hours a day and three hours per evening for lawyers to meet with clients, that a space be provided for "confidential" if not totally private meetings, and that prisoners be produced within thirty minutes of attorneys' requests.[31]

"The good news is, lawyers are complaining because they can't get enough access to their clients," says Tulane Law School's Pam Metzger, explaining that before the hurricane, public defenders hardly bothered about access to their clients in jail, mostly talking to them on the fly in open courtrooms. "The bad news is, there is such resistance from the sheriff."

And in Louisiana, sheriffs have extraordinary clout. "The two most powerful people in any parish in Louisiana are not the mayor and city council chair, but the sheriff and the district attorney," says Loyola Law School's Steve Singer. That's because in New Orleans, for example, there are term limits for the mayor and city council but not for the sheriff and DA—so they can often just ride out the storm of an unruly city council or combative mayor. Indeed, Charles Foti Jr., who served as sheriff until 2003, held the post for almost three decades (after a short interim sheriff, current Orleans Parish sheriff Marlin Gusman was elected in 2004). The district attorney, Harry Connick, was there from 1973 to 2003.

Meanwhile, a battle rages over construction of a new jail facility—and how big it will be. "The sheriff wants this massive jail so he can have his own fiefdom," insists Norris Henderson, one of the few folks willing to speak on the record against the sheriff. The jail in the pre-Katrina days housed 6,700 inmates, by 2012 that number was approximately 3,500,[32] and in February 2011, the city council passed an ordinance agreeing to cap the number of beds at 1,400.

This is going to require a massive and coordinated rethinking of how business gets conducted by the police, district attorneys, and sheriff. In an effort to get more nonviolent offenders released on their own recognizance while awaiting trial, the New Orleans sheriff finally agreed to allow the Vera Institute of Justice, a national nonprofit, to start a pretrial release program in the jail in spring 2012. When I visited the jail, three weeks after the introduction of the program, pretrial release staffers were interviewing newly arrested men, collecting data on their history, education level, criminal background, employment situation, and so forth to assess whether the person was going to be a danger to the community or a flight risk. For example, pretrial folks might verify an inmate's employment status—and if the person has a job and has worked consistently for more than two years at the same job, statistical analysis tells us she or he would be more likely to show up for court. This would be considered a positive point and be factored into a simple, total score. New Orleans joins 400 other pretrial programs in the country in using an empirical, evidence-based evaluation of defendants to come up with a score for judges to use in deciding whether or not to release defendants when they first appear before them. Aside from the huge cost saving to taxpayers by cutting down on the number of jailed defendants awaiting trial, it strengthens rather than severs a defendant's ties to the community. If a defendant is released pending trial, he or she can still go to work or school, keep up with rent or a mortgage, make car payments, and pay child support. (For example, one 19-year-old I spoke to in the New Orleans jail had been arrested for marijuana possession. He was in a GED program and would lose his slot if he failed to attend class—not to mention falling behind in his studies.) While such programs have the potential to shift the lay of the land in the criminal justice world, they meet with resistance from different quarters, including the bail bonds lobby, which stands to lose millions if the programs are widely adopted. But advocates say such programs have a host of advantages, not least among them leveling the playing field between rich (who simply post bail and get out) and poor (who frequently can't raise the necessary funds, some 53 percent of those arrested for felonies, according to a 2012 report by the American Bar Association[33]). In another important discrepancy designed to be addressed by the pretrial release program, black defendants awaiting trial in New Orleans on nonviolent felonies in 2010 averaged 54 days in jail while white defendants averaged 31 days according to a 2012 report, "Important Trends in Jail and Pretrial Release" by pretrial consultant James Austin, PhD. These discrepancies can have a huge impact on communities.

In a May 2012 *Times-Picayune* article, reporter John Simerman drew on a 2009 Columbia University study of the small inner-city neighborhood in New Orleans called Central City. It had 4 percent of the overall population before Katrina, but 8 percent of its residents were imprisoned. Further, Simerman observed, cops regularly did "sweeps" in the neighborhood. In a single, small "sparsely populated four-block area" of Central City, they made ninety-eight arrests in the last two years (60 percent of them for drugs). The Calliope Projects, where Greg Bright was arrested in 1975, sit just outside the edge of that neighborhood.

"When I went to prison, I could hardly read my name," says Gregory Bright today. He had dropped out of school in sixth grade to help take care of his sisters and his father, who was disabled by arthritis and bedridden. "When he took ill, I used to read the Lord's Prayer to him. He would help me and I could stumble through it." While he sat in jail at "Tulane and Broad," which had no library but had some magazines and "lots of religious stuff," he slowly taught himself to read *The Watchtower*. "I began to underline all the words I recognized from the Lord's Prayer." After being found guilty in 1976, he was moved from the New Orleans jail to Angola Prison. There, he found a pile of law books that were being thrown out. "I got some of those books, set on my locker, and read them books. Read 'em and read 'em. That's how I come to read, and how I come to know the law."[34]

The more he discovered about the law, the more indignant he grew about the way his case was handled. "I'm watching my twenties, my thirties, my forties disappear," Greg says. "I'm in prison year after year, and in the presence of guys who been there twenty years before me. So I know it's a reality that a life sentence in Louisiana is a life sentence. I could see that."

At the time—and this remains true today—indigent "lifers" were not entitled to an attorney for post-conviction proceedings in state court. While there is more rigorous attention to this in death penalty cases, in Louisiana and other states, lifers have no right to counsel. Instead, what the state of Louisiana provides is what one attorney characterized as "authorizing the unauthorized practice of law by prisoners." In essence, the Department of Corrections will appoint an inmate who is typically self-educated in the law. A guard will give him a typewriter, a computer (without Internet access), some paper, a day or two of training, and a certain amount of freedom to talk to "clients." Called inmate counsel substitutes, they are required to have a GED and attend twenty-four hours of training. (A previous paralegal training program was defunded.) In addition to handling minor, simple legal matters, they also take on hugely complicated cases and appeals. Calvin Duncan, a counsel substitute at Angola for twenty-three years until he was freed in 2011, was described by Emily Bolton, director of an organization called Innocence Project New Orleans, as a rare and skilled exception to the otherwise undereducated jailhouse lawyers. Duncan entered prison with a ninth-grade education when he was nineteen and notes proudly that he initiated certain noncapital appeals in fellow inmate Juan Smith's case, which included a first-degree murder conviction that went all the way to the Supreme Court in 2012, where it was overturned in an 8-1 decision.[35] Still, as Bolton notes, such good legal representation is extremely rare—and real lawyers took over the Smith case. Currently, at Angola Prison, sixty-one counsel substitutes practice law for their five thousand incarcerated clients.

In this manner, but largely through his own initiative, Greg Bright appealed his conviction and tried desperately over the years to procure the documents he knew would help prove his innocence. Between them, he and Earl Truvia made dozens of requests for documents—such as copies of the original police report, the coroner's report, and trial transcripts—from every conceivable government body in the state of Louisiana, including the Department of Agriculture.

Very quickly on the heels of the trial, Earl's attorney appealed the conviction. But no appeal was filed for Greg, because his original attorney Robert Zibilich missed the deadline. According to court documents, Zibilich sent a one-sentence letter to the court saying that Gregory Bright "adopted" the appeal of "Carl Truvia" (sic). But on March 15, 1978, the state supreme court upheld the convictions.

Greg went on to use the knowledge of the law that he gleaned from his prison studies to represent himself in two post-conviction applications. In 1982, he tried to claim ineffective assistance of counsel and denial of compulsory process. He lost that, as did Earl. In 1991, he again argued that he had ineffective counsel, that there was insufficient evidence, and that the jury had received the wrong instructions. He lost that. He also filed a federal habeas corpus application by himself (as had Clarence Earl Gideon some thirty years earlier, similarly insisting he had been wrongly imprisoned), again arguing he'd received ineffective counsel. A certificate of probable cause was granted, but only on the narrow issue that his attorney had failed to call any alibi witnesses. There was a hearing on the issue in May 1982 in which Haggerty and Zibilich were called to testify. Haggerty, who had himself been an assistant district attorney for more than eleven years, clearly did not believe for a minute that his client was innocent. Testifying in 1982 that he saw Sheila

Robertson's name on the witness list and questioned Earl about her, Haggerty said: "He feigned complete ignorance of Sheila Robinson [sic], claimed he didn't know anything about it."[36] By arguing that their failure to call any witnesses was a tactical decision—and a wise one, at that—the two lawyers managed to protect their reputations and tossed Greg and Earl to the wolves.

Meanwhile, Greg kept requesting copies of the police report, which he knew existed in fairly detailed form since on the stand at the trial a detective had been handed a copy of it by the prosecutors to help refresh his memory. In 1994, after eighteen years of asking for it, Greg finally got a copy of the original fifteen-page police report. He found what he had suspected all along: Multiple witnesses fingered two others for the crime, explaining that it was a drug deal gone bad when Elliot Porter skipped off with $300 from two customers but failed to produce the marijuana they thought they were purchasing. Several witnesses named the buyers and insisted that the buyers sought revenge by shooting Porter. But the two people named in the police reports had apparently skipped town and headed to Thibodaux. Cops pursued this a bit and then, suddenly, when Robertson came forward out of the blue, the detectives simply dropped the investigation, arrested Greg and Earl, and closed the file—keeping it from Greg for almost two decades.

Unfortunately, it was not enough to prove the cops were on the trail of other suspects but withheld this information from the defense. Greg—functioning as his own attorney—also had to prove that this information and additional evidence gathered might have caused the jury to deliver a different verdict. But from prison, he couldn't pursue any leads, interview witnesses, access most documents, or properly investigate his case. He was growing increasingly despondent. His chances of proving his innocence were dwindling as the years passed. There was a sign over the majestic stone courthouse in New Orleans that haunted him. "This is a government of law not of men," it said. But Greg was discovering that men—in particular, the influential white elite of New Orleans—had complicated backstories and powerful allegiances. The obstacles this created for a poor black man were nearly insurmountable.

Earl's attorney, Edward Haggerty, for example, had been an assistant DA in the city for eleven years and then a judge in Orleans Parish Criminal District Court for fourteen years.[37] He was booted from the bench in 1970 for "willful and intentional" misconduct "so seriously delinquent as to bring disgrace and discredit upon the judicial office." In fact, he had been caught in a vice raid at a local motel that year. "Haggerty has described the occasion as a before-the-wedding bachelor party," reported the *New Orleans States-Item* in November 1970.[38] "The state contends admission was charged and prostitution was to take place." Porn is euphemistically described as "stag films" and fourteen people were arrested in the raid, including several prostitutes. Police seemed as surprised as anyone to find Judge Haggerty there; Haggerty allegedly resisted arrest, slugged one of the officers, and had to be subdued. Haggerty defended his actions at the time, insisting that such stag parties were an old New Orleans tradition, while his attorney told the *States-Item* that "if all men in the city who had attended such functions were placed on the police blotter, it would read 'like a telephone directory.'" His attorney in the case? Robert Zibilich. The judge in the criminal case was Matthew Braniff, the same judge who would later preside over Greg and Earl's case (argued by Haggerty and Zibilich). Braniff threw out the criminal charges against then-judge Haggerty due to insufficient evidence, but the state's judiciary commission ordered Haggerty removed from the bench.

Such overlapping histories and allegiances would trip things up for Greg Bright—and ultimately for indigent defense reform in the city. Consider this: two prosecutors tried Greg's case, one of them would go on to become the judge hearing all his appeals (i.e., the judge was empowered to weigh in on accusations about his very own prosecutorial misconduct). How could this happen? In Orleans Parish, post-conviction appeals are heard by the same section of the court that heard the original trial. If the original judge left or died, whatever judge was elected to that section (courtroom) to replace him would hear the post-conviction appeals. In Greg's case, the judge who heard the original case, Judge Braniff, was no longer on the bench. His successor was a judge named Patrick Quinlan, who was also the assistant district attorney who prosecuted Earl and

Greg's case. When Greg and Earl filed their post-conviction applications themselves, they automatically went to now-judge Patrick Quinlan. He should, of course, have recused himself from their case as he prosecuted it. He did not. If there had been the right to counsel in noncapital post-conviction appeals in Louisiana, the lawyer representing them would have known Quinlan was now on that bench and have moved to have him recused. The case would have been randomly reallocated to another courtroom—and judge. But Greg and Earl, representing themselves, did not know who the new judge was in that section of the court. Finally, Greg saw Quinlan's name on some court documents and once that happened, he tried to figure out what he should do. It didn't seem fair, but what were his options?

Consulting the law books, Greg learned he could take a writ to the Louisiana Supreme Court saying that his and Earl's post-conviction appeals had been denied by a judge who had originally been a member of the team that prosecuted them. The state supreme court agreed that Judge Quinlan should have recused himself, overruled his denial of the appeal, and ordered that the cases be randomly reallocated. They were, and then strangely, ended up in different courts.

Today, Greg insists there were some shenanigans going on with the "random" reassignment of his case. His appeal was randomly reallocated to Judge Charles Elloie's section. But then he was brought into Judge Dennis Waldron's court in error. Judge Waldron, says Greg, was Quinlan's supervisor in the DA's office. "So then he's denying my appeal," says Greg. "That went on and on till I felt like [I was] boxed in."

Greg was deeply discouraged. For years, his mother had regularly buoyed his spirits with her visits to the prison. "It's painful to watch someone else's pain," Greg says. "So we're both trying to cheer each other up. I tried to always have something positive to tell her when she came. I'd say, 'Mom, I just found this out [with my case]. It's a huge discovery right here.' Or I'd say, 'I'm going to file this or that.' She'd say, 'I don't really know what you saying, but it sound good.'" But good news about the progress of his case had ceased. And his mother had died the year before. Greg found himself in deep despair, ready for the first time to give up on his case, and the chance of freedom.

The right to counsel in a criminal case seems so fundamental, most Americans would be shocked to learn the extent of constitutional lapses that continue to exist. But consider how the kind of problems Greg Bright had with getting effective counsel span the decades—and spill into contemporary New Orleans.

On April 18, 2011, New Orleans police arrested Clarence Jones, a forty-one-year-old African American man. Clarence contends that he was walking with his cousin Keitha Hyde, running some errands around 11:30 A.M., when he ducked into an alley to relieve himself. "It was just an empty house, so I went in the backyard out of sight," he says. When the cops turned the corner, he looked guilty. But police assert that Clarence was climbing out of a window with pliers in his left hand, apparently scrapping for metal or copper wiring in the gutted building. The cops arrested him and his cousin and took them to the Orleans Parish Prison. On May 13, nearly a month later, Clarence finally appeared before a magistrate in Orleans Parish Criminal Court, who arraigned him on the charge—simple burglary—and set his bail at $10,000 (before raising it four days later to $20,000).

More than sixteen months later, Clarence is still sitting in jail waiting for an attorney to be assigned to represent him. "It's been hell back here," he says, explaining that he is living, along with approximately four hundred other prisoners, in one of the "temporary" tents.[39] "It's like we animals," he tells me via phone one afternoon in June 2012. "They're just packing more and more people in. They got us packed to capacity. Lots of us have no attorney," says Clarence. "Can't do nothing but sit back here. We're just stuck."

As an impoverished, incarcerated defendant in a criminal case, Clarence has a guaranteed right to free counsel. But in Louisiana, even today, such rights are routinely flouted. Indeed, Clarence was one of 230 defendants sitting in limbo at the Orleans Parish Prison in June 2012, as a $2 million budget shortfall forced the Orleans Parish public defender's office to lay off twenty-seven employees, twenty-one of them lawyers. Hundreds more defendants are out on bond, trying to make sense of the court documents being sent to them and wondering whether they will ever be assigned a lawyer to help. As post-Katrina federal dollars dry up and the fiscal crisis forces drastic budget cuts at the state and local levels, one of the areas hardest hit in New Orleans—and in the nation at large—has been public defender offices. When money gets tight, the lawyers charged with protecting the rights of the poor in criminal cases are considered expendable.

Describing the situation as "dire," Norman Lefstein, a member of the American Bar Association's Standing Committee on Legal Aid and Indigent Defendants and the author of several books on the topic, says the system was already severely overburdened prior to the current economic crisis. "Now, across the country, these strapped public defender offices are seeing freezes and outright reductions in their budgets," says Lefstein, "resulting in even fewer lawyers available to provide services."

The stories mount. A 2011 Justice Policy Institute report cites example after example: California cut costs by implementing low-bid contracts for public defense (the aforementioned fraught arrangement where the winning attorney has to take on hundreds of clients for a flat fee); in Kentucky, the state cut the Department of Public Advocacy budget by $500,000 and, with deeper cuts expected in 2012, anticipated a reduction in services; Minnesota lost 15 percent of its public defender staff due to layoffs.

Something very similar happened in New Orleans. Squeezed by budget shortfalls, chief public defender Derwyn Bunton announced that he was laying off nearly a third of his lawyers. Bunton cut the entire staff of his conflicts division, the department responsible for representing additional defendants in cases with more than one person charged. (An example of a conflicts division case: two people rob a liquor store and one of them shoots the cashier. Each of the men points to the other as the shooter; they'll need two separate lawyers.) As a result, a slew of people suddenly lost their lawyers.

If these conflicts division defendants aren't provided with an attorney and a "speedy trial" can't proceed, by law they ought to be released from prison. But most of them aren't released, despite this clear violation of their constitutional rights. Why? For several reasons. First, it's a catch-22 for the jailed defendants: most of them need a lawyer to fully grasp how their rights are being violated and help them make that argument in court. Second, there is some linguistic fudging going on: it's not that they're being *denied* representation; these defendants are simply "on a wait list" for private, pro bono representation. (Since February 2012, the number of defendants on the pro bono wait list has shot as high as 543.) Third, due to quirks in Louisiana law, folks can be held up to four months (depending on the alleged crime) before the district attorney decides whether or not to pursue the case. It's possible that some particularly proactive judge could step in and start setting these jailed defendants free—but it had better be someone who doesn't mind losing the next election for being "soft" on crime.

Meanwhile, the poor languish in jails. For example, on June 11, 2012, I spoke by phone to Willie Cheneau Jr., a thirty-two-year-old unemployed handyman who'd been sitting in Orleans Parish Prison for nearly two months, ever since his arrest for possession of a nickel bag of marijuana on April 24. The fact that this was his second arrest for possession bumped the charge up from a misdemeanor to a felony. Although he is very poor and qualifies for a public defender, Willie had no attorney assigned to represent him. His friend had been picked up in the same bust and merited a public defender, so Willie's case was relegated to the now-defunct conflicts division. The judge set Willie's bond at $1,000; to bail him out, someone would have to pay 13 percent plus fees, or $180.

Willie is single and had been living with his mother. When she was contacted by a bail bondsman to show up in court with the $180, his mom refused, according to Willie. She figured he needed to get his life together. "She tired," Willie explains. "She tired of me. She's turning fifty, all her children are grown. She's been raising kids since she was sixteen, and she says, 'Y'all grown—now I'm going to live my life.'" He isn't angry with her for not coming up with the $180 bail, but he desperately wants out of the Orleans Parish Prison, where he's housed in a tent with eighty-eight other inmates. "It ain't no place to be," he says. "There's a guy in here trying to see the nurse. He hasn't eaten in eight days, coming down off heroin. They won't medicate him. Just stick him in here and make him go cold turkey."

Willie doesn't deny that he had the weed or pretend that he hasn't been in trouble before. (As a teen, he was convicted of stealing a car and then, a few years later, on a burglary charge.) But he doesn't understand why he should sit in jail for two months without being able to talk to a lawyer. He'd like to plead guilty to the marijuana charge—but he can't even do that without a lawyer to represent him and get him into court.

Willie's pretty typical of the people who flood the public defender's office, and the folks waiting for attorneys to represent them. But his plight doesn't generate a lot of sympathy.

Chief public defender Bunton has tried, but it's hard to rally support for the program. The state is funding 53 percent of New Orleans's budget for public defense, while the city pays 1 percent. "And the remainder we pray for," Bunton says, explaining that the rest of the budget for the forty-seven-person office depends on traffic tickets and court fees or fines from the mostly poor folks processed by the courts here—a practice not unique to New Orleans, but one that makes the funding variable and unreliable.

Today, public defenders in the city represent more than 28,990 criminal defendants each year. But even as the 2012 Orleans Parish public defender's budget shrank from $9.5 million to $7 million, there was an uptick in the number of cases prosecuted by the local district attorney: 30 percent more felonies alone than the preceding year (arrests during the same period held steady).[40] The district attorney's budget—$14 million—is far larger than the public defender's $7 million, giving prosecutors a serious manpower advantage. Add to the mix the national economic crisis, the local public defender budget cuts, and new super-aggressive Orleans Parish district attorney Leon Cannizzaro, who has been criticized by public defenders for accepting more cases, overcharging for crimes, and bringing more defendants to trial—and the confluence of events produces a disaster.

Here's what is supposed to happen: municipal, traffic, and criminal courts all collect fees from convictions. Every time a person is found guilty or pleads guilty, they pay a fee, and $45 of that fee goes to fund indigent defense in that jurisdiction. Also, ironically, they are charged a $40 application fee to apply for indigent status; this too goes to the public defender's office. (While this could be viewed as an abrogation of *Gideon* and the promise of *free* counsel to the indigent, the fairly common practice goes largely unchecked.) If a district has an interstate cutting through, it can fund fairly robust indigent defense services by passing out speeding tickets to out-of-towners (area law enforcement is sensitive to sheriff reelection campaigns and treads lightly on locals), but if there is no interstate in the parish, the income stream slows to a trickle. Such traffic-based financing creates huge funding imbalances, and huge discrepancies in the quality of defense a client gets around the state. Worse, Bunton insists, is the fact that "there is absolutely no correlation between this [traffic- and court-fee-based] income source and a district's criminal arrests—and many indigent programs across the state are severely underfunded." A troubled urban district like Orleans Parish, which has a high volume of serious cases—eight hundred armed robberies, for example, in 2011—makes defense time intensive and expensive.[41]

There is also an inherent conflict of interest with a system that pays its public defenders from the kitty of fees and fines paid by those found guilty. Fees and fines can range from $35 to several hundred dollars. "How would you feel if you hired a lawyer and he asked you to sign a contract that said, 'You only have to pay me if you lose'?" says Katherine Mattes, who directs Tulane University Law School's Criminal Litigation Clinic. Mattes challenged this funding mechanism as conflicting with the Sixth Amendment right to counsel in 2006, insisting the amendment meant "conflict free" counsel. The trial court in two sections of Orleans Parish Criminal Court agreed. However, because the state's attorney general never appealed the ruling up to the Louisiana Supreme Court, the impact was limited to two local courtrooms. Otherwise, it is business as usual. And that puts Louisiana's public defenders in a jam. One public defender, who did not want her name used, says she regularly asked that her clients' fees be waived due to their poverty. But under the budget crisis, the marching orders are different. "Now we're supposed to say, make my client pay because that funds me and my salary," she says. "That's not advocating for the client, that's advocating for us."

Bunton, who in May 2012 found himself in the uncomfortable position of urging the state legislature to increase the indigent defense fee from $35 to $45 or face another year of budget shortfalls and layoffs, recognizes the conflict. "It put us in a trick bag where we need, in the short term, an additional infusion of money, but as a long-term solution to the question 'how do you fund public defense?' it's a poor one."

Even collecting the money owed poses big problems. In the last five years, the Orleans public defenders and the Louisiana Public Defender Board, created in 2007, have stepped up efforts to track the revenue stream—and discovered they've been shortchanged. "When you start pulling up these rocks, things begin to scurry," Bunton says, and notes that they've ended up suing judges, auditing traffic court, and investigating collection procedures.

On December 20, 2010, the state and local public defender boards joined forces to sue twenty-three New Orleans judges in the Nineteenth Judicial Court in East Baton Rouge Parish for failing to assess the then-$35 fee from guilty defendants.[42] State board chairman Frank Neuner announced the suit in a press release, declaring that he was reluctant to sue judges but, "If judges are not assessing the amounts that the Legislature intended, the costs of representation fall heavily upon Louisiana's taxpayers."

Then in May 2012, auditors hired by the Orleans public defenders discovered that Orleans Traffic Court had failed to give the public defenders their share of traffic ticket revenue. In the two-month window auditors investigated, the public defender's office was shorted $84,000.[43] Extrapolating from there, it could be owed as much as $500,000 a year for who knows how many years. The *Times-Picayune* reported on May 14, 2012, that "the judges also keep hundreds of thousands more for the court by reducing traffic violations to contempt violations or other tickets on which the court collects a fee for itself but isn't required under state law to pass along money to other agencies." The court disagrees and the battle is still raging.

Meanwhile, Bunton turned to the city council, itself strapped for cash. The public defenders banked on the city council to make up the shortfall, but got squeezed between the state, which had cut their budget by $2 million, and the city, which said indigent defense was a state responsibility. Ultimately, the city council kicked in $1.2 million, but that left the office severely underfunded for the year, thus the twenty-seven people laid off.

"Now we're back to square one, begging people for money so public defenders can do their jobs," says Norris Henderson, of Voice of the Ex-Offender and Resurrection After Exoneration, worried about the recent backslide. "The criminal justice system can't work without the defendant having an attorney."

It was in this desperate context that, in February 2012, Criminal District Judge Arthur Hunter Jr. took the radical step of appointing a group of high-profile lawyers to represent thirty-two criminal defendants pro bono in his courtroom. These defendants were among the 543 people who were left without attorneys to represent them on the heels of the public defender layoffs. The judge, insisting that he was merely acting to appoint lawyers in this "constitutional emergency," named state legislators, the head of the local crime board, and other high-powered attorneys—whether or not they had ever practiced criminal law.

Democratic state senator Karen Peterson learned that she had a twenty-two-year old client who'd been charged with possession of marijuana and alprazolam and possession with intent to distribute hydrocodone. She quickly filed a motion to withdraw from the case, according to the *Times-Picayune*: "I've never, ever appeared or represented anyone in criminal court. I practice commercial transactions."

Many of those asked to take on these cases pro bono are attorneys at big law firms with expertise in civil suits, not criminal cases. Some of these private attorneys admit to being out of their depth— and several have contacted Mattes at Tulane's law clinic for advice and assistance. "Having tax attorneys and property lawyers tackle criminal cases is far from ideal," says Mattes. "You don't ask the cardiologist to do your brain surgery."

Other judges in the city have asked the laid-off public defenders to remain on their cases. But these are folks who are scraping by, having been laid off with only two weeks' notice from a job where the annual salary was in the $40,000 to $60,000 range. It's fair to wonder how much work someone in that situation will do when they're ordered to defend a client without pay. (In fact, the laid-off lawyers I spoke with are ethical professionals and deeply committed to their work; one who consented to be interviewed on the condition that I not use his name, says he's remained on several cases at judges' requests. "I can't afford to work for free," he says. "But whether I'm rehired or working as a private attorney, I'm likely to be arguing a case in that judge's courtroom in the future. I don't want to burn any bridges with him.")

Henderson insists that this breakdown in public defender services threatens the criminal justice system as a whole. "If you're sent to battle with five hundred soldiers and find out you need five thousand, you're going to take on a lot of casualties," Henderson says. "You simply don't have the same resources the other side has." And prior to the reforms, there were a lot of casualties—thus, Louisiana's extraordinarily high exoneration rate. Henderson, who is meeting with me in May 2012 at the Resurrection After Exoneration office, sweeps his hands around the room. The walls are lined with portraits of people exonerated in Louisiana in the last decade, and Henderson summarizes each of their stories, intimate and friendly with the men whose stories he tells. They are not statistics; he knew almost all of them in prison before he himself was exonerated after twenty-seven years. He gets to the oversize black-and-white photograph of a man in his fifties, his face gaunt and lined, and launches into the story of this man's twenty-seven-year prison stint at Angola. Minutes later, this same man steps through the front door, ready to slink into the back office where he is doing some work for the organization. It is Gregory Bright.

"I didn't want to concede defeat," Greg Bright says today, casting his eyes back on his darkest days in 2000, his twenty-sixth year behind bars. "But I was kinda in a hopeless situation."

Unknown to him, help was about to arrive from an unexpected quarter. In 2001, Innocence Project New Orleans opened its doors in Louisiana. The director, Emily Bolton, had just graduated from law school and launched the project with a fellowship from Equal Justice Works (for two years of salary at $32,000 per year) and a $10,000 grant from Columbia Public Interest Law Foundation for expenses. The project perched in borrowed office space, and relied on law student volunteers for extra labor, as Bolton was the only staffer. Once word got out about the project, it was flooded with requests for help from the state's prisoners. Bolton decided they would exclude inmates on death row, since these men were already guaranteed legal representation, and accept cases only from prisoners who were sentenced to life. These "lifers" had no right to a post-conviction attorney. Speaking to me via Skype in May 2012 from her new home in England, she insists the difference between these cases is mere semantics: "After all, the lifers were going to die there, too, they just didn't have a specific date set." She figured her organization could tackle a very narrow class of people. "How about if we start with the smallest possible group, the innocent?" she thought. "How many can that be?" She was shocked. "Ha, ha! Turns out there was a lot." There was "a huge floating mass" of folks serving life sentences in the state—4,900 prisoners—and within a year, 2,000 of them had sent letters to the Innocence Project asking for help with their cases.

Most of these pleas for help were not from prisoners saying they were actually innocent. Contrary to the mythology, Bolton says plenty of prisoners acknowledge their guilt—but ask for help with problems as diverse as an unfair sentence, denial of access to public records about their cases, or simply help ascertaining whether their mother is still alive when prison mail goes astray. But there was also a disturbing number of letters from prisoners stating that they were actually innocent. So Bolton turned for help to the sixty "counsel substitutes" across the state, the inmates who were, in essence, deputized to provide legal advice to other prisoners. "We took care not to make them the sole gatekeepers to prisoners reaching us with their cases, but as people who lived around the applicants; inmate counsel were giving me some insight as to whether this was the real deal or what," she says. She recalls one inmate counsel mentioning Greg and Earl, who "had been boring the pants off their dorm mates for twenty-five years about their innocence." Bolton asked for some information on the case, slowly collecting documents—while steadily cautioning Greg, via phone or letter, that she wasn't promising anything.

In February 2001, she agreed to represent him at least temporarily in getting his case moved back into the section of court that it was supposed to be in. As she prepared, she delved deeper into the court papers surrounding Greg's case. The more she read, the clearer it became that something had gone terribly wrong here. Meeting him for the first time that February, as the two of them walked down long courthouse corridors from the wrong courtroom to the reassigned one, she considered him. Greg was tall, lanky, careworn, soft-spoken, and shackled, shuffling along in his orange prison jumpsuit with a guard beside him. Bolton was short, white, young, fast-talking, and looked like a suffragette with her dark hair swept into a massive, loose bun as she hopped along beside him. "How do you feel about being represented by someone who was five years old when you went to jail?"

"Okay," he said.

But he didn't mean it. He wasn't sure he trusted her. He wasn't even sure he understood her. "I was just devastated," Greg says describing their first meeting. "She has this heavy British accent and I could barely understand every other word she was saying, she just so excited and stuff." He sweeps his hands up around his head, trying unsuccessfully to describe her "huge, big, huge, big thing of hair," and admitting that her appearance alone left him deeply troubled. How was this petite British woman who looked like she stepped out of another century going to stroll into a Louisiana courtroom and take on the Southern good old boys in a murder case? Like Clarence Earl Gideon before him, Greg was terribly worried about the efficacy of an out-of-town lawyer; unlike Gideon, he was poised to take a leap of faith.

His friends thought he was crazy. "That a crippled filly," they warned. "You need a horse that would finish." They were skeptical, Greg recalls, "because she a woman and British and she looking so timid and looking so like they're going to walk all over her." They repeatedly warned him. "'Slim,' they say, 'don't do it. Scrape you some change together and get someone else.' But it ain't always the strong, it's not always the cannon that wins." Could be some pre-cision artillery was called for at this point. "I thought about it and talked about it and prayed about it. I mean, it didn't make no better sense to try to hire someone than it did to let this woman take this case who had a genuine interest." And really, it's not like lawyers were banging down his door asking to represent him. "I told them guys, 'You look here. I been in prison twenty-five years and in all this time this is the first time that someone has taken an interest in my case. I'm going to let her ride.'" He turned over more and more of the papers to her, the documents he'd painstakingly collected over the years. "'Damn,' she said. 'Didn't nothing look right.'" Here was something; that's what he'd been thinking all these long years. He smiles: "She just took it and ran with it."

In the days ahead, Greg and his best friend in prison, Bo White, took to calling her Butcher Knife Shorty. "She may be little, but she cuts some tall lumber," they'd say.

The first thing Bolton did was a take a little ride, a quarter mile down the road from the courthouse to the scene of the crime. This was something Greg's attorney Robert Zibilich should have done twenty-five years ago, days after he accepted the case; had he done so, the case may well have fallen apart. Bolton discovered that there was no way the state's primary witness could have seen what she described taking place on the sidewalk, no way she could have seen the hole in the fence, no way she could have seen Elliot Porter where she said she did. Beneath Sheila Robertson's third-story bedroom window was a porch roof that completely obstructed her view of the sidewalk.

Then Bolton studied the woman's testimony and noticed how her sequence of events shape-shifted over time. First she said the two men broke into her apartment and threatened her. Later, she would say they choked her. By the time she got to the trial, she said they had a gun—and they threatened to kill her baby. Robertson also testified that she could see "pretty good" and therefore had no trouble identifying the men who broke into her house because she had the bathroom, kitchen, and hall lights on. In fact, the kitchen and the bathroom were on the floor below the bedroom. Other incon-sistencies began to pile up. She said that she reported the break-in to the Housing Authority; the Housing Authority, which kept very detailed tenant records, especially of crimes, had no record of such a complaint.

And finally, when Bolton acquired a copy of the original autopsy report, she discovered that the coroner's report noted that rigor mortis had not yet set in when the body was autopsied at 9 A.M. that day. She spoke to the original forensic pathologist who conducted the autopsy. He confirmed that the time of death had to be between 5 and 8 A.M. There was no way the boy could have been killed at 1:30 A.M. as Sheila had testified.

Bolton was puzzled that Greg was convicted without a shred of physical evidence tying him to the crime. No gun was ever found. No blood, fingerprints, footprints, hair, or anything else was collected. None of the victim's clothes or possessions were found in Greg's possession, despite the fact that some things had been stolen from Elliot Porter. The police were clearly on the trail of two different suspects, when Sheila Robertson surfaced with her eyewitness statement.

But why would Sheila, who didn't even know these guys, lie? It didn't make sense. Bolton knew she had to have a conversation with Sheila Robertson. She was steadily gathering such public records as were available on the woman, from the courts, the Department of Motor Vehicles, and the police. Strangely, on one state document printout she noticed an "aka" next to the name. She investigated further and made a startling discovery. The witness's name wasn't Sheila Robertson at all. She was Shelia Caston—and Shelia Caston was a "career criminal" who, with her multiple aliases, had been arrested for shoplifting, theft, forgery, prostitution, drug possession, and distribution.[44]

There were so many unanswered questions about Caston's testimony, Bolton knew she had to talk to her. But where was she? All of the addresses Bolton and her team could find for Caston were old; she was transient, impossible to track down. "We were always looking for her," says Bolton, explaining that they took to entering her name and her various aliases into the jail computer whenever they had a quiet moment, thinking a career criminal was likely to resurface in jail. One day, they got a break. She had been arrested.

Bolton paid her a visit at the Louisiana Correctional Institute for Women. She spent two hours talking to Caston, who "cried quite a lot" and said she couldn't really remember events from back then. Caston shared snatches of her past—abused as a child, sent off to the State Industrial School for Colored Youth, addicted to heroin as an adult, ill and hospitalized for long stretches of time on the third floor of Charity Hospital—but Bolton left no more enlightened than when she arrived. "Her life story was rough, traumatic, and tragic," Bolton said. "It still didn't make sense, though. Why would you lie about something that would send someone to prison for life?" She wanted a "Miss Marple moment of motive," she says, but it eluded her.

Still, she kept thinking about her interview with Caston. There was something odd about her phrasing: *third floor of Charity*, she'd said. Strange. Who says, "I was ill and hospitalized on the *seventh floor* of Union Memorial"? She turned the phrase over in her mind as she left the prison, figuring it a local euphemism, but for what? She set the thought aside. A few days later it came back to her, *third floor of Charity Hospital. Third floor?* Suddenly, it clicked. She looked it up. Sure enough, it *was* a euphemism. The third floor of Charity Hospital was the psych ward.

Gregory Bright's twenty-six-year stretch of bad luck was about to change.

Bolton got a court order for Caston's hospital records, and those under her alias Robertson. To her surprise, she learned that the state's only witness was a paranoid schizophrenic. In fact, she was experiencing hallucinations at the time of the murder and alleged break-in of her home. Hospital records revealed that she had been admitted in January 1975 for psychotic depression. According to documents filed in the case, "[s]he had a previous diagnosis of paranoid schizophrenia and sociopathic personality disorder on admission, from her treatment at Center City Mental Health Clinic." She was brought to the hospital when her two-year-old son was hospitalized after she allegedly abused him.[45] A doctor had noted in her file: "She was depressed, crying and experienced auditory and visual hallucinations (voices telling her she was going to be killed or to kill her second child)." Because of the accusations of child abuse and the intervention of Child Protective Services, it wasn't even clear that any of her children were actually living with her when she testified that Greg and Earl held a gun to her baby's head. There are multiple mentions of hallucinating in her hospital files, which also note that she threatened to burn down a cousin's house and her mother's house. She also suffered from something called pica. In her case, it manifested itself by her compulsion to consume cloth towels almost every day, beginning in her childhood. "This condition is more usually seen in third world countries," Bolton would later explain to a judge, "and is a primitive human response to malnutrition; in Ms. 'Robertson' it persisted into adulthood perhaps because she remained malnourished as a heroin addict."[46] From the pieces of documentation that Bolton and her team began accumulating—gathered from hospitals, probation, child welfare, police—it emerged that Caston, at the time she was testifying in Greg's trial, was a drug addict (heroin, marijuana, and amphetamines), had a long history of psychiatric problems that had her in and out of treatment since she was sixteen years old, and was intermittently on an antipsychotic medication called Mellaril (thioridazine).

"This was seven months before she was approached by the police and told them she had seen Elliot Porter's murder," Bolton wrote in a new, amended application for post-conviction relief that she was drafting on Greg's behalf over the summer of 2001. "The fact that the only witness against Mr. Bright was medicated in an attempt to reduce incidents of psychosis was information that would have been critical to his defense," she adds in her understated, British way. "But it was kept from Mr. Bright by the State."

Finally, it turns out that Caston was a sort of "professional witness" and had helped put away at least two other men, one for heroin distribution and one for murder. There was a confused—though never substantiated—reference by Caston herself that she may have been paid some "Crime stopper" money in exchange for her statement to police.

On the day that Greg and Earl's trial had been scheduled to begin in June 1976, it had to be delayed for a month because Caston was at that very moment hospitalized at Sara Mayo Hospital for mental health services, and therefore unable to testify. This would seem to indicate that the state was well aware of the star witness's questionable credibility, yet prosecutors declined to share this information (or even Robertson's real name, which would allow Greg's attorney Zibilich access to a completely different person's rap sheet) with the defense.

On August 20, 2001, Bolton, along with local attorney Jason Rogers Williams, filed a 148-page amendment to the application for post-conviction relief that Greg had written on his own behalf in 1995. The amendment cited twenty-three reasons why Greg's conviction should be overturned. Then, on February 8, 2002, and again on February 22, 2002, Greg finally had his day in court. In these two evidentiary hearings, Bolton and her team presented 150 documents and testimony by twenty witnesses—all the new facts they had collected in Greg and Earl's case.

The judge chided the DA for the shoddy prosecution of this case, particularly the withholding of crucial evidence. "The court finds that the district attorney's office was aware of these facts about its eye witness, including the false identity of the eye witness and her problems with the law and with the courts, and that this evidence is Brady material which, if presented to the jury, was reasonably likely to have produced a different result in the trial," Judge Charles Elloie wrote on March 11, 2002. "For these reasons, the conviction herein is vacated and set aside and a new trial is ordered."

The district attorney's office appealed this, but after many months, the Louisiana Supreme Court turned down the state's appeal. The judge set the date for a new trial. Meanwhile, a new assistant district attorney, Robert White, was assigned to the case. Bolton describes him as "an ex-navy man with a keen eye for injustice, and probably the first person in the district attorney's office to actually read the entirety of the material filed on Greg's behalf." Bob White decided that the charges should be dropped in the interests of justice, and his boss agreed to do just that. The charges were dismissed, and on June 23, 2003, Greg and Earl walked out of Angola as free men with nothing but $10 and a garbage bag full of legal paperwork. Earl did not even have shoes.

Poor defendants in New Orleans today continue to fight for basic rights in the criminal justice system. The case of Clarence Jones, the

New Orleans man accused of burglary, is complicated but instructive. At his May 17, 2011, arraignment—almost a month after he'd been arrested—the judge agreed with Clarence's assertion that he was indigent and qualified for a public defender. (Clarence is a day laborer in construction, mostly with hazardous material—including, in the aftermath of Katrina, such things as mold remediation, lead paint, and asbestos removal. At the time of his arrest, he was out of work and qualified for food stamps.) Because his co-defendant in the case had already secured a lawyer from the public defender's office, Clarence was appointed someone from the conflicts division, LaShanda Webb.

Then on June 27, 2011, Clarence was sent over from the jail to the courthouse for a preliminary hearing. But his attorney, likely busy in another courtroom, never showed up. The hearing was rescheduled for July 11. Clarence's lawyer and a police officer showed up for that and probable cause was found for the burglary charge. (The judge found no probable cause for Clarence's cousin, Keitha Hyde, and reduced her charge to trespassing.) The judge set a trial date of July 25.

On July 25, the state asked for a postponement. The court granted the request and set a new trial date, September 22. On September 22, the court docket says simply, "Defendant, Clarence Jones Jr did not appear for trial. Defendant in custody and not brought into court." This would become a refrain in the records; Clarence has lost track of the number of times the jail neglected to bring him to court or, having transported him to the building, left him sitting in the "docks," a holding pen for inmates waiting to be brought by sheriff's deputies into their respective courtrooms. Sometimes, the attorneys are simply filing routine papers and don't need their clients to be present in the courtroom, but sometimes clerks or understaffed sheriff's deputies simply fail to get it together. One public defender insider said mildly that such snafus were "not completely uncommon." In Clarence's case, the docket notes that deputies failed to deliver him to the courtroom twelve times in a sixteen-month period. Because a trial cannot go forward without the defendant in the courtroom, the delays piled up.

Meanwhile, Clarence's attorney also failed to show up on September 22. The judge postponed the trial, and a hearing was set for September 29—at which point the judge set a new trial date of December 7. On December 7, she set a new date for a pretrial conference of December 12. On that day, Clarence had a newly appointed attorney, Leigh Ann Rood, show up in court on his behalf; unbeknownst to him, his original lawyer, Webb, had left her job at the public defender's office. Clarence says Rood never met with him. Not that they had much chance to build rapport. Clarence's trial was rescheduled for March 1—but by then, Rood had become a casualty of the mass layoffs at the public defender's office. She lost her job, and Clarence became one of the 543 indigent defendants in the city of New Orleans, people charged with everything from possession of marijuana to murder, who were suddenly without a lawyer.

A year passed, slowly.

Clarence spent it in the Orleans Parish Prison tents. "I never been appointed another lawyer," he told me in June 2012. "They call me to court, I sit back in the dock, and they never let me in." He tried to educate himself on the law: reading some books from the prison library, talking to other inmates, and doing some seat-of-the-pants legal work on his own behalf. "I'm not the only one back here don't have a lawyer," he says. "We get law books, so I read a few pages to see what fits my case." He tells me that he filed a motion for "discovery and inspection" to see what kind of evidence might be introduced during the trial and a motion to "squash" (meaning *quash*) based on a violation of Louisiana's Code of Criminal Procedure, which says he has a right to a speedy trial. And while Clarence may be a bit off on the lingo, he's correct on the essence: "The trial of a defendant charged with a felony shall commence within one hundred twenty days if he is continued in custody." Clarence is doing the best he can, but after spending so many months in jail, he is growing discouraged and starting to wonder if he will ever get out. "I think it sucks," he says. "I think if I had an attorney, I would have been home."

Not that Clarence Jones has spent his life treading the straight and narrow. Indeed, he's been arrested five times in his life and convicted twice: once in March 2004 for a misdemeanor (possession of marijuana) and a second time in May 2004 for a felony (distribution of marijuana). It's not inconceivable that he did attempt a burglary and is lying about what he was doing in that alley. The point is, who knows? Without a trial, and without an attorney to help him navigate our complicated legal labyrinth, he is languishing in jail, his constitutional rights clearly violated. (Case in point: I personally had to consult three local attorneys to "translate" the docket master and comprehend the loopy history of his case.)

Almost fifty years ago, an indigent man who shared the same first name—Clarence—and the same charge (he was accused of burglarizing a pool hall in Panama City, Florida) helped establish the right to counsel in *Gideon v. Wainwright*. Like Clarence Jones, Clarence Gideon did not have a lawyer and wrote to the court himself. "Petitioner cannot make any pretense of being able to answer the learned attorney General of the State of Florida because the petitioner is not a attorney or versed in law nor does not have the law books to copy down the decisions of this Court. But the petitioner knows there is many of them," Gideon wrote to the U.S. Supreme Court in April 1962 from his jail cell. "All countrys try to give there citizens a fair trial and see to it they have counsel."

In March 1963, the U.S. Supreme Court agreed. Writing for the majority, Justice Hugo Black stated the obvious: "[R]eason and reflection require us to recognize that in our adversarial system of criminal justice, any person haled into court, who is too poor to hire a lawyer, cannot be assured a fair trial unless counsel is provided for him." Echoing Clarence Earl Gideon—in corrected syntax and spelling—Black further insisted, "The right of one charged with crime to counsel may not be deemed fundamental and essential to fair trials in some countries, but it is in ours."

Is it? When I speak to retired Judge Calvin Johnson in April 2012 at his Common Street office in New Orleans, it is clear that he has a profound understanding of how the legal system fails poor people in Louisiana. He is the judge who decided, in *State v. Peart*, that the state legislature must properly fund indigent defense, and the one who, as chief judge, spearheaded public defender reform in the aftermath of Hurricane Katrina. He sees the interconnectedness of the personal, political, and legal—and the value of working all three angles at once. At sixty-five, with cropped gray hair, a mustache, and a colorful pink-and-white striped shirt, he has left the law for a new job heading up New Orleans's Metropolitan Human Services department. But his heart—and hand—are still in the criminal justice arena.

Over the years, he has been a public defender in the city. ("Those who know me well say I left because I wasn't very good at it," he says. "I say I left because I was overwhelmed by it.") Then he ran the criminal law clinic at Loyola University Law School for a decade. In the '90s, he became a judge. "Full disclosure," he says. "It was apparent to me in 1979 that the way the system operated here was not in the best interest of those who needed representation. That's what generated *Peart*." Johnson thinks back to the 1993 case *State v. Peart* and says he'd like to correct the record on that. "One of the misnomers about *Peart* is that it is always associated with capital cases or serious matters," he says, explaining that the defendant, Peart, was charged with rape and murder and, due to the seriousness of these charges, was actually quite likely to get some attention as the public defender involved triaged cases and the most serious rose to the top of his to-do list. "But what about all the other people Rick [Teissier] could not represent properly because he had to focus all or most of his attention on cases like Peart?" Those charged with low-end, petty crimes, "these are the guys getting screwed," he says. "Getting convicted of a misdemeanor or low-level felony could be a life sentence in Louisiana. Here, it's a life sentence [to have that conviction on your record] because you are banned from some schools, some houses, some jobs. You can't, can't, can't." The conviction can be for a minor case. Maybe a person was convicted and got probation, but it still stays on his or her record. "The conviction is a life sentence. That conviction will go with you till the day you die."

What he hoped would happen with *Peart* was that the legislature would take decisive steps to fund public defense adequately. In fact, they made some funding increases but remained troubled by lack of sufficient resources. In 2007, legislators passed the Louisiana Public Defender Act, which created a statewide board to oversee public defender services in the state, and gave them a budget to disperse. But it remains terribly difficult to persuade the general public that this is a budget item worth funding. Politicians, then and now, recognize this is not a popular cause. "It's difficult in America to talk about this, to really engage people in a conversation about public defense," Judge Johnson says, explaining that even his own mother used to say back when he was lawyering, if they're not guilty, how come they got themselves arrested? "That notion still prevails. People believe that individuals who go to jail ought to be there. You have that kind of stigma attached to those folks, but also those folks who are defending them." That makes it hard to muster up the political will for reforms, especially when budgets are tight. "We have a state like so many in America that is having revenue shortfalls," Johnson says. "So how do you make determinations? You look at all of the needs around the state, again triaging, to decide, whom do you fund first and foremost? Public defense is obviously not going to be that high up on the totem pole. That's just the reality of that."

How do you make the general public understand the value of the right to counsel for the poor? Johnson says you have to make it personal for people, to say, "let's talk about your own life and your family and community and those you know and love—and invariably you find, regardless of their station in life, that they have friends or family who have gone through the justice system." He says he asks these questions: "Should they be represented by someone who can't even go and speak to them in jail, interview them, think about them?"

Pair that educating with the force of the law, he says, which is what he tried to do with *State v. Peart*. The way he sees it, "changes in the law don't happen because a case is filed, but because there is a bubbling up of things." Around the country now, that bubbling is beginning to happen. "It takes one case and then another case and another [challenging the system]. That's how we finally get to *Gideon* because of lawyers constantly pushing the envelope and making judges deal with these issues, until finally there are the right facts and circumstances and you get that landmark decision."

Seen that way, *Peart* is one tiny bubble that rose to the surface and everyone in state and local politics could see it. And the decision, demanding that the legislature do its job and fund what is constitutionally required, flowed seamlessly out of Johnson's life history. Johnson, growing up as a black man in the South in the fifties and sixties, was intimately acquainted with the way the law was used to force change. His father was a plaintiff in a lawsuit filed by Thurgood Marshall in 1949 to equalize teachers' pay in Louisiana and a plaintiff in lawsuits to integrate schools. Johnson himself met Thurgood Marshall when he was eight years old and figures he met "damn near every black lawyer in Louisiana in my living room" during those years. He laughs, "not that there were that many." His dad was the third black man to register to vote in Plaquemines Parish, Louisiana, a feat he accomplished by having the woman with the finest minute handwriting in the community transcribe the Bill of Rights up his hand; he could recite it, even if his memory failed during the voter test requiring it. Judge Johnson himself was arrested and convicted of inciting a riot in 1964 when he was seventeen, after a civil rights protest—inadvertently proving his point that one doesn't have to look too far to find someone who has been jailed, hauled into court, and desperately relied on the skills and attention of a lawyer.

Greg Bright was finally released from prison on June 23, 2003, thanks to the herculean efforts of a team of lawyers who, working for a tiny nonprofit, randomly stumbled on his case and agreed to work his appeal. According to the parameters established by *Gideon*, he had been given a lawyer for his initial trial. But regardless of how ineffective his counsel was, he had no right to an attorney to represent him in most of the complicated legal processes that followed. The fact that there was no possible way for him to do the legwork necessary to investigate the case—visit the crime scene, interview witnesses, secure documents, obtain witness rap sheets, consult psychiatric experts—is considered inconsequential by the government. Making matters worse, Louisiana joins Michigan, Arkansas, and Washington in limiting felons' access to public records, including police reports and DA files. While the federal government recognizes the absolute necessity of a lawyer for appeals in the federal courts, at the state level, where most cases are tried, there is no such right. In Louisiana, prisoners have this right if they get a hearing—

which usually means the judge assigns the court public defender to do it on the fly, or a private lawyer unfortunate enough to be in the room at the time. But in federal court, an inmate will get dedicated counsel for a hearing that will do more than this, thanks to a much better funded federal public defender system.

What this means is that we as a public assume our justice system is foolproof and never errs. Or if it does, the indigent client who is convicted ought to be able to navigate the appeals process on his or her own.

If Emily Bolton and Innocence Project New Orleans hadn't taken on Greg Bright's appeal, he likely would now be looking at his thirty-seventh year in jail for a crime he didn't commit. Bolton wonders how many more like Greg are out there. Within a year of opening their doors in Louisiana, Innocence Project New Orleans had received more than two thousand requests for help with appeals from the guilty, the innocent, and the vast swath in between. The organization exonerated twenty-one clients. It has taken a decade, Bolton says, for legal representation for post-conviction appeals to evolve from "just a fuss to a credible fuss to a fuss which we must do something about."

Meanwhile, New Orleans is backsliding on providing the most basic right to free counsel for the poor in the original criminal case as well. As the summer of 2012 drew to a close, Willie Cheneau Jr., the man arrested and jailed for marijuana possession, was finally appointed a lawyer, who promptly got his charge reduced from a felony to a misdemeanor. Willie pleaded guilty to possession of marijuana and was released within two days—after two months in jail. Clarence Jones finally got a pro bono attorney who specializes in tort, product liability, construction, and insurance law. The attorney, Kirk Gasperecz, said that he was already "up to his armpits in alligators" at work, but nonetheless agreed to take Clarence's case when a local judge told him Clarence had been sitting in jail for more than a year. Gasperecz says he will work closely with colleagues who have criminal experience to get Clarence out of prison. Also, the Orleans Parish public defender's conflicts division was finally revived in August, but is struggling along with only three attorneys.

A weak public defender system has societal impact above and beyond the personal impact on folks who are wrongly convicted and
spend years of their life behind bars. Katherine Mattes, of Tulane's
law clinic, calls it the "trickle-down theory of community safety."
"The public defender system is one of the most important public
safety systems we have—a strong public defender who challenges
the prosecutor ensuring that the prosecutor can make his case,
forces the prosecutor to make sure that the police are investigating and making solid arrests based on evidence, not bias, attitude,
or laziness; this in turn leads to a safer community," she says. "In a
community without an effective public defense system, as has been
the case for decades here in New Orleans prior to Katrina, the prosecutor doesn't need to worry about whether his cops are bringing
him well-investigated, solid cases, and if the prosecutor isn't worried, then the police have no systemic incentive to investigate thoroughly and confirm that their arrest is solid. I think it's essential for
the public to understand this relationship between effective, well-
funded public defense systems and their own safety."

Case in point? Whoever killed fifteen-year-old Elliot Porter remains on the loose.

Today, Greg Bright, fifty-six, sits on the cement porch of his yellow
clapboard house in New Orleans's 7th Ward and rests his hand on
the head of his yellow dog, Q. It is 2012, and he often finds himself
musing over the notion of time—time past, time lost, time wasted.
"It feels like a minute since I been out here," he says. It took some
time to adjust to life on the outside, he admits, and once, on a dark,
rainy morning as he found himself biking seven miles in the rain to
his miserable job working the line in a chicken plant in Mississippi,
he felt real despair—just recognizing that he was forty-seven years
old and had never owned a car. He tried hard to dismiss the sobering thought that, arrested at age twenty and doing twenty-seven
years of time, he'd been "seven more years in prison than I was on
the streets." Sometimes, he says, "it's little things like that" that really threaten to drag him down into sorrow.

So he chose to do something that both keeps those wasted years
fresh in his memory yet also mitigates the sense of powerlessness

he sometimes feels. He helps to educate others in the hopes that his story will spur reforms. He is not an educated man—his formal schooling stopped in sixth grade—but he is one of dozens and dozens of ex-cons who form a vital link in the post-Katrina criminal justice reform efforts through various organizations such as Resurrection After Exoneration, the aforementioned holistic reentry program for ex-offenders, and Innocence Project New Orleans. Greg tells his story to students, activists, politicians, church groups, friends, strangers—anybody with time to spare and an inclination to listen—doggedly putting a face on an abstract idea, injustice.

On this particular afternoon in May 2012, he tells his story to me. For a fourth time. He is deeply preoccupied with the judge who repeatedly denied his requests over the years (the same one who was on the team prosecuting his murder case in 1976). The very month that Greg was released in 2003, the judge died. Greg goes into his house to retrieve the judge's yellow and tattered obituary that he has kept these nine years. He reads it—as he has done hundreds of times. The obituary, like all obituaries, says nice things.

"The judge may have been a good man," Greg muses. "He might have been a good husband, a good father, a good friend to many people—and I'm sure he was. But people may be saying the same thing about me." Q, the dog, who lies panting at Greg's feet, lifts his head for a moment to look around, as if considering the matter. Then he lowers his head to rest his muzzle on Greg's shoe. "But because I'm not a lawyer, but because I'm the little guy, man, you step on my head and crush me. I don't have money or influence or even God on my side." Interestingly, he saves most of his venom for the judge and the old boys' network that got him a lawyer, but one friendly with the judge and disinclined to even work up a sweat when it came to Greg's case. *Gideon* guaranteed him an attorney, but a flawed indigent defense system and a lackluster lawyer rendered that almost meaningless. "But why?" he says. "You know, why? Sometimes I think about it." He wonders what the solutions are to the troubled criminal justice system here, to the high incarceration rates in the black community, to the racism and power imbalance. He talks on and on, indignant, furious, rambling—but right. He grows heated. Mostly he wonders how one draws attention to these problems, how change happens. "Sometimes I think about, what is it? This Mahatma Gandhi thing, this passive resistance," he says. "They crack your head to the skull. You get up and say to the man, 'Thank you.' He cracks your head again. You got to be an animal to continue that. That's what I felt like the judge was doing to me every time I came forward. It's an outrage." He pauses, inhales, collects himself. "But I'm not talking from bitterness." He says this, and yet, how can he let go of bitterness? Like a dog licking a wound, keeping it open and raw, Greg Bright revisits his past, alternately trying to decide whether he—and the city of New Orleans—get to have a happy ending or whether their shared story is a tragedy. Is it a happy ending because he now sits on the porch of the modest little yellow house he owns in New Orleans's 7th Ward—"my pot of gold at the end of the rainbow," as he once called it after finally receiving $190,000 restitution in 2011 for being wrongly imprisoned? Or is it a tragedy because he wasted twenty-seven years of his life behind bars?

The criminal justice system in New Orleans—indeed, the nation—seems similarly poised between plot twists, an ending that could go either way.

CHAPTER 4

Rodney Young at his capital murder trial in February 2012. The jury had to decide whether his school years in special ed meant he was "retarded" and thus ineligible for the death penalty. Photo courtesy of *The Covington News.*

DEATH IN GEORGIA:

A CAPITAL DEFENSE

At 11:20 P.M. on the night of March 30, 2008, a 911 operator in Covington, Georgia, took a call.

The woman on the other end of the line was sobbing—almost unintelligible—as she stood at the end of her driveway in the eerie pitch-black silence of a warm spring night. The operator tried to calm her down, get some information.

"What's the address?"

"Sixty-five Benedict Drive," the woman said. "My son is in the house. He tied up to the chair. I just came home for work . . . I don't know. Help me, Lord. Help me."

"Ma'am—"

The woman's sobs interrupted her.

"Ma'am, you came home and your son was tied to a chair?"

"Yes."

"How old is he?"

"Twenty-eight."

"Is he hurt?"

"Yes, yes. He's out."

"Sixty-five Benedict?"

"Yes, please help. Please help."

"Your name?"

"Doris Jones. Help! Oh, God. Oh, God. Oh, God."

"Did you go in the house?"

"Yes."

"Did you see any blood?"

"Yes, all over. Oh, God. I need help."

"What kind of vehicle are you in?"

"A Chrysler. I been calling him all day long."

"You been calling all day? When was the last time you talked to him?"

"This morning."

"This morning?"

"Yes." Doris Jones began moaning, sobbing.

"Talk to me," the operator says.

"I can't go back in—"

"Don't go back in! Just stay right here and talk to me. They are on their way."

"Can't you please hurry up. I'm scared. Oh, Lord. Please God, I need someone to help me."

"What's his name?"

"Gary Jones."

The operator tried to calm her, to keep her talking, her questions now on repeat. "How old is he?"

"Twenty-eight . . ."

"Ma'am, is anybody else there with you?"

"No, I open the door and everything is knocked off . . . the chair . . . he there . . . he still has his church clothes on."

"Where are you?"

"I'm across the street. I'm so scared someone still there. Oh, God." Doris Jones's primal terror fueled her voice. It rose and swelled and spilled out into the night in a gulping horror at what she'd seen.

"Hold on," the operator says. "There someone I can call for you?"

"My family all in New Jersey."

"A friend?"

"I can't think of anybody right now. Help me, Lord. Help me, Jesus. Oh, Lord, help me. Tell them to hurry up and get here. Oh, Lord, tell them to hurry and come."

"They are coming."

". . . Last night when I came home from work, he called me and said . . . the window broken. . . ." She remembered that he told her the window in the laundry room looked tampered with, as if someone had tried to break in. She remembered that they found the window's screen tossed in the woods at the edge of the house. She remembered that he was concerned about a robbery. "Oh, oh, Lord, help me . . ." Doris spied a police cruiser approaching. "They're here."

"They're there?"

"Yes."

"They see you?"

A cop approached Doris. "Listen. Stay right here." He asked about the situation, her son inside. "He in trouble?"

"I don't know. I think so. He been there all day long."

The line to the 911 operator goes dead.

Cops rushed the home she shared with her son. They found his body, bloody and battered, tied to a chair.

Gary Jones was dead.

Four years later, in February 2012, Doris sits in a Covington court-room testifying against the man accused of murdering her son. Her ex-boyfriend, a forty-four-year-old African American from Bridgeton, New Jersey, named Rodney Young, is on trial for Gary Jones's murder. Doris, also African American, had dated Rodney for seven years; the romance had gone sour several months before the murder and she had fled New Jersey to live with her son in Georgia. Prosecutors allege that Rodney killed Doris's son in order to get to her, to scare her back into his arms by making her think that roving, violent gangs were out to get her in Georgia. Rodney was extradited from New Jersey, hauled down to Georgia, and faced the death penalty.

Technically, as the district attorney plays Doris Jones's recorded 911 call for the jury, she is trying to persuade the jury that Rodney is guilty of murder in this first phase of the trial. In reality, his public defender, Joseph Romond, acknowledges in opening arguments that Rodney likely committed the murder. However, Romond insists his client is mentally retarded and thus ineligible for the death penalty; the U.S. Supreme Court ruled in a 2002 decision, *Atkins v. Virginia*, that people with mental retardation were not morally culpable for their actions and thus could not be executed. Unfortunately, the Court didn't define mental retardation. Nor did it spell out what kind of proof was required—beyond a reasonable doubt? a preponderance of the evidence?—to make the determination of mental retardation. As a result, Georgia is the only state in the nation that requires evidence "beyond a reasonable doubt" that a defendant is mentally retarded.

If the jury finds that Rodney is guilty but mentally retarded, then he'll be sentenced to life without the possibility of parole. If the jury decides he is guilty but *not* mentally retarded, the trial goes into a second phase. At this point, the jury gets a second chance to decide on the appropriate sentence for him: should he be put to death or should he be sent to prison for life, without the possibility of parole?

The jury deciding Rodney Young's fate in this February 2012 capital case joins thousands of other juries in the United States over the last fifteen years in determining whether a person convicted of murder should himself be killed—943 of these juries returned a death sentence.[1] In Georgia, this particular capital trial is business as usual—just one of the 94 death penalty cases sitting on the desks of the public defenders at the Georgia Capital Defenders office that same week in February 2012. But in Georgia such "business as usual" is deeply tangled in the politics of race, power, and money. Being poor, black, and accused of a crime in this country always increases a person's chances of conviction. But here in Georgia—at the far end of the punishment spectrum where the stakes are highest—the right to counsel, and the funding so crucial to mounting a defense equal to that of the well-funded, well-resourced district attorney's office, is in daily jeopardy. Indeed, justice is not necessarily the principal *business* of business-as-usual in the Georgia courts; justice is too expensive.

I arrive in the Covington, Georgia, courthouse on Tuesday, February 14, 2012—Valentine's Day. It is the first full day of Rodney Young's murder trial, and there is a lot of red. Bloody weapons. Bloody clothing. Bloody flesh displayed in oversize slides. As the jury returns from lunch at 2 P.M., the state calls Dr. Jonathan Eisenstat, a Georgia medical examiner, to talk them through the autopsy he performed on Gary Jones's body, and to share the pictures documenting the event. It is a gruesome scene.

"Can you tell us what is depicted here?" asks Layla Zon, the trim thirty-something district attorney, as she strides across the courtroom to dim the lights and direct the jury's attention to photos projected from an overhead projector. She sets a photo down on the machine, adjusts the focus, and turns her attention back to the medical examiner.

"It's a photo of the body," Dr. Eisenstat says, "just as it comes out of the bag."

"I'd like to enter into evidence state's exhibit number 301," Zon says as she puts down another photo. Then another. Then another. On the huge screen, in slow succession, thirty-two images of a mangled man lying face up on an exam table flash by. The series of photos changes perspectives and moves closer and closer, from a bird's-eye view of the man's chest and head to a close-up of a bruise, a laceration, a rope burn. Jurors see that the corpse, in repose, has one eye closed and one eye open, staring straight ahead in startled surprise that death caught him—and possibly at the form and person it arrived in. The button-down oxford that clothes the corpse is so drenched in deep red blood that it is impossible to detect what color it might have once been.

"Now we see the body before it has been cleaned," says Eisenstat. "The right side of the face and upper chest." He points out a rip and explains that the "defects" in the shirt are "consistent with traumatic injury." He borrows a pointer from the judge and steps out of the witness box to help the jury focus on the details. The camera had zoomed in so that every pore in the dead man's skin was visible as an unseen lab technician used tweezers to fold his ear into a gruesome carbuncle, squeezing and pulling it forward to show a mark behind the ear. The technician pinches again with the tweezers to pull the eyelid back, to point out the lacerated flesh beneath. The medical examiner had cut into the body and peeled back the flesh, and he narrates his process as dully as someone sharing vacation photos of the Jersey shore. The photos flicker by, on and on.

A blond woman in the front of the jury box puts her hand over her mouth and folds her head down to stare at her lap. The woman next to her looks away, away from her neighbor, away from the photos, away from the defendant, Rodney Young, who prosecutors say committed this murder. She digs into her purse for a pink tissue and blows her nose.

The district attorney plows ahead. "Can you give me an opinion as to whether Gary Jones was alive when those ligature marks were made?" she asks.

"We have a bruise in the line of a ligature which indicates he had blood pressure and therefore was alive when the marks were made," he answers, explaining that the victim had been tied to a chair in his home and likely beaten to death with a hammer.

Zon abruptly turns on the lights. "Overall, did you make a determination as to cause of death for Gary Jones?"

"Blunt force injuries of the head and neck," Eisenstat says.

Zon sits down next to her co-counsel, Melanie Bell, crosses her legs, and gives a satisfied nod to those at the defense table.

None of the three attorneys there moves.

For his part, the defendant Rodney Young had declined to look at the photographs that appeared on the screen almost directly above him. He sits, a hulking man in a beautifully pressed yellow shirt and creased trousers, hunched over. He keeps his head down in his hand—unwilling or unable to look. It is a posture he will maintain for much of the trial.

Next to him, the three public defenders from the Georgia Capital Defenders office take a moment to collect their thoughts, shuffling through papers to prepare their cross-examination. Thea Delage, on a yearlong fellowship at the Capital Defenders, is a slight, young white woman in a gray suit who sits next to Rodney throughout the trial, occasionally leaning over to whisper an explanation or answer a question. Teri Thompson, a bone-thin, stylishly dressed black woman, sits next to Delage. As the attorney with the most experience, she is senior counsel. However, having just completed another murder trial two weeks earlier, she has not had adequate time to prepare for this case, so instead, Joseph Romond takes the lead on this one. A young, white man who joined the Capital Defenders office in 2008, Romond is trying his first death penalty case. He wants very much to win. He barely stands a chance.

Like many public defenders—and certainly like most who work on capital cases—Romond is deeply passionate about his work. He is both typical, in his way of obsessively working excruciatingly long hours, and atypical, in that he came to this work in an unusual way. Romond grew up in Morristown, New Jersey, and moved with his parents to Chicago when he was sixteen. He spent the last two years of high school at a Christian evangelical boarding school and, being "not very academically inclined," decided against college in favor of vocational school. He learned to be a mechanic. After working at the local Goodyear for a mediocre year and a half, he realized he probably did not want to do this for the rest of his life. He decided it was his "calling" to go into the ministry and so he enrolled at Messiah College, a Christian evangelical college outside Harrisburg, Pennsylvania, where he majored in religion. Somewhere during his first semester's Bible class he had an epiphany. "I realized how big a farce this was," he says, vaguely referring to a loss of faith, or at least disenchantment with organized religion. He decided he did not want to be a minister after all.

Romond spent a semester abroad, arriving in Cairo, Egypt, at the end of August 2001. He had been there two weeks when the September 11 attacks occurred. When folks in the United States worried about his safety and urged him to come home, he was blasé. "Hey, nobody is flying planes into buildings over here," he said. Pro-Palestinian, he spent a month in the West Bank and discovered his position was fairly unusual among evangelical Christians. When he returned to Messiah College, an indignant critic of the widespread brutality and injustice he'd witnessed in the Middle East, one of his professors scoffed, "You're so outraged about the Palestinians, but take a look in your own backyard."

In fact, Romond had been active in his "own backyard" as well. He had marched against the death penalty at various protests, but felt "pretty impotent" when it came to impacting death penalty policy. Toward the end of his senior year, a friend suggested applying his resistance to the death penalty in a more practical way by becoming a lawyer. Romond went online to find out how to register for the LSATs on what happened to be the final, late-filing day for taking the upcoming test. He signed up, took the test two weeks later, applied to one law school—Howard University in D.C.—and got in.

Howard, a historically black college, was an unusual choice for a white kid from the Midwest. "I wanted to learn the perspective of the law from those most mistreated by it," he says. "I never thought about being a lawyer one day in my life until then. I showed up for my first day of law school with a pen and some paper in my hand." All around him were students who had been groomed for this their whole lives, armed with laptops and law books. He felt similarly outmatched when he applied to intern at the public defender's office in D.C., almost universally touted as the best one in the country (thanks to the proper funding it gets from the federal government). "I showed up and here were all these kids from Harvard and Yale and Princeton," he recalls.

But he persisted, successfully finishing his internship there and then scoring another coveted internship at Georgia's Southern Center for Human Rights. It's easy to see how Romond, with a round, guileless face, scruff of beard, and cropped dark hair, who is quick to laugh, with others and at himself, managed to navigate the terrain between privileged law students and underprivileged clients. His decision to become a lawyer may have been fairly random, but he is clearly suited to the work and passionate about his clients. "When I started in the Capital Defenders office in '08, I was reluctant," he says, "because I was so young and inexperienced. But there is so much need. It's just so wrong, what goes on, on so many levels. I understand what many of my clients have done. I don't deny that some have done awful, horrific things. But I have yet to have a case where there is not a compelling, sad, abusive, or turbulent growing up," he said.

As he sits talking to me one day in February, sipping mimosas in a dark bar and brooding about his profession, he runs a finger around the collar of the brown fisherman's sweater he wears as if it itches or irritates him and admits he always "gets a lot of shit" about being a public defender. "That's true of every public defender," he says. "Someone will say, 'How do you defend *those* people? I don't know how you can do that.'" Romond has a couple of different responses, depending on his mood or patience. "Sometimes I say, 'How could I *not* defend these people?' I love what I do and I'm passionate about it and I want them to understand why, but somehow my engagement or passion doesn't really change minds." When he's feeling flip, he'll respond to someone's moral outrage—"How could you defend someone who is guilty of something so heinous?"—by reminding them, "I don't represent people who are guilty; everyone in this country is innocent until proven guilty." In his more Socratic moments, he has some success by asking people to consider the alternative, no lawyer to defend "those" people. "Imagine some poor, uneducated guy or someone mentally retarded who is standing there in a courtroom facing all the power of the government alone. It's Orwellian, horrific."

"I've become somewhat of a libertarian," he jokes. "I enjoy getting up each day, knowing that I'm working to keep the power of the government in check. I don't vote libertarian, but I *feel* libertarian."

Romond is fervent about his defense work, but he has a casual, light touch. During the Rodney Young trial, he moves fluidly between types of people, chatting as easily with co-counsel about voir dire as he does with sheriff's bailiffs (whom he's troubled to know by name) about his cell phone accidentally going off in the middle of the trial, and as he does with his client, Rodney, who was more preoccupied with the color of the pressed shirt Romond would bring him to wear in court each day or the gummy worms he begged everyone for than legal strategy.

When it is his turn to question the medical examiner at the trial, Romond buttons his jacket and rises. The pictures the jury has seen are horrific, and he is stuck doing damage control. "I believe what you said was, either of the injuries to the neck would have been fatal in themselves?"

"Yes," Eisenstat agrees.

"There's no way to really tell the order of the injuries, correct?"

"Yes."

"Sometimes you can tell, but not in this specific case?"

"Correct."

"You mention the person was still alive because he had blood pressure?"

"Correct."

"That doesn't mean the person is conscious though, correct?"

"Correct."

"Is it reasonable to say that a person could be unconscious from injuries to the head [like this]?"

"From the totality of head injuries, yes."

Romond sits down, reduced to mitigating the cruelty by suggesting that the victim might at least have lost consciousness.

And things are about to get worse for the defense. When the medical examiner leaves the stand, the state calls the victim's grandmother, sixty-four-year-old Annie Sampson. She is dressed in a prim navy-blue dress, her gray hair cinched in a tight bun atop her head. She clutches a cardigan tight around her, toddles a bit on her heels, and looks like she just stepped out of church. When she speaks, her voice unwavering but soft, she explains that Doris Jones is her daughter and that she has raised Doris's four boys for her, including Gary, since they were babies. "He called me *mommy*," she says.

Zon takes her back to the day of the murder.

"Gary called me as he was leaving out the church," Sampson says.

"Any idea where he was?"

Sampson says he was calling her on his cell from his car as he drove home from church. "He was talking about the service the whole ride home. And he asked me, did I go to church? I said, yes, with Aunt."

"What time was this conversation?"

"A little after 1. He was on Salem Road and getting close to home. But he had gotten a call from [his girlfriend] and said, 'Hold on.' Then he got back on the line and said he was going to go to dinner with [his girlfriend]. He was going to go home, take a shower, pull his suit off and then go with them. He was on the outside of the house, fumbling with his key, getting ready to walk in. He hung up." He called right back, she says, because he forgot to talk to his niece. He asked to talk to her and wished her a happy birthday.

"Did he mention anything about a screen?" Zon asks.

"Yes, he said the screen was away from the window, [thrown] back in the woods. I said, 'be careful.' He said he would. He said he would call back in fifteen minutes." She pauses. "And he didn't."

"Did you ever talk to him again?"

"No."

Rodney Young worked in a factory in Bridgeton, New Jersey, putting labels on cans, before he was extradited to Georgia for his trial. Neither he nor his family had the money to pay for a private attorney, so he was assigned a public defender to represent him. But the history of indigent defense in the state of Georgia is a long and troubled one. As in so many states, funding problems have hobbled Georgia public defenders. As the local district attorney offices collected money from the federal government, the state, and the county, public defenders limped along begging for handouts.

Ironically, in the late '70s, Georgia had tried to position itself in the lead on the provision of counsel for the poor. In 1979, Georgia passed the Indigent Defense Act, a series of sweeping reforms that, on the surface, looked promising. Prior to that, Georgia left indigent defense up to its many counties. This was a complicated, hodgepodge system in which county governments cobbled together representation based on what they decided they could afford. The quality of representation was vastly uneven across the state. Georgia has 159 counties—second only to Texas with 254—and no single agency coordinated indigent defense for the state. Attorneys who practiced in small towns at the time recall judges simply going through a list of local lawyers to appoint attorneys randomly. (This would be the Atticus Finch model, familiar from *To Kill a Mockingbird*; lucky is the defendant who gets an Atticus type, pity the defendant who gets the tax attorney down the street.) This meant a real estate practitioner could be required to take a felony case, an attorney with no criminal experience might be dealt a murder case. Worse, it was not uncommon for the accused to sit in jail for months waiting for an attorney to be assigned, oftentimes languishing in pretrial confinement longer than a maximum sentence for his or her crime would have merited. Many lost their jobs, their homes, custody of their kids.

The 1979 Georgia Indigent Defense Act attempted to address these disparities in quality of representation, grouping the counties into forty-eight judicial circuits, establishing a statewide Indigent

Defense Council, and creating a three-part system where county commissioners, the local bar association, and the judges of superior court all had a voice in determining what kind of provisions would be made for the defense of poor people in each jurisdiction.

It looked good on paper—and for a brief moment, the legal community around the country lauded Georgia's reforms—but it had one major flaw. The state legislature failed to set aside money to implement the changes. Each county still had to pick up the tab for indigent defense—and many failed to provide adequate funds.

Wycliffe Orr, a Gainesville, Georgia, attorney who served on that first Indigent Defense Council and went on to push for reforms over the next three decades both as a state legislator and as a council member, asserts that passage of the 1979 reforms changed little.

"All the council could do is issue guidelines as to caseload limits and such and try to work with local lawyers to improve things," he says when I talk to him in his Atlanta apartment in February 2012, in the midst of the Rodney Young trial. He explains that the council had a single part-time director of indigent defense for the entire state. Still, he says, "We went all over Georgia and said [to county commissioners] that you *have* to do this under the constitution, so step up to the plate." Orr and the council argued that it was the right thing to do, the ethical thing, the fair thing, the constitutional thing. "It fell on deaf ears," he says. Local elected officials simply refused to get behind the issue. The reality, Orr insists, is that "nobody is going to get elected campaigning with a stump speech about the poor receiving ineffective counsel."

So reformers switched tactics, to money. "We finally realized that we should go all over the state and talk with county commissioners, saying, 'Tell your legislators, "how 'bout you pick up some of this tab for indigent defense?"'" Eventually, the Indigent Defense Council made some headway. County commissioners who were reluctant to get behind any change that would cost money, agreed they would be happy to spend state money to improve defense—and they told their state legislators as much.

It took ten years of agitating, but in 1989, the state finally agreed to chip in $1 million annually toward indigent defense. It was a paltry sum, but it grew, incrementally, until it reached approximately

$5 million in 2000. The money made a slight difference. It was progress, certainly. But the amount couldn't begin to address the problems that plagued public defense in forty-eight separate circuits across the state. For example, private attorneys were winning low-bid contracts to represent all of a district's poor for annual salaries in the $25,000 range, Orr says. On top of that, the lawyer necessarily juggled those duties with a private practice. Hundreds of defendants languished in local jails waiting for an attorney to be appointed or received slapdash defense by an overworked, underpaid defender whose caseloads skyrocketed.

In 2000, as the crisis in public defense grew too large to ignore, the state supreme court established a Blue Ribbon Commission to study indigent defense. Comprised of judges, lawyers, legislators, and others, the commission heard horror stories from more than sixty witnesses in the criminal justice system over two years. As a result of that investigation, in 2003 the legislature passed the Georgia Public Defense Act, which established a new, uniform statewide public defense system in Georgia. For the first time, public defenders would work out of central offices—as district attorneys had long done—with staff investigators, paralegals, law libraries, and, significantly, colleagues who could mentor newcomers, share knowledge, offer tips, refer experts, advise on case law. The public defenders would be governed by the Georgia Public Defender Standards Council.

What made reformers truly ecstatic, however, was the promise of dedicated state funds for public defense. Even for death penalty cases. "One of the last-minute tradeoffs done to get counties to support this was the promise that the counties would no longer be responsible for capital cases," says Chris Adams, the public defender appointed to head up the resulting, newly created Georgia Capital Defenders office. Death penalty cases were time-consuming and expensive. "The counties signed on to this, in part, so they could get out of the burden of capital cases."

As the Rodney Young trial begins, Joseph Romond has nine open death penalty cases on his desk. This fact torments him. The stakes are so high, yet he knows Rodney's case has faltered because of lack of resources. "If we had enough time and energy to adequately prepare, things would look very different," he says.

Romond's old boss, Chris Adams, tried very hard that first year of the Capital Defenders office's existence to keep cases at four per lawyer. "Especially because I had a lot of new lawyers," he says, explaining that more experienced lawyers may be able to take on five cases as they gain skills and get faster, but there are practical and emotional challenges to this work that are unique. "Even pleas," he says, can be tough. "Getting emotionally to the point of being able to plead a case to life without parole feels like a terrible defeat. It's weird to say, but it can feel like you're giving up on your client." Adams, who has been doing this work for twenty years, says it could be that he is jaded—and perhaps new lawyers struggle with this. But when there is, say, a videotape of your client shooting the police officer by the side of the road or a taped confession or other incontrovertible evidence, a plea can make sense. "You don't have to litigate everything under the sun. Rather than being jaded, it might mean that with experience, you learn to trust your intuition."

But even with pleas, it takes some serious work to find out whether they make sense. And, because one never knows at the onset whether there will be a plea or a full-fledged trial, Adams was committed to capping caseloads for attorneys in the Georgia Capital Defenders office at four. Once, a few years earlier, while working for the Southern Center for Human Rights, he was doing a capital trial in Alabama. "I thought if I had to work on eight cases at a time, I would have lost my mind," he says—and this after twenty years' experience and twelve capital trials under his belt. "I had responsibility for three active, full-on cases and I was losing my mind anyway."

Lack of funding has continued to plague public defenders there, though in the beginning it seemed as if the legislature had developed some promising solutions. In 2000, the Georgia legislature deftly skirted the thorny issue of "my hard-earned tax dollars paying for criminal defense" by eschewing the use of tax for the venture. Instead, it created an Indigent Defense Fund, whose coffers were filled via court filing fees from civil cases. For example, if a Georgia resident filed a civil case, $15 was added to the processing fees. The fund quickly swelled to more than $40 million, and the state began to pick up more and more of the cost of indigent defense services.

The new system became operational in 2005, and for the first two years, things went well. "But there were telltale signs early on that the state was not making a full-fledged commitment to it," said Orr, explaining that several million a year started being diverted from public defense into the state's general fund. "The effect on the system over time because of lack of funding was dire indeed. It created a situation where various cases, including capital cases, were essentially stopped due to lack of funding."

And then there was the Brian Nichols case. Nichols, who was on trial for rape, escaped from the Atlanta courtroom where he was being tried, killing a U.S. Customs agent, the judge, the court reporter, and a sheriff's deputy. The Fulton County district attorney took this horrific but fairly straightforward murder case—there were plenty of eyewitnesses to the crime, so the guilt-innocence phase of the trial was not overly complicated—and charged Nichols with fifty-four counts, listing 478 potential witnesses—a daunting number to defend against. The Capital Defenders office was hard-pressed to respond in kind; to do so would cost almost $2 million. When the press and politicians got wind of that, and took to calling it the "Cadillac defense," public support for indigent defense plummeted. At the same time, with the Capital Defenders office having used up almost half of its budget on a single massive case, the remaining seventy-five death penalty cases in the state ground to a near halt due to lack of funding.

But it wasn't just lack of money that plagued the system. After two years of operation, politics struck. Fueled in part by legislative dissatisfaction with the progress of the Nichols case, the legislature began to chip away at the public defense system. Historically, since the 1700s, things to do with the courts had been handled, naturally, by the judicial branch. In 2007, the legislature moved oversight of the Public Defender Standards Council to the executive branch. While the council was under the judicial branch, the legislature had little control over its funding. It could reduce the judicial budget as a whole, but its ability to dictate how the judicial branch used those dollars was limited or nonexistent. But with the council under the executive branch, the legislature could chip away directly at the budget for indigent defense.

And it did. Consequently, the budget crisis for indigent defense played out across the system with layoffs and cutbacks. Its impact was particularly dramatic in the Capital Defenders office, even though this new office held a lot of promise. In 2004, Chris Adams was appointed to take over a small Georgia legal organization called the Multi-county Defenders that would morph into the Capital Defenders office the following year. Adams needed to come up with an estimate regarding costs and staffing needs. In Georgia, the average cost of a capital murder trial was $360,000. Based on historical averages, he knew they would be carrying about a hundred cases at a time, with approximately forty new cases a year.

"If you do that math, forty new cases times $360,000, it comes to—" I can hear Chris Adams over the phone line checking his math on a calculator to double and triple check that he's got it right even all these years later. "—$14.4 million a year. I had just come from a small nonprofit [the Southern Center for Human Rights] and I could not even say $14.4 million a year out loud in a request. Phenomenal. That was just a stunning number for me." Because the Georgia Capital Defenders would be gradually accruing new clients as the system changed over and all of the state's death penalty cases were sent its way, the office began with $7.2 million for the 2005–2006 fiscal year. "I thought it was a good starting point," Adams said.

And it was. Midyear expenses were running about a million under budget, Adams said. But then the director of the state's larger indigent defense took that million out of the Capital Defenders' budget midyear to funnel it to other public defenders in the state. "That would have been fine if it was just for the five remaining months of the year and we went back up for next year, but it didn't [get restored]," Adams says. And most of the new cases were not yet at the trial phase, so costs were still low. But the budget was cut to $5.1 million the next year. Then it went down to $4.1 million. At that point, the Georgia Capital Defenders had approximately sixty-five death penalty cases. "At that point, we couldn't survive on that money," said Adams, insisting that approximately $9 million was needed to properly fund that number of cases.

That year, 2006, the Brian Nichols case came along, and it was clear the coffers would be drained. The Capital Defenders were trying to handle sixty-five open cases on a budget of $4.1 million. "At this point, I'm looking at our budget and all our cases and saying, no way," Adams recalled. "The only way it would work is to sacrifice our clients' constitutional rights, and I can't do that. I felt like it was at a crisis point."

"We had been told to ration resources," Adams said. If a case really urgently needed some expenditure, it would get approved, they were told, but if it could wait a year, wait. "I've been doing capital work long enough to know that the only way to get good results is to jump on it early and work it hard," Adams said. Wait, and evidence vanished or witnesses forgot or documents were tossed. "You can't win if you wait."

Because efforts to procure adequate funding from the legislature had been repeatedly thwarted, Adams thought he should attempt to engage the judiciary. What would happen if he simply refused to take more cases? "I don't know if the judge can order the state to pay more—or whether that would violate separation of powers—or whether the DA could push for fewer death penalties, don't know if you can do that, but we've got a problem," Adams said. He hoped to send a strong message through the judges. But Adams's boss refused to let him take his funding issue to the courts.

So, in September 2007, Adams resigned.

"Was he good to you in the beginning?" assistant district attorney Melanie Bell asks Doris Jones, the victim's mother.

Doris, in her forties but looking much older, walks into the courtroom carrying the weight of her past relationship with Rodney Young as if it were a heavy burden that has physically worn her down. She climbs the step into the witness box after a lunch break and settles into the seat, smoothing her dress over her thighs and then plucking at the sleeves busily—lint? dog hair? a stray thread?—and manages to avoid eye contact with anyone for a few moments. The assistant DA repeats the question. Doris looks up. Her face is lined and her eyes overflow with tears. Between her cautious movement as she ascends the stand and the tight, matronly bun she wears, it is clear that the last few years have taken their toll. She looks nothing like the fun-loving party girl who met Rodney Young seven years ago at a bar in Bridgeton, New Jersey.

Doris considers this question for a moment. *Was he good to her?* She glances at Rodney Young, who sits in front of her, just to the right. His head is down, never meeting her gaze as she speaks. He looks at the carpet. She looks at him—and then away.

It is a hard question.

Ultimately, Doris will tell the jury what she saw the night her son was murdered, about the threats that were scrawled on the walls of her home—"Wes will get you too" and "Wes know what you look like," the semiliterate culprit had written, likely meaning "We's" or "We"—about her sneaking suspicion in the days to come that her semiliterate ex-boyfriend up in New Jersey might be behind this, about the love letters this same ex had barraged her with begging her to come back, about her fear that this man might have come down to Georgia to try and scare her into returning to Jersey with him, about the terrible toll her son's murder had taken on the family.

Was he good to her?

The attorney repeats. "Was he good to you in the beginning?"

"Yes," Doris says, but explains that they argued a lot.

"Can you give an example of the things y'all argued about?"

Doris says they argued about her smoking, which Rodney hated. They argued about money. They argued about friends.

"Did you argue about infidelity?"

"Yes," Doris says.

"Would you break up?"

"Yes."

"For long?"

"Couple months."

"Who was pursuing who?"

"He was."

"Did he give you any gifts?"

"Yes, and he would buy me groceries."

"So, he was trying to woo you back?"

"Yes."

Rodney lived in the basement of his aunt's house in Bridgeton, while his aunt's family and Rodney's daughter lived upstairs, Doris tells the jury. The prosecutor walks Doris through the history of her relationship with Rodney. Doris says she left him many times over the years, twice going as far as Georgia to live with her family there. Then Rodney would call and send letters, begging her to come back.

"And after these phone calls and letters, y'all would reconcile again?" Bell asks.

"Yes."

"That pattern existed throughout your relationship with Rodney?"

"Yes."

"Would he get you back with those nice gestures?"

"Yes."

"And then it would deteriorate again?"

"Yes."

"Then, in November 2007, did the defendant come see you [in Georgia]?"

"Yes."

"You aware he was coming?"

"Yes."

"Did anything out of the ordinary happen during that November 2007 visit?"

"Yes, he proposed to me. Everyone knew [he was going to do it] but me. We were all at my sister's house. He came in and got on his knees and proposed to me."

"Did you think the relationship was going to improve when you married?"

"Yes."

Doris agreed to move in with him after that. But she had to deal with her job. When she left New Jersey, Doris had taken a job in Georgia assisting mental health patients in supervised living apartments with grocery shopping and other chores. After Rodney proposed to her, she went back to New Jersey and was able to get her old job back. But Rodney did not seem happy to see her when she returned, and they fought immediately and repeatedly. In January 2008, she says, she left him for good, clearing out so quickly she came with only the clothes on her back and returned to Covington, Georgia, where she moved in with her son, Gary Jones.

Rodney, she says, begged her to come back and sent her multiple letters. Beneath the bright fluorescent lights of the courtroom, the prosecutor places a handwritten letter—carefully printed but rife with errors—dated September 6, 2007, onto an overhead projector and reads it aloud.

Dear Doris

Doris I really miss you and I want to be with you for the rest of are's lives I love you I miss you I love the way you walk I love the way you Dress for me I love to look at you naked I just love the total packet about you it can't get no better than that Doris. So I hope you want me too. I don't want to be with out you. I got my hope up high being with you so let that happen lets me, you and Aaliyah [Rodney's daughter] be the family were proposed to be Okay. You said one thing wright to my mom that I'm the boss of AalihyaH and that all matter. . . . All I want from you is love and to treat AaliyaH like the mom she never had. And I believe that can happen. I Promise I will never hurt you and I will try to take care of me, you and Aaliyah the best way I can. I Just want Wive that love me and I love her I don't need nobody Else. That my worD. I need you Honey Cause I love Doris M Jones. Your mother said something that made me mad But I got over it. So call me or write me back. . . . Remember what you told me about if your family dn't like me Ownly matter that you love me. Remember that saying Cause I love you and I don't Care what nobody Else say. Remember that. Doris this is my life and you are my life Okay. And I Care What happen between me add you. So you can tell anyone else or tell anyother Negro that Im not going to let you go. That not easy so don't forget that you love me and I know you do.

love
Rodney R. Young

The prosecutor removes this letter from the overhead projector and puts down another one. And another one. And another one.

Alternately threatening and cajoling, the letters paint a picture of a severely dysfunctional relationship, one that bears many of the telltale signs of a classic case of domestic violence. (Indeed, later in the trial it would come out that Rodney had twice punched Doris.) On the heels of this is a display of raw sexual or emotional need. "Please come back, I'm sorry," he writes in another undated letter. "I just want you to show me love Doris meaning give me Sex and I will try to cover everything until you get back on your feet." The correspondence, seen together, is full of the wild mood swings in their troubled and confusing relationship. Throughout the reading of the letters, Rodney stares down at the floral carpet, absorbed in the endlessly repeating pattern of beige and green petals, flowers unfolding in orderly, predictable rows.

Moving forward in time, the prosecutors direct Doris's attention to the week before the murder. In what has to be the most curious aspect of this murder, she tells the jury that she discovered signs of breaking and entering through the laundry room window several days before Gary was killed. Prosecutors return to this somewhat bizarre fact several times over the course of the trial, first while questioning Doris. Gary was killed on a Sunday, after returning from church, but Doris says that a strange thing happened on the Friday night before when she got home from work. "I washed some clothes and went to bed," she says.

"And you woke up on Saturday?" Bell asks.

"Yes."

"Anything unusual?"

"My laundry was all folded up and set on the couch in the living room."

Someone switched the loads, waited for the dryer to finish, folded the garments. Gary had spent the night at his girlfriend's, so it couldn't have been him. Doris was puzzled the next morning. She went into the laundry room. That's when she discovered the window had been tampered with and alerted Gary that it looked like there had been a break-in. Someone had broken into the house, she believed, but they had merely switched the loads and folded the batch in the dryer.

"Did you see Gary that day?"

"Yes."

"Any more conversation regarding the broken window?"

"Yes."

"What?"

"The screen was out to the woods," Doris says, explaining that it looked like it had been thrown there near the edge of their property. "Around the window it looked like someone chopped away at the wood and the hole was a big one." She told Gary, "Let's get that fixed and fix the alarm." They had a security system in the house, but it wasn't activated at the time.

Two days later, someone broke in and murdered Gary.

"At the time period when Gary was killed, would you say the defendant was angry with you?" Bell asks.

"Yes."

"Did you think of that at the time?"

"No."

"Why?"

"Because he was in New Jersey and I was in Georgia."

The prosecutor returns to questions about the night of the murder. "Did you notice anything of yours missing?"

"My social security card."

"Anything of Gary's missing?"

"Gary's cell phone."

When it was time for the defense to cross-examine her, Romond stood up, buttoning his beige suit jacket as he walked around the defense table to stand closer to the wood-paneled witness box. "Miss Jones," he said. "We are very, very sorry for your loss."

He had no further comment.

Over the next few hours and days, the prosecution continues to build its case against Rodney Young. A handwriting specialist testifies that the letter writer who penned the love notes to Doris—"I got my hope up high being with you so let that happen lets me, you and Aaliyah be the family were proposed to be"—is the same (semiliterate) person who scrawled threats in marker on the walls of Gary Jones's house the night of the murder—"Wes know what you look like."

Another witness, like a character straight out of the old TV hit *Heat of the Night*, happened to be passing the time on the tailgate of his truck in the Covington town square at 7 P.M. a few nights before the murder. A guy fitting Rodney Young's description pulled up next to him in a car with Jersey plates and asked for directions to Salem Road, the turn-off before Gary and Doris Jones's street.

A local gang investigator from the Newton County sheriff's office, James Fountain, offers his expert testimony regarding the writing on the wall at Gary Jones's home the night of the murder. "Do you know anything about 'ATL mob'?" Zon asks him, referring to the graffiti scrawls that were scribbled around the various rooms.

"No," he says.

"And did you reach out to other experts to see if they had heard of this gang, ATL mob?"

"No intel anywhere that I could find of a gang going by the moniker of ATL mob."

Then, AT&T mobility engineer David Walker takes the stand and produces Rodney Young's phone records. The itemized list reveals which cell towers his calls were bouncing off on the days before, during, and after the murder. Walker charts a damning path from Rodney's home in New Jersey on March 25, 2008, all the way south down Interstate 95 and on into Atlanta, Georgia. He talks the jury through records showing that Rodney Young made a few phone calls that bounced off the cell tower less than a mile from the Joneses' house on Friday, March 28, on Saturday, March 29, on Sunday, March 30—the night of the murder.

A co-worker of Rodney's from the canning factory in New Jersey testifies that he loaned Rodney his TomTom (GPS) the week before the murder. The TomTom is in evidence and one of the recent trips is to Salem Road, the road that leads to Gary Jones's subdivision.

A detective tells the jury how he found duct tape (like that used to bind Gary Jones), magic markers (like the kind used to graffiti the walls in Gary Jones's home), and a cell phone (registered to Gary Jones) in Rodney Young's basement bedroom in New Jersey a few weeks after the murder.

Things look very, very bad for Rodney Young. It seems clear that he did, in fact, brutally murder Gary Jones. And, on the morning of February 16, the prosecutors begin the day by playing a tape of an interview cops conducted with Rodney Young several weeks after the murder. There is no lawyer present to advise Rodney as they push him to confess. Rodney admits he went to Georgia to visit his sister in Atlanta.

"I got these phone records that indicate you were down there," a cop says.

"I hadn't done anything," Rodney says.

"I understand you maybe didn't do anything, but were you down there that weekend?"

"Yes."

"Why didn't you tell me the truth the first time?"

"Because I was scared. I didn't kill anybody. I didn't have nothing against him."

"Yes, everybody loved Gary. . . . You need to understand where this evidence is going. We have you picked out of a photo lineup, asking directions to that road on that day. . . . At the time that Gary was killed, your cell phone was pinging to a tower a mile from that house. You were at that house when he was killed. . . . Rodney, you're down there and go inside that house—"

Rodney tries to interrupt to say something.

"Listen to me. Listen to me, Rodney. Give me a chance to talk, then . . . you go in the house to scare her and want her to come back. You don't expect him to come home till 4:00 or 4:30, and you're writing on the house and Gary comes in. . . . Or the only alternative I see is you went down there and murdered him. You waited for him to come home and murdered him in his church clothes. Either you didn't plan this and it was a spur-of-the-moment thing, or you thought about it."

"I never kill him."

"You were there."

"No, I wasn't."

"You were there," he insists. He asks a few more questions, then returns to the crime scene. "It often happens that victims bring things on themselves by their lifestyle and the decisions they make.

Gary wasn't one of them. He was coming home from church. He was in his church clothes. A good-looking guy trying to do the right thing and murdered right in his house." He mentions the writing on the wall. "'Get out of town. Get out of the state.' No gang-banger writes that on the wall. I cringed when I read that on the wall. It was almost painful to look at how someone was trying to make it look like something it was not. Just tell us what happened."

"I didn't kill him."

"You lied about being there. It doesn't make sense."

"I didn't have no beef with him. . . ."

"Why didn't you tell us you were down there?"

"Because I was scared."

"That doesn't make sense."

"I gave you a swab and everything," Rodney says, referring to the DNA swab he'd agreed to. (No DNA evidence ultimately connected him to the crime.)

The two detectives questioning him circle around with their questions for several minutes, growing increasingly volatile, raising their voices, and then calming down to try and coax him into a confession. "You are responsible for a death. I'm not characterizing it as a murder. I don't know when he came in and what kind of misunderstandings might have taken place. . . . You, based upon everything we know, you are not going anywhere except to Georgia. Do you understand that?" he says. The specter of the death penalty—illegal in New Jersey, handed down with frequency in Georgia—hangs heavy in the room. "At this point, I want to know the truth. . . . You need to have your side of the story out because this is your opportunity. . . . You're a man, a big man. . . . I'll tell you what a jury's going to think. . . . A jury is going to say you were waiting for a moment to strike, and then you struck. It is you. The only thing left is for you to say to me, man, I didn't mean to do it."

"I ain't kill nobody. I ain't kill nobody."

"You did."

"I didn't kill nobody."

The detective, yelling now, interrupts him. "You killed him and you know you did. . . . You know he was a good person. You regret this ever happened, but you need to say it."

"I didn't. . . ."

"You did it, and I just want to know why."

"I didn't. Why you say I did it?"

"You!" *Bang on the table.* "Were!" *Bang.* "There!" *Bang.* Silence. "I feel sorry for you."

"Why you feel sorry?"

"You are no less of a person or no less valuable in the eyes of God. I'm not a perfect person. I made a lot of mistakes. And honestly, this is bigger than you and I. You know there is a God and I know there is a God. And he is looking down on us right now." He says he knows Rodney, after doing this, can't live with himself, can't sleep at night.

"I ain't kill nobody. Why wouldn't I go to sleep? I sleep every day. . . . I didn't kill nobody."

"Your life will never be the same. . . . It gets down to you. It gets down to Rodney. It's about why something like this happened. At the end of the day, Rodney, when we go back to Georgia, you have to answer for it. . . . You and I, you and I are going back to Georgia. You understand that?"

There is a moment during the two-hour taped recording, as investigators cajoled, harangued, coaxed, and urged Rodney Young to confess—and he denied committing the murder, repeatedly—where doubt enters the mind of listeners.

What if he really was innocent?

It is obviously illogical. Overwhelming evidence indicated he committed the murder. Yet, he does not admit it. What is the psychology behind this? listeners speculate. Is it because this is an act so profoundly abhorrent that he cannot admit it to himself? Or what if he really cannot understand that he committed the crime? In arguing for clear procedures to determine mental retardation, the authors of a 2005 Constitution Project report called Mandatory Justice: The Death Penalty Revisited argue that the reason mentally retarded people are not "morally culpable" is in part because they simply do not understand the consequences of their actions: "Persons with mental retardation suffer from substantial disabilities affecting moral reasoning, cognitive functioning, control of impulsivity, and understanding of the basic relationship between cause and effect."[2] Probably this is what is going on. But what if he was telling the truth? Is there any chance at all that he did not commit the crime?

Listening to the recording, jurors were no doubt waiting for the admission of guilt to come, the aha moment that comes at the end of every *Law and Order* episode to clarify motive and method. We have come to expect such things, steeped as we are in tight episodic narratives of crime and punishment. One assumes the reason the prosecutors are playing the audio is so that jurors will hear the suspect break down and spill all. All this questioning by detectives, the voices spilling out into the dead silence of a courtroom four years later, presumably, was leading up to Rodney's spectacular confession.

But as the tape winds down, the conversation repeats. "Ain't nothing happen," Rodney insists. "I said, 'Ain't nothing happen.'" The recording hangs on a question about Rodney's cell phone. "Then why on Sunday, during the homicide, was your phone in Covington the better part of six or seven hours?" the detective asks. "Did you get a flat tire? What made you stay there?" Moments later, the tape dribbles off into a heavy silence. The cursor on the blue screen above the jury's head just comes to the end of its trajectory and stops. And jurors blink out of their reverie, suddenly alert, shifting in their chairs, stretching, glancing at the clock. *Is it lunchtime yet?*

And the thought—what if he is innocent?—nudges, insistent and awful in the stale air of this Covington, Georgia, courthouse. Or, more likely, what if, given his extremely limited mental abilities, he cannot even acknowledge—let alone comprehend—the nature of what he has done? Under those circumstances, what is the function and role of our justice system? And does a defendant like Rodney actually need extra help from the government, via an adequately funded public defender, to protect his rights?

These thoughts gather steam in the afternoon when a parade of teachers, coaches, and social workers from Rodney's Bridgeton, New Jersey, high school are put on the stand to testify about his mental acuity. The defense addresses a skeptical jury, and will have a tough time painting a portrait of Rodney as mentally retarded in the eyes of the law. After all, jurors knew that he held a job, lived more or less on his own, moved through the world like the rest of us. But the teachers tell a different story.

The defense team brings down twelve teachers and others to talk about Rodney Young as a student so that the jury can see him in an expanded way. The big question hanging in the balance is whether or not Rodney is mentally retarded and thus ineligible for the death penalty. Secondarily, the tactic is a way of pleading for mercy in sentencing—a way of setting up phase two of the trial (in case Rodney is found guilty and *not* mentally retarded). Revealing who he is as a person with very low functioning mental abilities and a troubled childhood becomes a way of asking the jury to recognize his humanity and spare his life.

To prove that he is mentally retarded, his attorneys must rely loosely on the American Psychiatric Association's *Diagnostic and Statistical Manual of Mental Disorders*, which defines someone who is mentally retarded as having an IQ below 70, being diagnosed with the condition before age eighteen, and having deficits in adaptive functioning (daily living skills). Before the trial began, an independent psychologist evaluated Rodney, without his attorney present. However, the psychologist was given leeway by the court to question Rodney about the crime itself. Without knowing what he said, the defense attorneys worried to the judge in advance that admitting this expert's testimony, wherein Rodney was asked details about the crime, was a violation of Rodney's Fifth Amendment right against self-incrimination. The day that jury selection began, the judge agreed to seal the psychologist's evaluation, which was not released to either side. In order to keep it sealed, however, defense lawyers had to agree not to call any expert witness to try and establish Rodney's retardation. They could present evidence of retardation through "lay witnesses" but not via experts. Reluctantly, Rodney's attorneys were forced to agree.

From the very beginning, this proves challenging, for all sorts of reasons. The defense calls twelve of Rodney's New Jersey teachers, guidance counselors, and coaches, who attest to the fact that he was in special education classes throughout his entire student life in the Bridgeton schools, and that to be in special education classes, students underwent an assessment, including an IQ test; all students in special ed had IQs under 70. However, in those pre-computer days, the school district threw out records after seven years. Nothing on paper from his school career proves definitively that his IQ was below 70. (In fact, the defense team had hired someone to do a current, adult IQ test on Rodney and he scored 77, classified by the Wechsler Intelligence Scale as "borderline mental retardation." They chose not to introduce that evidence.) But at the time, IQ tests put him below 70, according to twelve defense witnesses.

Wayne Hendricks, a small, precisely dressed African American man in his sixties, is the first to take the witness stand for the defense. He has been a teacher for thirty-eight years, teaching special education at Rodney's Bridgeton High School. He testifies that Rodney was classified as "educable mentally retarded" based on the standard IQ test, which means he fell between a range of 60 and 69.

"Could Rodney read?" asks defense team member Teri Thompson.

"He could read but not very well, third- or fourth-grade level when he was in tenth grade." Hendricks went on to say that he worried a lot in those days about whether African American students were rightly assessed and placed—or whether being disadvantaged and discriminated against, they were sometimes too quickly shuffled into special ed. His voice catches and his eyes fill with tears; Rodney is looking across the courtroom right at him. "I was certain that Rodney's placement was correct," he says. He describes a day when he was teaching and Rodney was really struggling with a basic math assignment. "Rodney was having some difficulty and I was trying to help him," Hendricks says. "We got into a conversation about football." Rodney was a running back and a powerful star player on the varsity team. "Then I guided him back to the activity and walked away. He was still having trouble." Hendricks's eyes fill again as he speaks. "I could see that he was beginning to cry and it was at that point I realized how very much trouble he was really having with this work."

Thompson points out that Rodney was actually accepted into college. He got a 220 on his SAT—you automatically get 200 for filling out your name correctly on the form. Still, he was admitted to

Norfolk State University and received a football scholarship. He went for almost two years and then went to a vocational school instead.

Hendricks says that a local man served on Norfolk's board and likely got him the scholarship.

Then the prosecution takes a turn. "Would it surprise you to hear that he got an A in psychology?" Layla Zon asks.

"Yes," Hendricks replies. "It could very well be that he didn't do the work himself."

"Would it surprise you that he kept down a job all these years?" Zon continued.

"That would not surprise me, no." Hendricks says Rodney worked in a summer youth program at the school every year where the kids did landscaping and construction work. Anything rote and straightforward, Rodney could do.

Next, a special ed teacher named Karen Denise Owens-Jones testifies. She taught for twenty-two years in Bridgeton and first had Rodney when he was fourteen years old and in ninth grade. "I'm not very comfortable using that term—educable mentally retarded—but at that time, that was the term that was used," she says.

"Did you ever see Rodney's [IQ] test results?" Bell asks when she cross-examines her.

"Yes, I saw them."

"What was his score?"

"It had to be in the range of 60 to 69 to be in that class, but I can't remember the specific score from thirty years ago."

"Were you in the room when the test was administered?"

"No."

"So you couldn't know whether [the tester] followed protocol?"

"No. Are you asking me, was she a professional?"

"No, I am asking, were you there?"

"No."

When Rodney's teachers speak, it is the only time during the trial when he looks up from his close study of the patterned carpet to meet someone's eye. All his teachers mention his wrestling and football prowess, and most say, because one year the team he was on went all the way to the state championship, that they saw every varsity game he played. They smile at him as they say this—and then look away when they say things, as Owens-Jones does, such as, "Rodney could tell me it was 1 or 1:30, but quarter of the hour . . . that he couldn't do. When digital clocks came out, I tell you, I was hopeful for those kids."

Another teacher, Jill Swaim, says that she taught remedial math to the special ed kids. "But Rodney didn't have the skills. He just couldn't do it, it was too advanced." She says that lots of the teachers were loyal sports fans, herself included, and went to all the football games. "We'd follow the kids and encourage them," she says. "They were so needy and some didn't have family. We were his family." She recalls getting a late-night phone call from him once. "'Miss Swaim, I need a ride,' he said. 'Okay, where are you?' I thought he was in Bridgeton somewhere. He was at a bus station in Delaware. I said, 'Give me your brother's number and we'll go down to get you.'" She doesn't know exactly what happened. "He could have gotten off the bus to get a drink of water and not thought that far ahead."

Layla Zon insists on facts, not anecdotes. "You specifically don't know what disability Mr. Young had because you did not test him, is that correct?"

"Correct," Swaim agrees.

"In all your years of teaching did you ever see a child who was misplaced?"

"How would I know?"

"You never saw a kid in a remedial class who should have been in another class?"

Swaim hestitates, but then admits, "Yes."

The defense team is trying desperately to show Rodney is mentally retarded, but they can't produce the evidence of an IQ test—and are banned from using experts, unless they want Rodney's Fifth Amendment rights compromised.

Another teacher, Mary Beth Galex, says Rodney reminded her of a big teddy bear. "A part of me always felt so guilty. He was so good, I was worried people would take advantage of him," she says. "He showed me not to give up. He didn't let his mental abilities hold him back. . . . Rodney was just a special person."

Later in the evening, at the Holiday Inn Express, seven of the Bridgeton staffers gather in the hotel lounge. I bring two six-packs and chips, someone brings a couple of bottles of wine, ice cream, lemonade, Doritos—and the Georgia Capital Defenders pick up the tab for dinner: pizza and wings from Domino's.

The teachers are excited, jazzed, a bit on edge as they ease down from the formality and high drama of the afternoon. Like most Americans, who rarely encounter the courts except on TV, they quickly sense the significance of trivialities as presented against the sharp backdrop of death. The mundaneness of our daily lives slips away for a moment and, as the stakes go up—*he could be put to death; death haunts us; we too will die someday*—there is nervous chatter. They want to unwind with a drink and talk about the trial, how they did, what they remember about Rodney, what they remember about their other students, what they remember about the year the football team went to state for the first time in twenty-six years, what they remember of that championship football game, what Rodney was like on the field—"three, four, five people couldn't pull him down," Jill Swaim marvels—and what they themselves were like thirty years ago when they were young.

Everyone has changed from their fancy court clothes—suits, jackets, ties, skirts, heels—back into the everyday—jeans, sweatpants, tennis shoes, T-shirts. The subdued voices of court go up several notches as they cut each other off and insist on being heard.

Romond is nowhere to be seen.

Finally, an hour or two later, he and his girlfriend, Jennifer, show up. She has driven down from Charlottesville, Virginia, where she is a week away from defending her PhD dissertation, to watch Romond's first capital trial. "After hearing him talk about this case for so long, it's exciting to finally see it happening," she says. She chats with all the witnesses, knows everyone's name, and they know hers.

Romond confesses that he went back to his hotel room and had a "moment," crying. He is under a lot of pressure and screwed up today in some way he is reluctant to reveal to a reporter. Some of the witnesses, too, threw him for a loop. He worries that he should have prepared better. He wishes he had had time to personally interview people before putting them on the stand. He knows that is good protocol—but he's also juggling eight other death penalty cases at the same time. The stakes are so high for Rodney—death—and that thought, Romond tells me, never leaves his head. Rodney is counting on him, and he is scrambling to do his best.

In some sense, the gathering has the kind of camaraderie of a team thrown together, an unlikely set of intimacies from folks who wouldn't ordinarily mingle. As they debrief, one of the teachers, Mary Beth Galex, slumps down in a chair for a moment and sighs. "It's just awful being up there on the stand saying he is retarded and incapable of this and incapable of that," she says. "After spending all these years telling these kids they can do anything and they are no different than anybody else." There are murmurs of assent and a hush falls as they wonder, they have hurt his feelings, but have they saved his life?

Covington, Georgia, is a curious place—a mix of old and new South, a mix of middle-class newcomers and strapped old-timers, a mix of black and white who only rarely actually mix. It is a town where the local paper, the *Covington News*, appears to finance its seven pages of news with thirty-two pages of classifieds—thirty-one of them relentless back-to-back foreclosure notices the week the Young trial began. While the murder of Gary Jones took place four years ago, a recent spate of violence, including a murder six days earlier, had editors pleading with locals to play nice, please don't murder each other. "Over the last couple of weeks our community has been rocked with one tragedy after another," editors wrote in their oddly pitiful February 15, 2012, editorial. "We understand that people in our community are going through some intense stress and pain because of the current economic situation we are in. . . . We can understand the fear that is brought about by the loss of a house or other property." Editors begged readers: "If you are reading this and feel you are at your wits' end, seek medical help. Don't let your emotions get the best of you and destroy or end someone else's life. You can also seek help from our creator at no cost. We are positive you will receive some comfort for your pain."[3]

The modest, low-slung *Covington News* office sits next to the courthouse, a modern building, only twelve years old. A bailiff tells me with some pride that the court has already outgrown its home—crime being what it is, apparently—and the five superior court judges have to share three courtrooms. The new courthouse sits a block from the old courthouse, which itself sits on the town square.

The old courthouse, a majestic brick building, anchors the Covington town square. The square, on this February dusk as the Young trial plays out, is a little downtrodden with a desperate, hopeful air. It is lined with locally owned businesses—Lee's Fashions, Pom Pom & Pirouettes, Fletcher's Jewelry—that were likely unable to spring for the higher rents at the new shopping center up the way. Faded awnings and hand-lettered signs on glass ("Bertha's Beauty Lounge, Hair Weeving, Styling, & Cutting") attract sporadic customers who languidly crisscross the square, never seeming to number more than six at any given time. They are a mix of black and white, like the county itself.

The stores flank a central grassy square with two magnolia trees, an American flag, and a giant statue of a confederate soldier. Erected in 1906, the marble soldier stares into the distance while resting his hand on the barrel of his musket. Beneath, under a relief of crossed swords, the inscription reads: "No sordid or mercenary spirit animated the cause espoused by those to whom this monument is erected, or inspired the men who bravely fought and the women who freely suffered for it. Its final failure could not dishonor it. Nor did defeat estrange its devotees."

In his memoirs, General W.T. Sherman mentions a march through this same Covington Square in November 1864. "[W]e passed through the handsome town of Covington, the soldiers closing up their ranks, the color-bearers unfurling their flags, and the bands striking up patriotic airs," he wrote. "The white people came out of their houses to behold the sight, in spite of their deep hatred of the invaders, and the negroes were simply frantic with joy."[4]

In the jury selection process, the deck is stacked against public defenders whose clients are primarily people of color. It takes a very experienced lawyer to finesse this issue. "We win and lose these cases in jury selection," said Chris Adams, former head of the Georgia Capital Defenders, who now does death penalty work as a private attorney in South Carolina. "And it is very different from ordinary voir dire. The case law is different and very complex."

As a result, both the ordinary rules governing jury selection and the special rules governing jury selection in capital cases both conspire against seating a jury that truly represents a fair cross section of the community. That is true in Georgia—and in plenty of other states. "There tends to be a whitening effect in voir dire," said Adams, explaining that by the time you've excused anybody with a record, you've often tilted the scales toward middle-class whites. "We know that police target public housing, which tends to be African American. If I am an eighteen-year-old drinking beer or smoking pot and I'm picked up by the police, I'm likely to get a ride home and cops will talk to my parents," said Adams, who is white. "Whereas an African American kid will be taken to the police station, arrested, charged—and end up in the system." Fifteen years later, that kid can be a pastor at a church and a pillar of the community, but he's not eligible for jury duty.

Economic disparities exacerbate this. The dismissal of potential jurors who are not able to afford time off work or can't serve because they have day care issues disproportionately affects people of color. "You can have a beautiful cross section of people that truly reflects the community when potential jurors are called in—and then the jury panel becomes significantly whiter than the community," Adams said. "That is true in all cases."

Add to this racially biased peremptory strikes where attorneys can exclude a juror based on the vaguest of reasons—*not the brightest bulb in the pack, too strident, wears a cross necklace, wears a nose ring, wears pearls, wears patchouli oil*—and things get tricky. Legally, jurors can't be excluded based on race or gender, but in fact peremptory strikes open a door for lawyers to do just that. According to a June 2010 study by the Equal Justice Initiative, a nonprofit law organization in Montgomery, Alabama, juries grow increasingly lopsided at this point.[5] The report, based on jury composition in eight southern states, found African Americans continue to be regularly excluded from juries for specious reasons. For example, the authors report that eight out of every ten qualified African Americans are struck from death penalty cases in Houston County, Alabama, while in Jefferson Parish, Louisiana, "there is no effective African American representation on the jury in 80 percent of criminal trials," since blacks are struck from juries at three times the rate of whites (and it only takes ten jurors to convict a defendant there). Further, they found several instances of all-white capital juries in majority-black counties.

However, proving racial bias in peremptory strikes is extremely difficult. Given the wide latitude prosecutors have for legitimately eliminating potential jurors, in the rare instances when they are called on to justify their strikes, they easily drum up race-neutral explanations. (The Equal Justice Initiative report even documented prosecutor training programs that teach how to deftly mask bias.) Some of the acceptable reasons "correlate strongly with racial stereotypes." The report's authors explained: "Prosecutors frequently claim to strike African Americans because they live in a 'high crime area' (meaning a predominantly black neighborhood); are unemployed or receive food stamps; or had a child out of wedlock."[6]

All of this is fairly well known in legal communities, but what is less understood is the additional tilt-toward-white that occurs in capital cases. In death penalty trials, jurors get asked a set a questions—called *Witherspoon* or *Reverse-Witherspoon*, based on a precedent-setting case of the same name—to affirm that they would impose the death penalty if the situation merited it or, conversely, to make sure they wouldn't automatically vote for the death penalty every time, regardless of the circumstances. This was designed to exclude those who would never vote for death and those who would always vote for death. Legal scholars believed this would skim 4 percent of those at the ends of the spectrum. But that's not what happened. According to Capital Jury Project research, more than 50 percent of jurors actually fall into those categories.

Over time, as feelings about the death penalty have shifted in the country so that fewer and fewer people support it, it has grown harder to pull together a "death-qualifying" jury. So, even while opponents of the death penalty are seeing successes in changing some hearts and minds in the public, defense attorneys are losing more cases to juries that are further tilted to the political right.

As a nation, that puts us in a tricky spot.

Once, when delivering a talk about the death penalty at the Washington College of Law at the American University in 1995, Stephen Bright, founder and director of Atlanta's Southern Center for Human Rights, mused about the evolution of morality.[7] "There is a debate about the evolving standards of decency—or even whether there are evolving standards of decency—that mark the development of a maturing society," he told the audience. "Are there some kinds of punishment that are beyond the pale: whipping, the stocks, capital punishment?" He told students that Alabama had recently brought back the chain gang, that the Commissioner of Corrections there spent $17,000 to buy three hundred pairs of chains. "You do not need to go to Singapore to find a chain gang. You can find one right there in Alabama." What does this say about us as a country? "I was in a debate with someone recently about the evolving standards of decency, and I said, well, now, boiling in oil, whipping, the stocks; do you think those are still appropriate punishments today? He thought about it for a minute, and said, well, boiling in oil, no; whipping and the stocks, yes. That is something to think about. Are there some kinds of punishment that we do not have because of questions of decency, because of questions of expense, because of questions of effectiveness?"

Because Bright knows the death penalty is not going away anytime soon, he has worked all his life to point out the flaws in the system. Interestingly, he explains the clamor for death as something elected officials—politicians, of course, but also elected judges—have generated themselves, fighting a fear of being perceived as "soft on crime." Before 1988, when George H.W. Bush famously used the Willie Horton ad (depicting a revolving prison door to show how his opponent let Massachusetts inmates out on weekend furloughs—and some committed further crimes) to help him win the election and portray Democrats as soft on crime, many Democrats, including presidential nominee Michael Dukakis, were opposed to the death penalty. By the time Bill Clinton rolled around, he was blithely trekking to Arkansas for Ricky Rector's execution. Bright tells the students:

Ricky Rector, a brain-damaged man who killed a police officer, put the gun to his own head and shot out the front part of his brain. Rector was tried by an all-white jury and sentenced to death. The logs at the prison show that in the days and hours leading to his execution, Rector was barking at the moon, howling like a dog, laughing inappropriately, and claiming he was going to vote for Clinton in the [forthcoming] election. . . . Ricky Rector had a habit of always putting aside his dessert until later in the evening, and then, before he went to bed, he would eat it. After they executed Ricky Rector, they went to his cell and found that he had put his pecan pie aside. He had so little appreciation for what death meant that he thought he was going to come back after the execution and finish his pie.

Even someone whose mental acuity was that compromised would no longer be spared—by either party. And that was a change. "The use of crime by people in both parties to get elected has resulted in a non-debate," Bright said. "In Texas, candidates argue about who is most for the death penalty. In Georgia, who is most for the death penalty. There is no one on the other side."

Bright insists this has spilled over into the judiciary and the legal system, ultimately corrupting our courts. It's an interesting argument; it goes back to the fundamental thinking behind our legal system, that truth emerges best in an equally matched adversarial system. Are the sides equally matched when it comes to public defenders (and their resources) and prosecutors (and their resources)? Are juries a representative sample of the American public and *both* sides of the death penalty debate?

Bright concluded his talk by telling the aspiring lawyers this story about Georgia:

> I recall a hearing in Coweta County, Georgia, in James Ford's case. The prosecutor had used most of his jury strikes to get all the African American people off the jury. The case had been remanded for the prosecutor to give his reasons for the jury strikes. . . . [He would be asked,] "Well, now, did race have anything to do with it?" And the prosecutor, under oath, would reply, "Oh, no, race had nothing to do with it."

I was struck by it. I thought, he knows he's lying. I mean, you don't strike nine out of ten black people out of coincidence.

He knows he's lying. The judge who was presiding had been a prosecutor himself. That's how he got to be a judge; he had struck all the black people from the jury when he was a prosecutor. He had taught this prosecutor how to do it. He knew the prosecutor was lying. He knew how the game was played, he had played it himself most of his career.

We know he's lying. Then I thought about the people out in the courtroom, whether they are white or black, everybody in that courtroom knew that the prosecutor was lying.

I thought this is not a court of justice. This is a court of vengeance. We are here not for justice, but for a different agenda. That is the thing we have to remember, that so long as we have courts of vengeance, we will never have courts of justice.

Because there is both anecdotal evidence and hard data indicating that African Americans in general are more likely to be against the death penalty, they are less likely to be seated for a capital trial. This, then, has the unintended result of tipping the scales in capital cases further toward a white majority. "While plenty of African Americans favor capital punishment, a significantly higher number of people in the black community mistrust the government or the government's use of the death penalty," says Adams. Indeed, a 2007 Pew Center study reported that 51 percent of African Americans opposed the death penalty, compared to 27 percent of whites. And, edging closer to an exploration of why that is, a 2008 American Friends Service Committee survey of African Americans in Missouri discovered that 90 percent "believed that the death penalty is unfairly applied based upon race and/or economic status of the defendant." This attitude is especially true in the Deep South, where the death penalty disproportionately affects people of color.

Whether it is their mistrust of the government or their deeply held religious beliefs opposing the death penalty, these folks' opposition makes them ineligible to serve on juries. "This creates an even wider rift between black and white in a death penalty jury," says Adams. The recent rash of well-publicized exonerations based on DNA has further eroded support for the death penalty among African Americans. "So the panel becomes even more skewed and even more evangelical and white and on the right of the political scale," he said. "So even in conservative counties like Newton, Georgia, a jury tends to be way to the right politically, compared to the community, and likely has fewer people of color."

As noted earlier, support for the death penalty has been eroding. Between the Innocence Project and many well-publicized exonerations based on DNA, public opinion is shifting. This is true based on data—but anecdotal experience is also telling. Adams, deeply absorbed in his death penalty work, talks to people about it all the time—in stores, on planes, standing in lines—and these days he's noticed a decidedly libertarian slant. "You talk to a lot of folks about the death penalty now who say, 'I just don't know if I trust the government,'" he said. "And a lot fewer people say to me, as they used to, 'How can you do that, defend those murderers?'"

In the Rodney Young trial, similar forces are at work. Despite the fact that Newton County, Georgia, is 41 percent African American, the jury had only two black members out of twelve—one male and one female. The minute this jury was seated, Young's chances of avoiding the death penalty plummeted.

Race matters. "If you have one African American male juror, the chances of the defendant getting a death sentence go down 40 percent," says Scott Sundby, a professor at Miami University School of Law and a Capital Jury Project researcher who has interviewed hundreds of capital case jurors in the aftermath of their deliberations. When I speak to him on the phone about the Rodney Young trial, he is intrigued. "Just to give you the counterpoint to that, if you have five white males on the jury, the chances of death go up 40 percent." With African American women jurors, the chances of a death sentence go down—but not as dramatically as with black male jurors.

"The reason this is true," he says, explaining the discrepancies in verdicts, "is we found African American jurors tend to be more distrustful of police testimony, so if there is a dispute over facts, they can be more likely to identify with the defendant's life story." He notes that it is often an African American juror who is making the case for life—as opposed to the death penalty—for an African American defendant in the jury room. "Sometimes the white jurors say, 'Come on, we all have rough childhoods,' or 'How did getting involved with drugs lead to murder?' But if an African American juror with knowledge of the neighborhood where the defendant grew up can and does step in and say something, it can lead the conversation down a different path. And white jurors often listen to that black juror. They say, 'Who am I? What do I know of that?'"

That said, the most powerful voices for death can be African Americans, Sundby says, so it's hard to make generalizations. A lot depends on where the minority juror's life lines up with the defendant's—and that can be a complicated pattern of cause and effect. "If the African American defendant's life really parallels that of an African American juror, growing up in this same neighborhood with gangs, and he is looking at this life of violence that led to killing, that juror could go, 'Hey, that was me and I didn't end up doing *that*!'"

Jury dynamics are complicated. Throw in the issue of mental retardation, and the outcome grows even harder to predict. In the last few decades, because of real progress in education for the mentally retarded and the success in teaching life skills, it has grown harder to prove mental retardation and to explain that the lapses in cognitive thinking really might mean this forty-four-year-old person is essentially thinking like a nine-year-old. "Advocates for mentally retarded people have been working hard to make their lives better, helped people get jobs putting labels on cans, gotten rid of the old language like 'imbecile,' and argued—and shown—a person who is mentally retarded can do the basics of life, meld into society," Sundby says. "But when a defendant in a capital trial is mentally retarded, this makes it hard to persuade jurors that a 'mildly mentally retarded' person can have a severe disability. Yes, they can drive, yes, they can put labels on cans, but their ability to think through things before acting is limited. Their disability affects their decision making." Sundby sees a deep irony here. "As we very admirably help mentally retarded individuals integrate into society, in a case like this, we lose sight of the true restrictions mental retardation puts on someone in terms of making them a follower, or leading them to rash decisions without being able to foresee the consequences."

As interesting as the Rodney Young trial itself is, the recesses between testimony also prove revealing. At one point, as district attorney Layla Zon finishes questioning a witness—and lets her response hang in the silence of the room for a few moments—a woman juror sniffles into a tissue. Noticing her weeping, the judge calls a brief recess and the jurors file out of the room.

Instantly, the formality of a trial, a life on the line, slips away as if this were a movie set and the cameras had just stopped rolling. The public defender, Romond, unbuttons his suit jacket and sighs, putting his hands behind his head to contemplate the many problems he faces here. An investigator pops a butterscotch candy in her mouth. The elderly couple who, as part of their religious mission attend every death penalty trial in the state of Georgia to support the defendant's family (lately, with the slew of capital trials, they have had to split up to cover all the bases), abandon the padded corduroy chair cushions they bring each day to soften the impact of the hardwood pews—and make a beeline for the bathroom. A bailiff slumps from his attentive, standing position into an office chair in the back of the courtroom, legs outstretched, rotating absently back and forth. The court recorder fishes her cell phone from her purse to show the prosecutors a photo on her screen. (A child? A dog? It's hard to tell.) "Idn't that cute?" she asks. The assistant DA Melanie Bell coos at the image. An officer from the sheriff's department chats with a local preacher watching the trial, questioning him about his burgeoning congregation, his plans for a bigger church. "Probably easier to move to an existing space than build?" he says. "For sure, that's true," the pastor agrees. "We'll find something. God is on our side." (Between God and the slew of foreclosures in financially hard-hit Covington, this seems likely.) Out in the hall, Rodney's mother sings the praises of the barbecue she just had for lunch to anyone who will listen. "Where did you go?" someone asks. "Can't recall," she says, fishing deep in her purse in case she saved the receipt.

It is a curious thing, as anyone who has watched a trial has doubtless observed, how fluidly people move from murder to the mundane. It's not, I suspect, the callous impulse that it seems on the surface, but rather a desire to return to the more manageable ephemera of daily life. Just as at a funeral or viewing, mourners maintain a grieving decorum for the requisite time, but then, naturally, compulsively, thankfully grasp at any strand of conversation that takes them away from the dreadful solemnity of the moment—the high price of gas, the new Lowe's going up on Route 1, the deceased who once penned the most beautiful thank-you note when he was six—those participating in such a capital trial are likewise relieved to abandon the drama and dreadful solemnity that *death* injects in the conversation.

This reaction could be viewed as incongruous, but it could also be seen in a different light—a sign of the natural goodness of people that they must struggle so hard to maintain the focused fury that drives a murder trial. The casual chitchat that punctuates the pauses in the formal record might be viewed as a sign that we can't live our lives on this heightened dramatic plane, that passionate love as well as passionate hate will wane. And as I watch those attending the trial file out the center aisle, I notice that Gary's grandmother Annie Sampson, teary eyed after her testimony, dropped a wadded tissue, and that Rodney Young's sister, who clutched a tissue of her own in one hand, bent to retrieve Sampson's tissue and hand it back to the elderly woman. Sampson thanks her, they smile, and I probably overinterpret this as a sign that our powers of empathy will ultimately overwhelm our desire for revenge. Will compassion, mercy, and politeness prevail here in the courtroom—and also in the jury room?

I began to wonder whether the death penalty is protection against that impulse, the natural impulse to let go of some of the intensity and fury that follows the death of a loved one. Maybe the death penalty itself is a formal way to gird ourselves against this instinct to forgive, and get on with things. We must do this, quickly exact vengeance—death for death—while the anger is still fresh and raw and sharp, knowing the danger of it fading with time.

Empathy is dangerous; it undercuts everything.

"We began this trial with the stark, sobering reality that Gary Jones was no longer with us," says public defender Teri Thompson as she stands to deliver the closing argument on Friday, February 17, 2012. Tall, slender, and elegant, she is composed and speaks without pacing. She looks at the jurors' faces one by one as she summarizes the defense, trying to read them, hoping to connect. "We began this trial with the sobering reality that Doris Jones . . . had to do something no mother should have to do: bury a child. We began this trial learning about the value of Gary's life and what he meant to those who loved him."

Thompson knows she must acknowledge the reality of the situation, and she does that forthrightly—quickly getting that out of the way. "And when we started this trial, Ms. Zon, the district attorney, showed you picture after picture for you to focus on the tragedy, on the horrifying last moments of Gary Jones. And never, ever, for one moment will we minimize this crime or what Gary meant." She pauses. "But it is with the lens of someone who is mentally retarded that we want you to see all of the evidence, the same tragedy, the same events. . . . And through that lens, you learned that when he began high school in the ninth grade, as all the kids shuffled to their new moments of high school, Rodney Young entered high school in the ninth grade but sat in a classroom on the Upper B Hall, reading from a third- and fourth-grade book." She reminds them that he was more than "just the kid that wasn't the brightest bulb, Rodney Young was referred to by that district as 'educable mentally retarded.'"

The defense's biggest challenge is the fact that Rodney went to college after high school. Teri Thompson wrangles with that in her closing, anticipating the state's arguments and trying to subvert them. "Now, I expect the state to tell you, to argue to you . . . he went to vocational school. No, he didn't. There is no evidence of that. Well, he went to college. College? College? Coach Cwik talked to us a little bit about college and what that looked like. He told you how that community of teachers that you heard from rallied around him and helped him do the application. He told you that in order to get into college, Rodney took the SAT, and he described for you that out of 1,600 possible points, Rodney scored 220 on verbal, and he got that for signing his name." She reminds the jury that, yes, Rodney got an A in psychology, but the semester before he took basic reading skills at college and got a D. "You see, when Rodney went to college at eighteen, he was still struggling to read. . . . So as college students do, as they do, bustle here and run to and from class, Rodney the football player, the star football player from Bridgeton, who that community of teachers wanted so much for him because he tried so hard, and it was that big, athletic football player that sat in a college classroom learning how to read."

She also anticipates his employment history will work against him. "I also expect that because he worked at Aunt Kitty's, he couldn't be mentally retarded. Well, the state's own witnesses just told us, it was a job putting labels on a can. He applied the glue. He took old glue off, and for eight hours a day, five days a week, he put labels on a can. Rote. Routine. Repetitive."

She hits a few more bases and then concludes simply, with their plea, "We ask you to find that Rodney is indeed responsible, but that he is guilty but mentally retarded."

"Ms. Zon," the judge says, turning to the district attorney.

"Thank you, judge," she says. "Members of the jury, what the state would ask you to do is look at this case through the lens of truth. The lens of the truth. Not the lens of a group of teachers who have come in, look back fondly twenty years ago, [to] what they knew of Mr. Young back then. We heard the testimony of all those teachers and coaches. And God bless teachers and coaches who invest in young people's lives. God bless them for spending the time that they did with each of these individuals that they had in their classes that had either special needs or disabilities or perhaps learning impairments or perhaps just emotional and just problems they have in their own life. . . . It's great that these teachers care about these young people. But this trial is about the truth. This trial is about the evidence. . . . What you should listen to is the evidence in this case, which means that we don't decide this case on emotion." She reminds them of the questions she asked during the jury selection process. "Could any of you, did any of you have a problem making a legal judgment? Not a moral judgment, but a legal judgment? And you all said you could. And that's the issue here. . . . And members of the jury, the evidence that has been presented in this case does not support the conclusion that the defense has in fact proved to you beyond a reasonable doubt that he is mentally retarded."

She pulls up a PowerPoint presentation—the time and energy and resources that the district attorney's office has are clearly apparent—and she runs through a definition of mental retardation and, as a foil, a list of Rodney's accomplishments. As she wraps up her closing statement, she admits, "There's a lot of things about that murder, about what happened in that residence that we are never going to know." The only person who knows is the defendant, she says. "He knows what happened in that house. He knows how many times he struck Gary, and he knows that he had no problem getting down here, committing that murder, that he planned it, that he waited outside that house, stalking them for the right opportunity to go in there and brutally attack Gary Jones with the force that everyone has described, the force of a man that it would take four men to take down. This man, Gary Jones, had no defense. He was brutally murdered in his residence. The state has proven that now beyond a reasonable doubt. So now it's up to you to decide if the defendant has proven beyond a reasonable doubt that he is mentally retarded, and we submit to you that he is not."

When the closing statements are finished, the judge instructs the jury, reminding them, "If you find the defendant guilty but mentally retarded, then you must specify it in your verdict." The jurors nod in assent and file out of court.

After they've left, the defense lawyers huddle around Rodney talking, while the judge prepares to question the defendant. As required by law, he asks him, "Are you satisfied by the defense provided to you?"

Rodney does not answer, looking over at Romond instead.

Thompson answers for him. "We have advised him not to respond."

"Do you understand what I've asked?" the judge says.

Again, Rodney stays silent.

"Well," the judge says, "we will again await a verdict." He gathers his papers and leaves the court.

The defense lawyers, likely trying to leave room for Rodney to appeal based on a claim of ineffective assistance of counsel or some related matter, seem willing to fall on their swords if it can help the client. And Romond frets constantly that the lack of funding for capital defense in Georgia is jeopardizing the quality of their lawyering. It will take some time, but eventually he will reveal the

behind-the-scenes machinations that are constantly going on regarding the fight for adequate funding in these capital cases.

It keeps him awake many a night, worrying. And now, as the
jury sits deliberating, Romond frets, not knowing how to read their
reaction to this, his first capital case. He has been working in the
Georgia Capital Defenders office since 2008, but clients in his other
cases have all settled, pleaded guilty, and avoided the death penalty.

For a while we stand around a small table in the miniscule witness room off the adjacent courtroom. This room is headquarters
for the defense team. One wall is lined with boxes of files. Another
wall contains bags, boxes, and briefcases. Crumbs are strewn on the
floor, and the table holds several legal pads, a jar of peanuts, a bag of
half-eaten pretzels, a pile of Peppermint Patties. As Romond and I
stand there talking—there is no room to sit down—the rest of the
defense team slowly drifts into the small anteroom. They listen and
nervously nibble on junk food, all bemoaning this judge who never
seems to rule in their favor.

"Wait a minute," the young lawyer on a fellowship, Thea Delage,
points out. "There was one time when he went our way."

"Right!" Romond says. He high-fives Thompson. "You got juror
number 25 dismissed!"

Indeed, moments before the jury was to begin deliberations, the
judge responded to a days-old request from Thompson to have one
of the jurors dismissed because of comments he'd made to the bailiff. The attorneys overheard him ask the bailiff if they were keeping an eye on the defendant. He looked agitated, the man said. He
was apparently worried that Rodney would snap and attack them.
(Chances are the aforementioned courthouse shooting by defendant
Brian Nichols was on his mind.)

"No," Delage says. "There was something else." She snaps her
fingers, trying to jar loose the specific memory. Everyone waits. No
one can think of it.

I feel optimistic.

They don't.

"There has never been a jury trial in the state of Georgia where
the jury decided a defendant was guilty but mentally retarded,"
Romond says.

"Really?" Delage says.

"I can't think of one in the last ten years," Romond says.

Thompson qualifies this: "There have been some habeas cases that have gone that way." She refers to cases that were appealed, and won on appeal.

"Yeah, but not jury trials," Romond says. "No juries have gone this way."

A silence falls on the room. This is a discouraging fact. They knew it before, but they had clearly tucked it away in the back of their heads where it would not get in the way of their hopes. They slowly drift out of the room—pacing the halls, checking their e-mail, texting, talking softly with Rodney's mother and sister—until it is only Romond and me in the room.

I apologize for asking Romond so many questions; I'm sure this is a stressful time.

"No, I'm glad of the distraction. Keeps me from thinking about the jury," he says. "Maybe someday—thirty years from now—I'll be some jaded old capital defender, but right now, I can't see that." He finds this whole process grueling and terrible. "The pressure of having someone's life in your hands . . ." His thoughts drift off. He doesn't finish his sentence. He mentions again that mistake he made yesterday that he does not want to elaborate on to a reporter, recalls that he yelled at a colleague about it. Several times, as he questioned witnesses, he knew he should have done better, could have known more, would have talked to them sooner himself. Coulda, woulda, shoulda. He tries again. "The stress—" he says, pausing, "I cried two hours last night."

Twenty minutes later, a court officer taps on the door. "Verdict," he says.

The jury has not deliberated very long; that is a very bad sign for Rodney Young.

For a moment, Romond doesn't move. He exhales a huff of breath and his hands curl around the armrests of the office chair he sits in. He sighs again, then steels himself and gets up.

Back in the courtroom, Rodney's mother, sister, daughter, and teachers stand on one side of the aisle as the judge enters. On the other side, the victim's family stands, Gary's mother, grandmother, girlfriend, and friends. The two elderly death penalty missionaries also stand; the woman holds a packet of tissues at the ready.

"Ladies and gentlemen of the jury, have you reached a verdict?"

"We have."

"Y'all can be seated," the judge says. "The verdict is as follows—" He announces to the silent courtroom Rodney Young has been found guilty on all counts, murder, felony murder, aggravated assault, and burglary. The words *mentally retarded* are not mentioned.

"Predicting whether a jury will sentence a person to die is a lot like predicting whether two people will fall in love," wrote Scott Sundby in his fascinating 2005 book, *A Life and Death Decision: A Jury Weighs the Death Penalty.*[8] Sundby, who has conducted more than seven hundred interviews with 165 jurors in forty-one capital cases in the aftermath of their deliberations, decided in 2005 to dig deep into one particular jury's decision-making process. He did an extensive postmortem of jury deliberations in a convenience store murder in California, and made some curious discoveries about group dynamics in the jury room. He found jurors tend to fall into certain roles and cites several predictable archetypes: the idealist, the chorus, the holdout. If there is an outspoken holdout on the jury—typically one person who resists the death penalty while everyone else favors it—the group is almost certain to wear that person down completely.

It is a deeply troubling revelation. After all, our judicial system is founded on the idea that these twelve citizens, representing the morals and values of society, will hold on to those notions. That they are swayed shifts our understanding of the process and ought to make us think. How random is a trial outcome when jurors are so easily manipulated by the larger group? This happens most frequently not during the first phase, where guilt and innocence are decided, but during the second phase where the death penalty is decided on. In an interesting 2008 paper presented by Sundby and two Cornell University law professors called "Competent Capital Representation," the authors break down the jury's thinking as they evaluate evidence and testimony during the trial (phase one) and the sentencing (phase two). During the trial, jurors are asked to make a fact-based decision. (Did he commit the crime or not?) During the sentencing, jurors make a moral decision. (Does he deserve to die for what he did?)[9] It is this latter question that jurors in Sundby's book struggled with mightily.

Studying the thinking of the "holdout," who is called "Peggy" in his book, Sundby says she interpreted the mitigating evidence differently. "Unlike the other jurors who saw individuals' acts as basically free will choices between good and evil, Peggy saw individuals almost as human supercolliders, their personalities buffeted and shaped in unseen ways by the numerous events, people, and influences that they come into contact with." This made her open to hearing about the defendant's childhood and other forces. When she saw a spark of his childhood self—and speculated about the trauma he likely felt after witnessing his brother's death at age thirteen—she was willing to consider his humanity, and the small possibility of redemption. But it is very, very hard for a lone juror to defend this position if the larger group resists. The impulse to conform is nearly insurmountable.

To understand why the holdout juror in this particular trial—as in most trials—capitulated to the majority, Sundby revisited the psychology of group decision making. For example, in experiments in the 1950s, Solomon Asch asked people to compare the lengths of lines on two chalkboards. He presented one length of line on a board and then three lengths on another board of distinctly obvious different lengths. Alone in the room, people were able to easily pick which of the three lengths matched the solitary length on the opposite board. When put in a room with a group of "fake" subjects who all voted for the incorrect line, the subject went with the group 75 percent of the time even though the answer was obviously incorrect. "Further research has identified additional situations and factors that increase the likelihood that an individual will adopt the majority's position and may help explain why so many holdouts eventually change their votes," Sundby notes in his book.

The Asch experiments document the powerful sway of the majority when it comes to factual decision making; the effect grows even "more powerful when the question to be decided is based on values, especially if frequent and open votes are taken," Sundby writes. "The psychological literature is rich with these types of findings about the human desire to conform, findings that often are counterintuitive. Most of us, for instance, when asked how we would respond if we were the test subject in Asch's line study believe that we would resist the majority's influence and give the correct response; yet research consistently shows that, in reality, most of us would yield to the majority's judgment."[10] Researchers, studying brain waves, speculate that the desire to conform is psychological, but also, perhaps, physical. People's brains respond to exclusion and rejection from the group the same way they do to pain from a physical blow, he writes. "As one of the researchers noted, it may be that as part of their evolution, humans developed a physical response of pain to the rejection by others as a self-survival technique to 'make sure we don't stray too far from the group.'"

This same powerful tug toward group conformity seems to play a role in Rodney Young's trial. At the same time, a similarly powerful factor, the character and circumstances of the victim, likely affect the jury deliberations. Romond, who has read Sundby's jury research, knows this will be a difficult challenge to overcome.

Sundby's 2003 *Cornell Law Review* article examined how capital juries weigh worthy and unworthy victims.[11] The Supreme Court established the role that victim impact evidence ought to play in the sentencing phase of a trial in the 1987 case *Booth v. Maryland*. Here, Justice Lewis Powell argued for the majority that "there is no justification for permitting [the death penalty decision] to turn on the perception that the victim was a sterling member of the community rather than someone of questionable character." In a footnote, Powell further observed, "We are troubled by the implication that defendants whose victims were assets to their community are more deserving of punishment than those whose victims are perceived to be less worthy." Sundby cites research indicating that, in the abstract, jurors were egalitarian and insisted the victim was not part of their decision. But when given hypotheticals—a child, a woman, respected person, stranger, troublemaker, criminal record, alcoholic, drug addict—they did make some distinctions. Fifty-three percent said they would be more likely to give the death penalty if the victim was a child. In contrast, only 3 percent said they would be "much more likely" to give the death penalty if the victim was a "respected member of the community."[12]

On the surface, Sundby wrote, this decision was good news. Juries truly are impartial. "Yet, as is often the case with empirical research, honest answers to hypothetical questions sometimes do not match up with how individuals put a particular principal into action." Indeed, Sundby says, "if we go a step further and look at what juries actually discuss in the jury room and how they focus on different victim attributes, it becomes evident that although jurors may value victim types equally in the abstract, when making the death penalty decision, they place great emphasis on the victim and his or her actions." Sundby refers to the "There but for the grace of God, go I" reasoning. "In other words, jurors may not care in the abstract whether the victim was a banker or a welfare recipient," Sundby explained. "They do care, however, if the banker was murdered while cruising a seedy adult bookstore late at night instead of during a robbery while honorably carrying out his duties at the bank."[13]

If they empathize or identify with the victim, they're more likely to push for death. "If the victim was just minding his own business, the juror is thinking, 'There, but for grace of God, go I,' and the jury is more likely to come back with a death sentence," Sundby says when I talk to him on the phone. The fact that Gary Jones was on his way home from church, "still in his church clothes" as the jury in the Rodney Young case hears repeatedly, can be a powerful influence on their thinking. "Whereas, if this was someone who was murdered when a drug deal went awry, or the victim was engaged in high-risk behavior, like prostitution, or hanging out at a biker bar, or whatever, those are the types of things where jurors say, 'What do you expect, if you're going to engage in this behavior?' They don't really identify with the victim," says Sundby.

If they identify with the victim, the defense team's job gets much harder. The lawyers must convince the jury that their client is a person worthy of mercy. The challenge is to create a fleshed-out portrait of a person, to tell the story of a life so well that someone—at least one person on the jury—can vividly see the defendant as a person (as opposed to the "animal" that the prosecution speaks of) and feels empathetic enough to suggest life in prison as a harsh enough punishment for the crime. But competent attorneys are not necessarily good storytellers. "If I was a defendant in this case," Sundby says. "I would much rather have Shakespeare than Blackstone as my lawyer."

Joseph Romond is not Shakespeare or Blackstone. He is a hard-working, smart, and dedicated lawyer who is trying his first death penalty case. He's a nice guy—the jury doubtless senses that—and he cares deeply about his client's fate. He asks all the questions needed to cast doubt and lay the groundwork for Rodney's appeal, but to the layperson, such questions occasionally seem scattered, hint that he is grasping at straws, and never quite cohere into the empathetic portrait of Rodney Young that the jury needs to see in order to feel merciful at the sentencing phase.

Throughout this trial, Rodney Young is a question mark. Who he is, who he *really* is, remains impossible to decipher as the witnesses talk around him and he sits, silent and hunched forward, staring at the ground between his two feet. Very rarely does he look up; he never makes eye contact. The defense lawyers, of course, won't let a reporter talk to him—who knows what he'll say?—and they will not jeopardize his case. Rodney won't take the stand either, likely for the same reason. Is he a sympathetic character? A monster? A loving father to his teenage daughter? A man who hits his girlfriend? A "man-child" who thinks like a boy in the body of an adult, as one of his old teachers insists?

This second part of the trial, the penalty phase, is all about telling Rodney's story so the jury truly sees him. It is not altogether successful. Romond admits he has not had enough time to question all of the witnesses as thoroughly as he'd like. His mitigation investigator, Felicia Sullivan, who tracks down the folks in Rodney's past and questions them about his life, has told him who has useful anecdotes and who is a good storyteller. But Romond admits funding limitations and a heavy caseload of similarly pressing, high-stakes capital cases mean that he didn't get to Rodney's defense witnesses as soon as he'd liked—some of them have forgotten details years after the incident—and late go-aheads from his office concerning travel and expert witnesses in all the cases he carries are an endless worry for him. He knows this compromises the efficacy of his representation. He has spent the weekend agonizing over this, understanding that he has already lost the guilt-innocence phase of the trial by failing to persuade jurors of Rodney's mental retardation, and he is determined to save Rodney from lethal injection. This is the part of the trial where, having dug deeply into Rodney's past, the defense counsel will try to show mitigating circumstances, to create a portrait of Rodney that forces jurors to see him as a human being, a person valued and loved by his family and friends.

But have they done enough prep work? Romond wonders. He knows they haven't.

His co-counsel, Teri Thompson, has been forced to prepare for three capital trials in the six months leading up to Rodney Young's trial. One client was tried in September and October. One trial was slated for November and, after doing all the preparation for it, was put off until a later date by the judge. She tried a third capital case in January. In February, the Rodney Young trial started. Meanwhile, Thompson had five other death penalty clients whose cases she was juggling and Romond had resolved three capital cases, while carrying five other clients himself. In the past few years, Romond has geared up to explain on the record to judges that the Capital Defenders office has been too financially strapped to represent all their death penalty clients adequately, but his boss forbids this frankness.

"Both Teri and I are mentally and physically exhausted from the workload," he will later confide. "If we had more lawyers and more money, we could divide up this work. It's impossible to do the job when money for experts, etc., is lacking." Romond describes the office as "triaging" capital cases due to the budget crisis. Whatever case is closest to trial gets resources for experts and witnesses, while others languish in a holding pattern. As cases drag on, witnesses forget details, move, fall off the grid, and sometimes die. "We're robbing Peter to pay Paul," he says, and the delays have all kinds of repercussions. First, investigations need to happen quickly when witnesses' memories are fresh—and so that the lawyers can begin to plan the best defense. Second, experts get booked months and months in advance. If the good ones aren't secured early, defense counsel is left scrambling at the last minute. Finally, when cases get delayed and delayed because they aren't ready, the judges grow furious—and sometimes take it out on defense lawyers and their clients. "The judge says, 'You've had this case for two years, why don't you have your experts lined up?'" reports Romond. "They don't want to hear about budget problems in your office."

Romond is squeezed between what he learned in law school were best practices and the reality of his work as a capital defender in the state of Georgia. This disconnect haunts him, along with the ever-present knowledge that someone's life hangs in the balance, there in that space between what *should* happen and what *does* happen in the courtroom. "Did Rodney's case falter because of lack of resources? Yes. If we had the time and energy to adequately prepare things, it would look different," he says. This weighs heavily on him.

And, while he likely wouldn't take much comfort in it, the problem of inadequate funding—or unequal funding, really, between the public defenders and the rest of the criminal justice system—weighs heavily on other public defenders across the country as well. One 2011 report by the Justice Policy Institute, a nonprofit advocating justice reform, notes that defense "receives less funding than the prosecution in many jurisdictions, leading to significant inequalities in resources and services to defend people who stand accused." Authors of the report insist that parity in funding, salary, resources, and workload "has been articulated in national standards by the Department of Justice, the Supreme Court and other experts," and yet, funding for "public defense often fails to keep pace with that provided for prosecution." For example, one 2007 study by the Spangenberg Group of Tennessee's expenditures found that the prosecution spent $130 to $139 million in a single year on public defense cases, while the defense had less than half that amount, or $56.4 million. And the disparities can be measured in personnel differences as well. The report cites public defenders in Cumberland County, New Jersey, for example, who handle 90 percent of all criminal cases, "but there are twice as many lawyers and more than seven times as many investigators working on criminal cases in the prosecutor's office than the public defender's office."

Such differences in funding levels have existed for years. Even when the salaries of prosecutors and public defenders are comparable—and they rarely are; district attorneys tend to make more than their counterparts across the courtroom aisle, especially when they stick around for several years—prosecutors spend more money overall on support staff, investigators, training, legal research, and costly expert witnesses. "Macro-level spending gives some glimpse of the lack of parity at the local and case level," Wake Forest University professor of law Ronald Wright wrote in an article in the *Iowa Law Review*, which studied Bureau of Justice data on this topic.[14] "A survey of 81 of the nation's most populous counties in 1999 shows $1.1 billion spent on indigent defense services and $1.9 billion spent on prosecution services."

Meanwhile, the Justice Policy Institute reports that over the last twenty-five years, "spending on public defense has increased, but it remains far below other criminal justice expenditures, including corrections and police protection." Noting that in 2008 taxpayers spent nearly $14 on corrections (prison) for every dollar spent on public defense, the JPI authors speculate that, "[w]hile there are many contributing factors leading to rising incarceration, underfunding of public defender offices may be one of these."

Even the Justice Department itself has long recognized this problem. "Indigent defense is an equally essential element of the criminal justice process, one which should be appropriately structured and funded and operating with effective standards," said former attorney general Janet Reno at a February 1999 national symposium on indigent defense.[15] She pointed out that public defense is *not* currently funded on equal levels with prosecution—and that creates huge problems. "When the conviction of a defendant is challenged on the basis of inadequate representation, the very legitimacy of the conviction itself is called into question. Our criminal justice system is interdependent: if one leg of the system is weaker than the others, the whole system will ultimately falter."

And the stakes can be very high. This was something Romond was acutely aware of. Now, in the penalty phase of the trial, he gets a second chance at saving Rodney's life. He has spent the weekend thinking about this, and when he arrives in court Monday morning to begin this phase of the trial, he looks haggard, as if he hasn't slept. "When you're attempting to get jurors to find the spark of humanity in someone, it takes an emotional toll," he says. "The weight of the family looking to you to get their life spared—." His voice trails off and, distracted, he hustles off to the defense table.

The district attorney begins the morning by explaining to the jury that she will offer aggravating evidence during this penalty phase and the defense will offer mitigating evidence. She tells them that this will be a very "emotional" day. "But we would ask that in the midst of that emotional evidence that you maintain a sense of objectivity as well and use your common sense and logic in sort of reconciling how this emotional evidence has any impact on the horrific crime that the defendant committed."

Teri Thompson then takes her turn in front of the jury, opening by assuring them that Rodney Young and the defense team accept their verdict. "By the very verdict of finding him guilty of malice murder and each of the other counts in that indictment, there's no question about whether he'll be punished," she assures them. "He will be punished severely every day, every hour for the rest of his life. . . . You will hear no excuses. There is no excuse. What happened to Gary Jones was horrific."

She reminds them that in the guilt phase they made a unanimous decision. "In the penalty phase, as we told you back then [during jury selection], two weeks ago now, it's about an individual decision based on your walk in life individually, your personal moral compass," she says. "That is where we are now. You now are the judges as you determine the sentence for Rodney. You are the individual judges."

The prosecution proceeds to call family members to read witness impact statements, explaining how the loss of Gary's life has affected them. The district attorney, Zon, also presents evidence of a history of domestic violence, drawing on police reports and testimony to show that an ex-girlfriend requested a restraining order against Rodney in 2000 for domestic violence. He had twice attacked the ex-girlfriend, repeatedly punching and kicking Wanda Wilcher, a corrections officer, one night on her way home from playing pool at a bar, the Elk's Home. A second time, he punched her in the face as she sat on a stool at the Country Bar in New Jersey. Doris Jones then testifies that Rodney once choked her, threw a brick at her car, and swung at her several times, to the point that she called the police. She too had asked for a temporary restraining order. (This is a common pattern in domestic violence situations in which the perpetrator begs forgiveness and swears it will never happen again. The victim withdraws the restraining order, reunites with the abuser, and then, often, the abuse happens again.)

"But you chose to dismiss [the restraining order]?" the assistant district attorney Melanie Bell asks.

"Yes," Doris says.

"Okay. Was that, again, because of the persistence and kindness and that sort of sweet version that he would show you?" Bell asked, alluding to the cycle of domestic violence to explain why Doris went back.

"Yes."

Bell then has Doris walk the jurors through family photographs depicting her son Gary as a child, a teen, an adult. In the church choir, his eighth-grade graduation, dressed for the prom, posing at his aunt's wedding, on his way to Easter Sunday service. She calls him by his nickname, G. "G was a strong believer in Christ," she tells the jury. "From the time I went back to Georgia until a few days before Gary's murder, he studied how to have an intimate relationship with God."

After Doris gives her witness impact statement about her son's murder, a church member does the same. Then Gary's aunt, his girlfriend, his grandmother. "I lived right around the corner on Bradley Street from Gary's house," his grandmother Annie Sampson says. "He came to see me every day and called me constantly. He was the light of my life. I have a hard time accepting—" She pauses, repressed sobs clogging her throat. "I have a hard time accepting the murder of Gary. My heart feels like it's been ripped out. . . . I have diabetes and neuropathy, and Gary would wash my feet. He would take blessed oil. He would anoint them. He would massage them. He would massage my back, my shoulders, my temples. He was very concerned about my health."

Three jurors are openly crying. The judge's clerk, a young woman sitting to his right at the bench facing the jury, is also crying. Romond stands and says simply, "I am very sorry for your loss. I don't have any questions for you."

When it is their turn, defense counsel is hard-pressed to counter these statements with a sympathetic portrayal of Rodney Young. And Rodney does not help his cause. According to counsel, he is hardly following the case. He is more concerned with the clothes he will wear each day than the impact of any testimony. His large frame, hunched shoulders, and impassive face only reinforce the image of an abusive batterer and killer. The defense team tries to subtly counteract this by having Thea Delage, the petite twenty-something lawyer who has a fellowship at the Capital Defenders office, sit calmly beside him, but Rodney's silence allows jurors to project their own ideas on him—and in this mostly white jury, racist stereotypes likely surface. This is the defense team's big chance to address that.

The first witness is Charlie Keats, a social worker at Rodney's school, who also grew up in the neighborhood with Rodney. Keats has known Rodney Young since Rodney was twelve or thirteen years old, and he tells the jury about the rough and violent neighborhood they lived in, alludes to his troubled home life with a single mom on public assistance with several kids. He speaks for all the teachers, Keats says, in saying that they feel terrible and keep asking themselves what happened, how can they match what they know of Rodney, of his teenage self, with this terrible crime. They can't reconcile the two images.

"Mr. Keats," Thompson says, "do you feel that Rodney should receive the death penalty?"

"No, I don't."

"And can you explain why?"

"Well, by saying that, by the jury saying that, giving him the death penalty, it would say to those that love him that he has no value, he can't be rehabilitated. And we feel that he can. We feel there's hope there."

The defense calls four more teachers and coaches from Bridgeton High School, a cousin, an in-law. Then the defense calls Rodney's mother, Sara Brihm, possibly to raise questions about her own mental acuity and parenting abilities in the minds of the jury. She tells the jury she was a single mother of five when she moved to New Jersey in the '70s. Among other jobs, she worked picking blueberries for commercial growers, and Rodney worked the fields beside her, starting when he was ten years old. "Well, life was a little hard back then," she says.

"And when you say hard, hard in what way?" Romond asks.

"You, if it ain't nobody but you trying to take care of your kids, it was hard for you because you wasn't getting much money and you wasn't making much money."

"Ms. Brihm, by now you know that Rodney has already been convicted," Thompson says. "Do you understand that?"

"Yes."

"Okay. And what is it you would like the jury to know?"

"I'd like the jury to know that Rodney, he been a good boy. And I don't know what else. And I think it can be more punishment without the death penalty."

"What would the impact of an execution of Rodney have on you?"

"It'll have a lot on me, just like there's a lot on me now."

"In what way?

"In all kind of ways. I miss my son every day."

Finally, Rodney Young's sixteen-year-old daughter, Aa'Liyah, takes the stand. She tells the jury that she has been living with her dad and her two great-aunts since she was two years old. Earlier testimony showed that Rodney had a basement room in the house where his two aunts lived upstairs with his daughter. Aa'Liyah tells the jury that she wanted to come today to talk about her dad. She says she has visited him in prison in Georgia a few times and that she still talks to him on the phone whenever she can. The defense enters five recent letters she sent to him in prison into evidence. She tells them that, as a junior in high school, she is thinking about college. "I want to go to Clark Atlanta University," she explains.

"And why did you pick that school?" Thompson asks.

"So I can be closer to my father."

"I just have one last question. Can I ask one more?"

"Yes."

"You know that your dad has been convicted. Is there anything else you'd like to tell the jury?"

Aa'Liyah nods. "Please don't kill my dad."

Rodney Young's life hangs with this jury of twelve men and women. As the group steps out of the courtroom to begin deliberating, the defense team returns to the topic of jury selection, worrying each call, second-guessing each decision, revisiting each choice. Two weeks ago, the judge, the district attorney, and these public defenders waded through a pool of 250 jurors in order to compile this particular "death qualifying" jury.

And, of course, race is a factor in this trial, just as it is a factor in all trials when the defendant is African American—and especially in all death penalty trials. By law, jury pools must reflect the latest available census data for the jurisdiction where the trial takes place. Here in Newton County, according to the 2010 U.S. Census Bureau, the population is almost 100,000 (a 61 percent increase over its population of 62,000 in 2000). It has a median household income of $52,361, with 12.7 percent living below the poverty line. Fifty-four percent of its residents are white, 41 percent black, 5 percent Latino.

Rodney Young's jury should reflect that same breakdown—but it doesn't. There are only two African Americans serving on the jury. Two weeks ago, one of them, Gwendolyn Butler (a pseudonym), stepped into the courtroom during jury selection to answer some follow-up questions. In the end, according to Romond, she would play a pivotal role; at the time, she was subjected to the usual collection of standard questions about the death penalty.

"Hey, Ms. [Butler], just have a seat and make yourself comfortable," the judge told her that afternoon. "As you were told, the death penalty may never be an issue in this case. However, if the jury determines that the state has proved the defendant guilty beyond a reasonable doubt of the offense of murder, the jury will then be called upon to decide whether the defendant will be sentenced to death, life without the possibility of parole, or life with the possibility of parole." Then he got right to the point. "Now, are you conscientiously opposed to capital punishment, that is the death penalty?"

"Not in all circumstances," Gwendolyn Butler answered.

"All right," he continued. "If the defendant should be found guilty of the offense of murder . . . do you think the death penalty is the only appropriate punishment?"

"No."

"So, in the event the defendant were found guilty, you would be willing to consider the punishment of life imprisonment as well as the death penalty?"

"Yes."

When it is the district attorney's turn, she asks her to describe her views about the death penalty in general.

"I do what I feel is right," Butler says. "I just don't think all circumstances require the death penalty. So I would have to kind of hear all the case. I wouldn't feel comfortable sentencing someone to death if, just depending on what the circumstance was . . . that I heard in the case. I mean, and I wouldn't oppose it at all if it was proven that they were guilty and they maybe killed a baby or a child."

"Right. So it just depends on the evidence and the circumstances presented."

"Mm-hmm."

Teri Thompson, the public defender, then takes a turn asking Butler a few questions. "I guess we all may have different views, you know, whether a person believes in it or doesn't believe in it and things like that. But my question's a little bit narrower." She goes on to explain a felony murder, how that means someone takes a life in the act of committing another crime such as robbery. "So in those kinds of narrow situations, can you tell me what your thoughts are about the death penalty as an appropriate penalty in that situation."

"I don't—see, it's really hard for me to say because I don't oppose the death penalty if the circumstances warrant it, just depending on the circumstances. But you know, I've always had a little feelings about, okay, is it man's right to decide if someone should live or not? But I think it's also my civic duty to do the right thing. And so from the question that you just asked, if I felt someone intentionally killed someone and it was a malice act of just, you know, disregard for human life and just, I could probably consider it."

"Okay. . . . You understand that you are entitled to, and the Court will instruct you that you are entitled to, your individual, moral assessment as to what the appropriate penalty is for you?"

"Yes."

"Okay, and how do you feel about that?"

"I feel okay."

"You know, coming up, hearing everything like you've already said, and making your own individual determination as to what—I think you used the word *comfortable*—"

"I wouldn't be swayed by the other jurors. Just, like, if morally I felt that no, the death penalty in this case is not warranted, I wouldn't just do it because everybody else is, like, let's go, we need to do it."

Both sides agree to seat Butler as a juror.

Deliberations in the penalty phase of Rodney Young's trial start on Monday at 1 o'clock. A half hour in, the jury sends out a note. "Is there an automatic appeal when the death penalty is given?" jurors want to know.

"That's terrible," Romond thinks. "That's bad, a bad sign."

The judge says he is going to tell jurors that "they are to decide this case based on the law and the evidence and not to concern themselves with matters of this nature." He tells the lawyers, "That's the only thing I know to do." The judge writes a note to this effect and sends it in to the jury.

Then, one hour and forty-five minutes later, jurors send out another note. One of the jurors has asked to be dismissed as a juror saying she has too many questions about this case, that she can't give the death penalty, that everyone else is in agreement but her.

The judge, who reflexively asks the prosecutor for input throughout the trial—and nine times out of ten, takes her advice—asks what she wants to say about this. "With respect to the Court's proposed solution that was discussed at the bench conference, which was to not respond or not address the note at this point in time, we have no objection," says Layla Zon. But she has two recommendations.

"One would be to bring the jurors out and ask the juror if he or she is still able to deliberate and then act accordingly or appropriately. Or B, send a note to the jury that would be something of the nature of . . . you're just to continue to deliberate, consider each other's opinions," an order known as the "Allen charge."

Scott Sundby, the professor of law at Washington and Lee University who extensively researched capital juries, says that the Allen charge is referred to as the "dynamite charge." Speaking to me on the phone, he recalls a juror he once interviewed who told him that the judge invoked the Allen charge by explaining they'd be there until the cows come home. "The judge says to the jury, you must abide by your conscience, of course, but you put in so much effort already and you need to listen to your fellow jurors and see if you can't agree. So go back in there. The dynamite charge is used when the jury is deadlocked and the judge hopes to blast out a verdict."

"Your Honor," Teri Thompson objects. "The note is clear. This juror, whoever the juror is, has reached his verdict." (The gender of the juror is not clear since the note was unsigned; in fact, it turns out to be a woman.) "The Court, I think, has the authority to sentence Mr. Young to life without parole based on this note. That is his verdict. He is not saying, he or she, whoever it is, is not saying they cannot deliberate. . . . He has made his verdict, and that should be—"

"So you want me to sentence the defendant based on a note from one juror?" the judge asks.

"Absolutely," Teri Thompson says. "This juror has made his vote. He's reached his verdict."

"So what do you want me to sentence him to?"

"I think—well, I can pull the law," Thompson says. "There is law that addresses where there is, if there is a lone juror, if there are eleven jurors voting one way—"

"We don't know what this juror is saying he or she is wanting the sentence to be."

Joseph Romond dives in. "Your Honor . . . our position on this would be . . . in the penalty phase of a capital trial, the decision by the juror is an individual moral judgment," he says. "That's the case law. This juror has made his or her individual, moral judgment as to what the penalty is, saying that, due to those questions, he can't say yes to the death penalty."

"Yes."

"So in that situation, that juror has reached their verdict," Romond says. "The statute allows the Court, in that event, to sentence the defendant either to life or life without the possibility of parole. I'll pull up that statute."

"I'm aware of the statute," the judge says. "I think it may be premature to make that leap based on one juror making this statement."

Romond disagrees, but the judge interrupts him.

"This juror does not say, we are deadlocked. This juror does not say that I am not listening to anyone else or anything else of that nature. I can't read into this one note what you're asking me to read into it. And I mean, I don't know what this juror is willing to impose. . . . Only one thing is mentioned that . . . he or she will not impose."

The prosecutor points out that they have not been deliberating very long, only two hours or so—and the judge agrees.

Romond tries again. "Our only point is that, a juror can reach their own individual, moral assessment about what the penalty should be in five minutes," he says. "And clearly this juror has, so our motion to the Court is to suspend deliberations based on the fact that this juror has reached their judgment and sentence Mr. Young according to the statute."

"What are you asking me to sentence him to?"

"Your Honor, the Court has the discretion—" Romond begins, scrambling for the legal language on his laptop. "I'll pull it up right now. The Court has the discretion to sentence Mr. Young in that event to either life imprisonment with the possibility of parole or life without the possibility of parole. As the Court is aware, a unanimous verdict is required for a death sentence. This note says that this juror cannot say yes to the death penalty. And in that event, the Court then has the discretion for either one, and so it's in the discretion of the Court."

The judge again refuses.

The judge and Romond go back and forth with this. Romond understands, in a profound way, that this juror holds tremendous power over Rodney's fate, but also is under tremendous pressure—and will likely succumb to the group. The stakes are high. He needs to act fast; research indicates holdout jurors resist only so long. He reiterates. "[O]ur position is this juror has reached their verdict, their individual, moral assessment. And as such, any further deliberations is simply beating, the other jurors beating up on this juror to try to get them to change their moral beliefs."

"No action is going to be taken by the Court at this time," the judge says.

Then, an hour later, the jury sends out another note. This one asks again for more information, a copy of the PowerPoint page that the State used in its closing argument. The section the jury is specifically requesting has to do with the *Diagnostic and Statistical Manual*'s definition of mental retardation, as well as a bell curve showing how the population falls in terms of IQ. The judge calls the jury in and shows them the slides again. They return to the jury room.

About an hour later, the jury sends out another note saying they cannot reach consensus, suggesting they are deadlocked eleven to one. What do we do now? they want to know.

The judge tells the attorneys that he intends to instruct the jury to "continue deliberations."

Romond objects. "It's clear that a verdict by one individual has been reached under the law and that any further deliberation would simply just be an attempt to coerce this one individual juror, and so we would object to any charge given," he says. "It's clear that the only purpose of this is to change this juror's individual, moral assessment, strongly-held belief . . ."

The judge is unpersuaded. "[B]ased on the note, I'm going to call the jury out and give them the instruction that I discussed with counsel," he says. When the jury reenters, he tells them that he received their latest note, but that he has something to say. "In order to return a verdict, each juror must agree to the verdict. Jurors have a duty to consult with one another and to deliberate with a view to reaching an agreement, if it can be done, without violence to individual judgment. Each juror must decide the case for himself or herself, but only after an impartial consideration of the evidence with the other jurors. In the course of deliberations, a juror should not hesitate to reexamine his or her own views and change an opinion, if the juror is convinced that it is erroneous. No juror should surrender his or her honest conviction as to the weight or effect of the evidence solely because of the opinion of the other jurors or for the mere purpose of returning a verdict." He then tells them to return to the jury room and resume deliberations.

At 6:30 P.M., he asks the jurors if they want to continue discussions—and, if so, if they would like to call family members to let them know what is up—or if they'd like to stop for the evening and continue the next morning. The jury says they need ten more minutes.

When the jury reenters the courtroom, the judge addresses them. "Ladies and gentlemen, have you reached a verdict?"

"Yes," the foreperson says.

The bailiff hands the form to the judge, who reads it aloud. "With reference to the sentence, we, the jury, fix the sentence at death," the judge reads. He then individually polls the jurors and turns to Rodney Young. "Mr. Young, you've been found guilty of the offense of malice murder. The jury, in its verdict, has found beyond a reasonable doubt the existence of statutory aggravating circumstances and fixed the sentence at death. I therefore sentence you to death by lethal injection. The execution shall be conducted between March the 28th, 2012, and noon on April 4th, 2012." As the jury listens intently, he concludes the trial. "Mr. Young, may God have mercy on you."

A few weeks after this trial, a disillusioned and dispirited Joseph Romond quit his job with the Georgia Capital Defenders, moved to California, and took a job as a bartender. He reports: "Despite my [new] profession, I drink a third of what I did as a lawyer."

CONCLUSION

The National Legal Aid and Defender's Association opened its one-hundred-year anniversary conference in Washington, D.C., in 2011, with the Reverend Michael Eric Dyson addressing the crowd of three hundred public defenders and legal aid attorneys scattered in a hotel ballroom with space for many more. "Does the rest of society demonize you? Of course. Do they suggest you are working for the wrong people? Of course they do. Do they say you are working for thugs and criminals? Of course they do," he said, working to rev up his tired audience with rhetorical flourishes. "But the work that you do is vital and critical, because the principles of democracy rest on the ability of ordinary citizens to get justice in our legal system."

His voice rose in volume and picked up speed as he told the audience that they ought to consider themselves superheroes. "Maybe you don't have an *S* on your chest," he said. No matter. "Each of you is a superhero."

It was an interesting observation, more desire than reality. The motley group of public defenders and legal aid attorneys sprinkled in the hall that day wore the resigned look and crumpled clothes of the system's legal workhorses. No power suits. No Brooks Brothers shirts. No Prada shoes. The men were the kind I had sat behind in too many courtrooms as a reporter over the years—worn tweed jackets sprinkled with a layer of dandruff that glinted under fluorescent lights, haircuts that might have been sharp three months ago but now curled into the collars of their blazers, wash-and-wear/no-iron shirts from L.L. Bean. The women at the conference also wore their standard trial attire—the jacket that told a jury this was serious work, though it came from Marshalls and had cat hair trapped in the nap, the practical if unglamorous Born clogs, the canvas book bag from Barnes and Noble with a faded, disappearing image of a gaunt Virginia Woolf.

It was possible that shiny spandex, superpowers, and the attendant glory lurked beneath these frumpy clothes, hidden by slumped and tired frames, but it was a stretch. What Dyson was up to, clearly, was trying to rally the crowd with a renewed commitment to this unpopular work, public-defender-as-martyr-to-a-losing-cause, the rights of the indigent.

This was a telling moment, indicative of the sense, from every single person I spoke to at this national conference (roughly fifty over the course of several days), that good work was possible for public defenders across the nation, but that the greater context in which they labored made it a herculean effort that few could sustain. Indeed, public defender systems regularly hemorrhage attorneys who left in a blaze of fury or slowly simmered with resentment until they burnt out after a few years on the job—and this inadvertently emerges as a theme among the lawyers I report on in the course of this book. Carol Dee Huneke is a vocal critic of the status quo in the public defender's office in Spokane and finds herself fired. Twenty-one hard-working public defenders in New Orleans are let go and Greg Bright's attorney at Innocence Project New Orleans returns to England after several years' immersion in the American justice system. Miami chief public defender Bennett Brummer fought a pitched battle to limit caseloads and reform the system, and after thirty years, decided not to seek reelection. Joseph Romond, a committed and passionate public defender in Georgia, quit in frustration after trying his first death penalty case before a jury.

In some ways, Dyson's speech has totally missed the mark. Most of the public defenders out there are not particularly interested in being vigilante superheroes acting alone to save the world from injustice. They want some backup. They want to work within the existing framework of the laws of the land to protect their clients' rights. And mostly, they want the time and resources to do their job right without having to resort to heroics. Over and over, public defenders said they needed more time with their clients if they were to properly represent them. "Clients don't trust the system," says Franny Forsman, a federal public defender for the District of Nevada for twenty-two years. "You can be the best smarty-pants lawyer out there, but the client doesn't know that or see it. There's a relationship of trust that has to happen because of the critical decisions that have to be made. Clients are asking, 'Do I trust you enough to tell you the truth of what happened?' And I need that information so I can see, for example, is this a self-defense case? There has to be enough time to create a relationship. That's where the difference is between rich and poor. The rich, because they're paying for their time, will have as much time with their lawyer as they need."

It is a curious thing that everyone at the public defender's conference knows the system is broken—and indeed almost everyone in all parts of the criminal justice system across the United States acknowledges deep flaws in the way representation is provided to poor people. Eric H. Holder Jr., attorney general of the United States, also spoke to the American Council of Chief Defenders in June 2009 about the urgent need to reform the system.[1] "The obstacles to representing the indigent are well-known," he said. "We know that resources for public defender programs lag far behind other justice system programs—they constitute about 3 percent of all criminal justice expenditures in our nation's largest counties. In many cases, contract attorneys and assigned lawyers often receive compensation that doesn't even cover their overhead. We know that defenders in many jurisdictions carry huge caseloads that make it difficult for them to fulfill their legal and ethical responsibilities to their clients. We hear of lawyers who cannot interview their clients properly, file appropriate motions, conduct fact investigations, or do many of the other things an attorney should be able to do as a matter of course. Finally, we know that there are numerous institutional challenges in public defense systems, like budget shortfalls." He acknowledged that the challenges the system faced were not new and quoted Justice Hugo Black, who saw the problems as long ago as 1963 when *Gideon v. Wainwright* came before the U.S. Supreme Court. "There can be no equal justice where the kind of trial a man gets depends on the amount of money he has."

"What can be done?" Holder asks.

The question resonates, echoing and bouncing off the walls of marbled courthouses all across the nation, where the players know what needs to be done in a technical sense to fix the problem but no one can generate the political will necessary to change things. Fifty years after *Gideon v. Wainwright*, equal justice for all eludes us.

AFTERWORD

David J. Carroll, Executive Director, The Sixth Amendment Center

"Liberty." For the signers of the Declaration of Independence, it is the universal notion that every person should determine their own path to happiness free from undue government control. Patrick Henry preferred death to living without it. In fact, liberty is so central to the idea of American democracy that the founding fathers created a Bill of Rights to protect personal liberty from the tyranny of big government. All people, they argued, should be free to express unpopular opinions or choose one's own religion or protect one's home without fear of retaliation from the state.

Preeminent in the Bill of Rights is the idea that no one's liberty shall be taken away without the process being fair. A jury made up of everyday citizens, protections against self-incrimination, and the right to have a lawyer advocating on one's behalf are all American ideas of justice enshrined in the first ten amendments to the United States Constitution. John Adams risked his reputation for these American ideals by defending in court the British soldiers involved in the Boston Massacre, recounting years later that a defense lawyer ought to be the last thing a person should be without in a free country.

In 1963, the United States Supreme Court agreed. "From the very beginning, our state and national constitutions and laws have laid great emphasis on procedural and substantive safeguards designed to assure fair trials before impartial tribunals in which every defendant stands equal before the law," the U.S. Supreme Court declared in the landmark case of *Gideon v. Wainwright*[1] before asserting that this "noble ideal cannot be realized if the poor man charged with crime has to face his accusers without a lawyer to assist him."

Without the aid of an effective lawyer, almost anyone stands the risk of going to jail when charged with a crime. To the *Gideon* Court, this seemed to be "an obvious truth." The majority of us would not know, for example, what is and is not admissible in a court of law, let alone how procedurally to convince twelve jurors that we are innocent. If this is true of even the most affluent and educated among us, is it then fair to let someone who has fallen on hard times or has been let down by our country's educational system or is not yet an adult face a loss of liberty at the hands of government, simply because they lack the guiding hand of counsel to navigate the complexities of our legal system?

The potential tyranny of government over the individual is mentioned throughout *Gideon*. For example, recognizing that governments "quite properly spend vast sums of money to establish machinery to try defendants accused of crime," the *Gideon* Court determined that "lawyers in criminal courts are necessities, not luxuries." And to those that would oppress individual freedom, the *Gideon* Court announced that the "right of one charged with crime to counsel may not be deemed fundamental and essential to fair trials in some countries, but it is in ours."

Over the ensuing fifty years since *Gideon*, the U.S. Supreme Court consistently determined that providing a lawyer to those of limited means is essential to preserve the fairness of the criminal justice system. For example, on the same day that *Gideon* was decided, the Court also mandated, in *Douglas v. California*,[2] that states provide lawyers during the first stage of the appeals process—the court hearing where a defendant may ask a court to set aside a trial verdict or imposed sentence—noting that "there can be no equal justice where the kind of an appeal a man enjoys depends on the amount of money he has."

Four years later, the Court again picked up the theme of potential government tyranny, this time in relation to children facing juvenile delinquency charges. "Due process of law is the primary and indispensable foundation of individual freedom. It is the basic and essential term in the social compact which defines the rights of the individual and delimits the powers which the state may exercise," the Court asserted in *In re Gault*, determining that children too were entitled to a lawyer.[3] To underscore the point that children needed more protections than adults, not less, the Court famously added "[u]nder our Constitution, the condition of being a boy does not justify a kangaroo court."

The 1972 decision in *Argersinger v. Hamlin* may have had the greatest impact on criminal justice systems in America.[4] The Court's *Gideon* decision had applied only to felony cases, but as of yet there was no similar right to counsel in misdemeanor matters. Because of the utterly massive volume of misdemeanor cases charged every year, the lower trial courts hearing those cases had developed "an obsession for speedy dispositions, regardless of the fairness of the result." And without publicly available lawyers to assist accused persons in their defense, misdemeanor courts became places of "futility and failure" rather than justice. "We are by no means convinced that legal and constitutional questions involved in a case that actually leads to imprisonment even for a brief period are any less complex than when a person can be sent off for six months or more," the Court confessed in *Argersinger*, extending the right to counsel to misdemeanor cases.

Rather than spend public funds on attorneys in misdemeanor cases, too many jurisdictions in America decided that the *Argersinger* mandate could be avoided. If the threat of jail time was not made imminent, perhaps the Sixth Amendment right to counsel no longer applied. A "suspended sentence" is a jail term that a judge delays imposing upon a guilty defendant in lieu of "probation"—or a set of conditions a defendant must fulfill under the supervision of a probation officer. The person only goes to jail if he or she fails to meet the terms of the probation. Some jurisdictions would tell defendants that they were only facing a suspended sentence and thus not provide a lawyer. Of course, without the aid of counsel, the conditions of probation were often so restrictive as to make it almost impossible to comply. Indeed, some states required impoverished defendants to pay a portion of the cost of their own representation, made repayment a condition of probation, and then sent them to jail when they did not make payments. Keeping up with payments, of course, is difficult to do when you are poor.

So in 2002, the U.S. Supreme Court asked: "Where the State provides no counsel to an indigent defendant, does the Sixth Amendment permit activation of a suspended sentence upon the defendant's violation of the terms of probation?" The Court concluded that it does not, and instead now requires that states provide access to effective representation even in those misdemeanors where the trial judge does not intend to impose a jail sentence right away.

The vast majority of criminal cases will never make it to trial, and instead will be resolved much earlier through pleas. But in the plea-bargaining process, the judge is not bound to impose the sentence negotiated between the prosecution and defense. For many years, states and counties would not provide lawyers to poor people who pleaded guilty to a crime but then wanted to appeal the judge's sentence resulting from that guilty plea. In *Halbert v. Michigan*, the Court determined that to be improper.[5] Recognizing that the majority of people facing criminal charges are indigent and that most people in prison are undereducated, mentally ill, or both, the Court reasoned that "[n]avigating the appellate process without a lawyer's assistance is a perilous endeavor for a layperson, and well beyond the competence of individuals, like [the defendant] Halbert, who have little education, learning disabilities, and mental impairments."

Although *Gideon* requires the "guiding hand of counsel at every step in the proceedings (emphasis added)," it took the Court a number of cases to delineate the specific "steps" in a case at which the right to counsel must be provided. Most people familiar with crime dramas know that when you are arrested you have the right to remain silent and to have counsel appointed for police interrogations. These are your so-called Miranda rights, established in the landmark 1966 case *Miranda v. Arizona*.[6] A year after *Miranda*, the Court also made attorneys available to those in police lineups in *United States v. Wade*.[7]

Once charges are filed, there are a series of events that generally occur in a criminal case prior to a trial (though these events often are named differently depending on the region of the country). Generally speaking, there is a "bail hearing" in which a defendant learns if he can get out of custody while awaiting his case to be heard. An "arraignment" is the court proceeding where the defendant hears the formal charges that he is facing (in some jurisdictions bail hearings and arraignments occur simultaneously). A "preliminary hearing" is the point when the prosecution makes its case that a crime has likely been committed and that the defendant likely did it. Usually "plea negotiations" occur to determine if the case can be settled without a trial.

In 1970, the U.S. Supreme Court made clear that a defendant has the right to public counsel at preliminary hearings (*Coleman v. Alabama*)[8] and during plea negotiations (*Brady v. United States*).[9] The question of counsel at bail hearings and arraignments is a little more convoluted. Even prior to the *Gideon* decision, the U.S. Supreme Court determined that an arraignment is a critical stage of the proceeding. Reasoning that what happens at arraignments can affect the whole trial and that "[a]vailable defenses may be as irretrievably lost, if not then and there asserted," the Court in *Hamilton v. Alabama*[10] required counsel be present at arraignments for those facing the death penalty.[11] However, it was not until 2008, in a case called *Rothgery v. Gillespie County*, that the U.S. Supreme Court clarified its position on the need for counsel at initial appearances.[12] The *Rothgery* Court concluded that "a criminal defendant's initial appearance before a judicial officer, where he learns the charge against him[13] and his liberty is subject to restriction,[14] marks the start of adversary judicial proceedings that trigger attachment of the Sixth Amendment right to counsel."

The United States Supreme Court has also sought to illuminate that the right to a lawyer means more than just the right to a warm body with a bar card. In *McMann v. Richardson*, the Court declared "the right to counsel is the right to the *effective* assistance of counsel (emphasis added)."[15] Two cases heard on the same day and announced on the same day in 1984 made clear what the Court meant by "effective" assistance of counsel: *United States v. Cronic*[16] and *Strickland v. Washington*.[17]

In *Cronic*, the Court determined that "if counsel entirely fails to subject the prosecution's case to meaningful adversarial testing, then there has been a denial of Sixth Amendment rights that makes the adversary process itself presumptively unreliable." The Court pointed out two ways to determine whether a system could fail to meaningfully test the prosecutor's case. First, if counsel is not present at all, of course, it is impossible to have effective representation. Secondly, they pointed to the systemic factors that led to the wrongful conviction of the Scottsboro Boys.[18] The so-called Scottsboro Boys were a group of eleven young African American men arrested for the rape of two white women in 1930s Alabama. They were tried and sentenced to death within a week of the alleged offense. Their attorney, who was hand-selected by the judge presiding over their case, was unfamiliar with criminal law, conducted no independent investigation, and had no time to properly prepare the case. When such systemic deficiencies occur in the present day, the attorneys in that indigent defense system should be presumptively determined to be ineffective.

Only when such systemic issues do not come into play can a two-pronged test be applied to determine whether an individual lawyer is ineffective, as set out in *Strickland v. Washington*. Under *Strickland*, a defendant must show on appeal that his attorney's representation fell outside of what object standards of reasonableness require, and that the outcome of the case would have been different had the attorney performed up to standards.

Several recent U.S. Supreme Court decisions have clarified the *Strickland* standard. For example, there are a number of potential collateral consequences of a criminal conviction, including loss of student loans, public housing, or even deportation. In 2010, in *Padilla v. Kentucky*, the Court determined that "[i]t is our responsibility under the Constitution to ensure that no criminal defendant—whether a citizen or not—is left to the 'mercies of incompetent counsel.' To satisfy this responsibility, we now hold that counsel must inform her client whether his plea carries a risk of deportation."[19] And in 2012, the Court made clear with two more cases—*Missouri v. Frye* and *Lafler v. Cooper*—that the right to effective assistance of counsel applies to the plea-bargaining process and not just to trials.

With this historical context, we can see that the United States Supreme Court has been nothing but consistent on the right to counsel in America. Yet, as we celebrate the fiftieth anniversary of the *Gideon* decision, violations of the right to counsel abound in America. Karen Houppert's *Chasing Gideon* shows that as a country we too often fail to live up to our own ideals. In far too many parts of the country, a poor defendant can sit in jail for three to four months before seeing a lawyer, while several hundred defendants may be vying for the attention of a single lawyer all at the same time. Attorneys may have a monetary incentive to do as little work as possible while being financially beholden to the presiding judge, in your case, and a defendant may have to reimburse the government the cost of his or her representation or face further jail time, a turn of affairs completely contrary to the spirit of the original *Gideon* decision. Poor people facing misdemeanor charges likely still will not receive a lawyer at all.

The United States Constitution is a living document whose rights must be continually fought for or be lost. As Benjamin Franklin once said, "They who can give up essential liberty to obtain a little temporary safety deserve neither liberty nor safety."

ACKNOWLEDGMENTS

This book would not have been possible without the many long conversations I had with defendants and their families—those mentioned in the book and many who provided background and insights, generously sharing their stories and their lives with me as we sat in courtrooms and talked on benches in the halls outside, plowed through court records, visited crime scenes, and rehashed events in living rooms and kitchens across the country. These folks gave me a front-line education on the intricacies of legal counsel for the poor and what it is like to experience a criminal trial from the perspective of the accused. Through their eyes, and through exchanges I had with public defenders who were all so generous with their time, frank in their assessments, and tolerant of my reporterly shadowing, I got a glimpse of what McJustice looks like in the nation today. I thank both the public defenders and their clients for their honesty and insights.

I received invaluable fellowships and grants from The Nation Investigative Fund, the John Jay College Center on Media, Crime and Justice, The Ford Foundation, The Latte Fund, and The Bridge Grant; so thanks to Esther Kaplan, Maurice Possley, Stephen Handelman, Cara Tabachnick, Fleur Edwards, Susan Breton, and Patricia Houppert for faith and funds. I was graciously housed and fed by fellow reporters and photographers—and a public defender—as I traveled around the country last year so thanks to

Sandra Lee Phipps, Russell Kaye, Wayne Curtis, and Louise Klaila for food, shelter, leads, backstories, fellowship, and cocktails. Ian and Barbara White-Thomson graciously lent me their Peaks Island seaside home for a two-week writer's retreat in January while Kathy Hanley and Will and Charles Winkleman provided respite and repast, ensuring that I didn't rattle around that "big ole house" all day writing nothing but "All work and no play makes Karen a dull girl."

Jennifer Walker helped research the book and did extensive reporting on the death penalty and the public defense crisis in Miami. Thanks to David Everett at the Johns Hopkins University MA in Writing Program and Sven Birkerts and Victoria Clausi of Bennington Writing Seminars who allowed me flexibility in my teaching and writing schedules to complete this project. Laura Wexler turned me onto a perfect source who opened doors and recharged my investigation. Andrew Hsiao talked me off a cliff at a critical juncture. Betsy Reed and Esther Kaplan at *The Nation* performed their trademark precision surgery on excerpts first appearing in the magazine. Cabin Creek Films' producer Suzanne Mitchell, cinematographer Gary Griffin, and soundman George Ingmire filmed sections of *Chasing Gideon* in New Orleans and also helped with reporting.

Franny Forsman and David Carroll read sections of the manuscript, explained byzantine concepts and legal histories, and offered expert opinions and sources for me along the way. Debbie Lee and Peter Chilson, members of my writers' group, read and critiqued early drafts, offering valuable input. Wendy Williams did some pinch-hit editing. My mom, Patricia Houppert, proofread final copy and fact-checked every single proper noun in the book—a huge task that she took on around the edges of her full-time workday, so I thank her.

At New Press, my editor Diane Wachtell cracked the whip, keeping me focused and on schedule with her swift, thorough, and insightful comments as the manuscript progressed. Thanks also to Kianoosh Hashemzadeh, Jed Bickman, and the entire staff. Their passion and dedication for social justice issues is palpable, contagious, and always exciting to be a part of.

Thanks, finally, to my son, Zack, who sacrificed many a game of Contract Rummy so I could report and write, and to Steve Nunns, my reluctant yet trenchant critic.

AMERICAN BAR ASSOCIATION'S TEN PRINCIPLES OF A PUBLIC DEFENSE DELIVERY SYSTEM

BY THE STANDING COMMITTEE ON LEGAL AID
AND INDIGENT DEFENDANTS

1. The public defense function, including the selection, funding, and payment of defense counsel, is independent.

2. Where the caseload is sufficiently high, the public defense delivery system consists of both a defender office and the active participation of the private bar.

3. Clients are screened for eligibility, and defense counsel is assigned and notified of appointment, as soon as feasible after clients' arrest, detention, or request for counsel.

4. Defense counsel is provided sufficient time and a confidential space within which to meet with the client.

5. Defense counsel's workload is controlled to permit the rendering of quality representation.

6. Defense counsel's ability, training, and experience match the complexity of the case.

7. The same attorney continuously represents the client until completion of the case.

8. There is parity between defense counsel and the prosecution with respect to resources and defense counsel is included as an equal partner in the justice system.

9. Defense counsel is provided with and required to attend continuing legal education.

10. Defense counsel is supervised and systematically reviewed for quality and efficiency according to nationally and locally adopted standards.

NOTES

INTRODUCTION

1. Pew Center on the States, "One in 100: Behind Bars in America," February 2008, p. 5.

2. Michelle Alexander, "Go to Trial: Crash the Justice System," *New York Times*, March 10, 2012.

CHAPTER 1: DUE PROCESS THEATER

1. Spokane Police accident report dated October 31, 2001, p. 6.

2. Material in this section is drawn from author interview with Judy Rodeen on January 11, 2001, and Judy Rodeen's witness statement to investigators, "Witness Statement, Judy Rodeen, February 2, 2002," p. 1.

3. Ibid.

4. Witness statement at scene of accident, "Witness Statement, Yvonne Belcourt, February 18, 2002."

5. Spokane Police report dated October 21, 2001, p. 113.

6. "Spokane Police/Sherriff Additional Report" dated October 31, 2001, and signed by Bryan Grenon, p. 1.

7. "Spokane Police Department Statement of Investigating Officer— Affidavit of Facts, State of Washington, County of Spokane," Report # 01-319110, p. 2.

8. "Spokane Police Additional Report # 01-319110," p. 2.

9. Ibid.

10. Center for the Study of Applied Legal Education, "Report on the 2007–2008 Survey," 2008, p. 10. www.csale.org/files/CSALE.07-08 .Survey.Report.pdf.

11. Laurence A. Benner, "Eliminating Excessive Public Defender Workloads," *Criminal Justice*, Summer 2011, pp. 25, 191.

12. The Spangenberg Group for the Bureau of Justice Assistance, Office of Justice Programs, U.S. Department of Justice, "Keeping Defender Workloads Manageable," January 2001, p. 7.

13. National Right to Counsel Committee and the Constitution Project, *Justice Denied: America's Continuing Neglect of Our Constitutional Right to Counsel*, April 2009. www.constitutionproject.org/pdf/139.pdf.

14. Ibid., p. 2.

15. Ibid.

16. Dan Gralike quoted in *Justice Denied*, which cites: Dan Gralike, "Living Double in a World of Trouble—The Indigent Criminal Defense Crisis in Missouri," *ESQ.*, June 3, 2005.

17. Laurence A. Brenner, "Eliminating Excessive Public Defender Workloads," *Criminal Justice*, Summer 2011, pp. 24, 190.

18. Washington State Office of Public Defense, "2010 Status Report on Public Defense in Washington State," January 2011, p. 5.

19. Based on multiple in-person interviews with Carol Dee Huneke during November 2011 and statement submitted in the Superior Court of the State of Washington in and for the County of Spokane, dated March 1, 2004.

20. Affidavit from David A. Carter submitted to Superior Court State of Washington in and for the County of Spokane, Document number 02-1-00721-1, February 27, 2004, p. 2.

21. Affidavit from John Stine submitted to Superior Court State of Washington in and for the County of Spokane, Document number 02-1-00721-1, February 27, 2004, pp. 1–2.

22. Affidavit from Kathleen Moran submitted to Superior Court State of Washington in and for the County of Spokane, Document number 02-1-00721-1, February 27, 2004, pp. 1–3.

23. Affidavit from Carol Dee Huneke submitted to Superior Court State of Washington in and for the County of Spokane, Document number 02-1-00721-1, March 1, 2004, pp. 1–4.

24. Kevin Blocker, "Judge Lays Down the Law to Attorney," *Spokesman-Review*, March 2, 2004.

25. Affidavit from Carol Dee Huneke, March 1, 2004, p. 4.

26. Affidavit from Carol Dee Huneke, March 1, 2004, pp. 1–4.

27. Ken Armstrong, Florangela Davila, and Justin Mayo, "For Some, Free Counsel Comes at a High Cost," *Seattle Times*, April 4, 2004.

28. Ibid.

29. Complaint: www.aclu-wa.org/sites/default/files/attachments/2004 -04-05--GrantComplaint.pdf.

30. Ibid., p. 3.

31. Officer Tom Sahlberg's accident report dated October 22, 2001 and attached diagram of accident.

32. Memorandum from Joanne Moore, Washington State Office of Public Defense, February 3, 2010.

33. Washington State Bar Association, "Suggested Standards for Indigent Defense."www.nlada.net/sites/default/files/wa_indigentdefense standards_proposed_10312011.pdf.

CHAPTER 2: "I HAVE NO COUNSEL"

1. Anthony Lewis, *Gideon's Trumpet*. New York: Vintage Books/ Random House, 1964, p. 4.

2. Quoted in Lewis, pp. 9–10.

3. U.S. Census Bureau, "Panama City (city) QuickFacts from the US Census Bureau." http://quickfacts.census.gov/qfd/states/12/1254700 .html.

4. Quoted in Lewis, p. 10.

5. Bruce R. Jacob, "Memories and Reflections About *Gideon v. Wainwright*," *Stetson Law Review*, vol. 33, no. 181, 2003.

6. From original copy of document dated October 16, 1961.

7. David W. Rintels, *Gideon's Trumpet*, film, 1979.

8. Quoted in "Gideon's Handwritten Response," *Gideon v. Wainwright: A 40th Birthday Party*. Dade County Public Defender, Federal Public Defender, S.D. Florida, Federal Bar Association, South Florida Chapter, and Dade-Miami Criminal Justice Council, n.d. www.rashkind.com/ Gideon/petition4.htm.

9. Lewis, p. 4.

10. Oliver Wendell Holmes Jr., *The Common Law*. Boston: Little, Brown, and Company, 1881, p. 1.

11. Quoted in Lewis, p. 43.

12. *Barron v. Baltimore*, 32 U.S. 243, Supreme Court, 1833.

13. U.S. Constitution, Amendment XIV, § 1.

14. "Ozie Powell, Willie Robertson, Andy Wright, and Olen Montgomery v. Alabama; Haywood Patterson v. same; Charley Weems and Clarence Norris v. same," 287 U.S. 45, Supreme Court, 1932.

15. *Johnson v. Zerbst*, 304 U.S. 458, Supreme Court, 1938.

16. *Betts v. Brady*, 316 U.S. 455, 1942.

17. Lewis, p. 53.

18. Ibid.

19. Wolfgang Saxon, "Carolyn Agger, 87, Lawyer and Widow of Justice Fortas," *New York Times*, November 9, 1996. www.nytimes .com/1996/11/09/us/carolyn-agger-87-lawyer-and-widow-of-justice -fortas.html.

20. Laura Kalman, *Abe Fortas: A Biography*. New Haven, CT: Yale University Press, 1990, p. 192.

21. Adam Liptak, "John Hart Ely, a Constitutional Scholar, Is Dead at 64," *New York Times*, October 27, 2003. www.nytimes.com/2003/10/27/us /john-hart-ely-a-constitutional-scholar-is-dead-at-64.html.

22. Information on Jacob primarily sourced from "Memories and Reflections About *Gideon v. Wainwright*."

23. Jacob, "Memories," p. 218.

24. Quoted in Lewis, p. 120.

25. Quoted in Lewis, p. 152.

26. Howard Ball, *Hugo L. Black: Cold Steel Warrior*. New York: Oxford University Press, 2006, p. 137.

27. Bernard Schwartz, "Justice vs. Justice," review of *Hugo L. Black: Cold Steel Warrior*, by Howard Ball, *New York Times*, October 15, 1989.

28. All transcriptions from the Supreme Court oral arguments. See *Gideon v. Wainwright*, The Oyez Project at IIT Chicago-Kent College of Law, October 21, 2012. www.oyez.org/cases/1960-1969/1962/1962_155.

29. U.S. Constitution, Amendment XIV, § 1.

30. Ibid.

31. Author interview with Bruce Jacob, November 3, 2011.

32. Bruce Jacob, "Letters to the Editor," *Harvard Law Record*, vol. 48, April 24, 1969.

33. *Gideon v. Wainwright*, 372 U.S. 335, 1963.

34. Ibid.

35. Ibid.

36. Lewis, p. 287.

37. See Lewis, p. 227.

38. Jacob, "Memories," p. 259.

39. All transcriptions from the oral arguments. See *Gideon v. Wainwright*, 153 So. 2d 299, Fla, 1963.

40. Lewis, p. 239.

41. Quoted in Lewis, p. 70.

42. Ibid, p. 74.

43. Ibid, p. 81.

44. See "Judge Joe Peel and the Chillingworth Murders," Crime and Investigation Network. www.crimeandinvestigation.co.uk/crime-files/judge-joe-peel-and-the-chillingworth-murders/crime.html.

45. "Ex-Judge Who Plotted Murder of Other Judge Dies of Cancer," *St. Petersburg Times*, July 5, 1982, p. 10.

46. "Peel Placed in Maximum Security Cell," *Ocala Star Banner*, August 9, 1963, p. 2. http://news.google.com/newspapers?nid=1356&dat=19630809&id=JAcTAAAAIBAJ&sjid=DAUEAAAAIBAJ&pg=1284,1650710.

47. Author interview with Bruce Jacob, November 3, 2011.

CHAPTER 3: A PERFECT STORM

1. Death Penalty Information Center, "State Execution Rates." www.deathpenaltyinfo.org/state-execution-rates.

2. Sentencing Project, "Throwing Away the Key: The Expansion of Life Without Parole Sentences in the United States," October 2011. www.sentencingproject.org/doc/publications/inc_federalsentencing reporter.pdf.

3. Ibid.

4. Death Penalty Information Center, "Regional Murder Rates 2001–2010." www.deathpenaltyinfo.org/murder-rates-nationally-and-state#MRord and www.fbi.gov/about-us/cjis/ucr/crime-in-the-u.s./2010/crime-in-the-u.s.-2010/tables/10tbl04.xls.

5. Laura Maggi, "New Orleans Homicides Jump by 14 Percent in 2011," *Times-Picayune*, January 1, 2012, p. 1.

6. This figure comes from the National Registry of Exonerations but could be somewhat skewed; some suggest the number locating Illinois at the top of the list could simply reflect the Center on Wrongful Convictions at Northwestern University School of Law's better recordkeeping in its own backyard. Also, the exoneration numbers could be a reflection of the robustness of the

innocence movement in that jurisdiction. Still, it's a rough snapshot of how badly justice fails state by state. See National Registry of Exonerations, "Exonerations in the United States, 1989–2012." www.law.umich.edu/special/exoneration/Documents/exonerations _us_1989_2012_key_figures.pdf.

7. Trial transcripts from *State of Louisiana v. Earl Truvia and Gregory Bright*, Criminal District Court for the Parish of Orleans, Section "B," Case No. 252-514, p. 21 and "Shots in Head Kill Calliope Project Youth," *Times-Picayune*, November 1, 1975.

8. Defense Exhibit 7 from trial: copy of Orleans Police Department statement from Sheila Robertson, taken November 10, 1975.

9. Ibid., p. 2.

10. Lindsey Hortenstine, e-mail message to author, June 11, 2012.

11. Pamela R. Metzger, "Doing Katrina Time," *Tulane Law Review*, vol. 81, no. 4, 2007, pp. 1191–1192.

12. Ibid., p. 1190.

13. *State v. Leonard Peart*, Nos. 92-KA-0907, 92-KD-1039, Supreme Court of Louisiana ruling, July 2, 1993.

14. "Left to Die in a New Orleans Prison," An Interview with Human Rights Watch by Amy Goodman of Democracy Now!, AlterNet, September 27, 2005. www.alternet.org/katrina/26073/.

15. Christopher Drew, "In New Orleans, Rust in the Wheels of Justice," *New York Times*, November 21, 2006.

16. Leslie Eaton, "Judge Steps In for Poor Inmates Without Justice," *New York Times*, May 23, 2006.

17. Pamela Metzger, "Doing Katrina Time," *Tulane Law Review*, vol. 81, no. 4, 2007, pp. 1204–1208. *Reprinted with permission.*

18. Trial transcripts from *State of Louisiana v. Earl Truvia and Gregory Bright*, p. 22.

19. Ibid., pp. 32–34.

20. Nicholas L. Chiarkas, D. Alan Henry, and Randolph N. Stone of Bureau of Justice Assistance National Training and Technical Assistance Initiative Project at American University, "An Assessment of the Immediate and Longer-Term Needs of the New Orleans Public Defender System," April 10, 2006, p. 8.

21. United States District Court, Eastern District of Louisiana Civil Action, transcripts from *Earl Truvia v. Frank Blackburn* consolidated with *Gregory Bright v. Frank Blackburn*, May 20, 1982, p. 72.

22. Marc Mauer, *Race to Incarcerate*. New York: The New Press, 2006, p. 33.

23. United States Sentencing Commission, "Report to Congress: Mandatory Minimum Penalties in the Federal Criminal Justice System," 2011, pp. 22–24. www.ussc.gov/Legislative_and_Public_Affairs/Congressional_Testimony_and_Reports/Mandatory_Minimum_Penalties/20111031_RtC_Mandatory_Minimum.cfm.

24. Jan Moller, "Attempts at Sentencing Reform Face Tough Opposition in the Legislature," Day four of eight-day series: "Louisiana Incarcerated: How We Built the World's Prison Capital," *Times-Picayune*, May 16, 2012.

25. John Simerman, "Prison Rips Up Families, Tears Apart Entire Communities," Day six of eight-day series: "Louisiana Incarcerated: How We Built the World's Prison Capital," *Times-Picayune*, May 18, 2012.

26. United States District Court, Eastern District of Louisiana, Class Action for Declaratory and Injunctive Relief, LaShawn Jones, Kent Anderson, Steven Dominick, Anthony Gioustavia, Jimmie Jenkins, Greg Journee, Richard Lanford, Leonard Lewis, Euell Sylvester, and Mark Walker, on behalf of themselves and all other similarly situated, *Plaintiffs v. Marlin Gusman, Sheriff, Orleans Parish, et al., Defendants*, April 2, 2012, p. 3.

27. Ibid., pp. 2–3

28. Ibid., pp. 15–16.

29. Laura Maggie, "Orleans Parish Sheriff to Close House of Detention Starting Today," *Times-Picayune*, April 10, 2012.

30. Copy of letter from Justice Department's Special Litigation Section-PHB to Orleans Parish Sheriff Marlin Gusman, April 23, 2012.

31. Richard A. Webster, "Gusman, Orleans Public Defenders Reach Pact on Jail Visitations Between Clients, Inmates," New Orleans City Business, May 3, 2012. http://neworleanscitybusiness.com/thenewsroom/2012/05/03/gusman-orleans-public-defenders-reach-pact-on-jail-visitations-between-clients-inmates.

32. Orleans Parish Sheriff's Office. www.opcso.org/index.php?option=com_content&view=article&id=145&Itemid=724 and author tour of Orleans Parish Sheriff's office, May 2012.

33. "Frequently Asked Questions About Pretrial Release Decision Making," American Bar Association, October 28, 2012. www.americanbar.org/.

34. Author interviews with Gregory Bright, April–June 2012.

35. Author interview with Calvin Duncan, June 12, 2012.

36. United States District Court, Eastern District of Louisiana Civil Action transcripts in *Earl Truvia v. Frank Blackburn* consolidated with *Gregory Bright v. Frank Blackburn*, May 20, 1982, p. 23.

37. Ibid., p. 31.

38. James Hearty, "High Court Votes 6-1 for Removal; Haggerty Ouster Ordered," *New Orleans States-Item*, November 23, 1970.

39. U.S. Department of Justice, Civil Rights Division letter to New Orleans Sheriff Marlin Gusman dated April 23, 2012, p. 6.

40. John Simerman, "New Orleans Judge Turns to Private Lawyers as Defender's Office Struggles," *Times-Picayune*, June 10, 2012.

41. Author interviews with Derwyn Bunton, April–July 2012.

42. Per Orleans Public Defenders press release dated December 19, 2010. www.opdla.org/docs/lawsuit.pdf.

43. Author conversations with Derwyn Bunton, April 30, 2012, and June 11, 2012, and John Simerman, "Audit: Indigent Defense Shorted," *Times-Picayune*, May 14, 2012.

44. *Gregory Bright v. Burl Cain*, Amended Application for Post-Conviction Relief, August 20, 2001, p. 16.

45. Criminal District Court for the Parish of Orleans, Criminal Docket Number 252-514 A, *Gregory Bright v. Burl Cain*, Amended Application for Post-Conviction Relief, p. 17.

46. Ibid., p. 31.

CHAPTER 4: DEATH IN GEORGIA

1. According to Anne Holsinger at the Death Penalty Information Center, no one collects the national numbers on how many death sentences are sought by district attorneys, only the number of death penalty convictions. Per author e-mail exchange with Anne Holsinger on August 4, 2012.

2. The Constitution Project, "Mandatory Justice: The Death Penalty Revisited," p. 23. www.constitutionproject.org/pdf/30.pdf.

3. "Our Thoughts: What a Tragic Week," *Covington News*, February 15, 2012.

4. William Tecumseh Sherman, *Memoirs of General W.T. Sherman*. New York: Library of America, 1990, p. 931.

5. Equal Justice Initiative, "Illegal Racial Discrimination in Jury Selection," June 2010. http://eji.org/eji/raceandpoverty/juryselection.

6. Ibid., p. 17.

7. Stephen B. Bright, "Capital Punishment and the Criminal Justice System: Courts of Vengeance or Courts of Justice?" Keynote at The Death Penalty in the Twenty-First Century Conference sponsored by the Criminal Law Society at the Washington College of Law of American University, March 23, 1995. www.schr.org/files/resources/justicesystem3.pdf.

8. Scott E. Sundby, *A Life and Death Decision: A Jury Weighs the Death Penalty.* New York: Palgrave Macmillan, 2005, p. 4.

9. John H. Blue, Sheri Lynn, and Scott E. Sundby, "Competent Capital Representation: The Necessity of Knowing and Heeding What Jurors Tell Us About Mitigation," *Cornell Law Faculty Publications*, 2008. http://scholarship.law.cornell.edu/facpub/172.

10. Scott E. Sundby, "The Capital Jury and Empathy: The Problem of Worthy and Unworthy Victims," *Cornell Law Review*, vol. 88, no. 2, January 2003, pp. 343–381.

11. Ibid., p. 358.

12. Ibid., pp. 346–347.

13. Ibid., pp. 358–359.

14. Ronald F. Wright, "Parity of Resources for Defense Counsel and the Reach of Public Choice Theory," *Iowa Law Review*, 2004–2005, p. 14. http://wakespace.lib.wfu.edu/jspui/bitstream/10339/15914/2/Wright%20Parity%20of%20Resources%20for%20Defense%20Counsel%20and%20the%20Reach%20of%20Public%20Choice%20Theory.pdf.

15. U.S. Department of Justice, "Improving Criminal Justice Systems Through Expanded Strategies and Innovative Collaborations," Report of the Symposium on Indigent Defense, Washington, D.C., February 25–26, 1999. www.sado.org/fees/icjs.pdf.

CONCLUSION

1. www.justice.gov/ag/speeches/2009/ag-speech-090624.html.

AFTERWORD

1. *Gideon v. Wainwright*, 372 U.S. 335, 1963.

2. *Douglas v. California*, 372 U.S. 353, 1963.

3. *In re Gault*, 387 U.S. 1, 1967.

4. *Argersinger v. Hamlin*, 407 U.S. 25, 1972.

5. *Halbert v. Michigan*, 545 U.S. 605, 2005.

6. *Miranda v. Arizona*, 384 U.S. 436, 1966.

7. *United States v. Wade*, 388 U.S. 218, 1967.

8. *Coleman v. Alabama*, 399 U.S. 1, 1970.

9. *Brady v. United States*, 397 U.S. 742, 748, 1970.

10. *Hamilton v. Alabama*, 368 U.S. 52, 54-55, 1961.

11. The right to counsel in death penalty cases was established thirty-one years before *Gideon* in the case of *Powell v. Alabama*, 287 U.S. 45, 1932.

12. *Rothgery v. Gillespie County*, 554 U.S. 191, 2008.

13. That is, an arraignment.

14. In other words, a bail hearing.

15. *McMann v. Richardson*, 397 U.S. 759, 1970.

16. *United States v. Cronic*, 466 U.S. 648, 1984.

17. *Strickland v. Washington*, 466 U.S. 668, 1984.

18. See *Powell v. Alabama*, 287 U.S. 45, 1932, the case in which the Supreme Court determined the right to counsel for death penalty cases.

19. *Padilla v. Kentucky*, 30 U.S. 1473, 2010.

CELEBRATING INDEPENDENT PUBLISHING

Thank you for reading this book published by The New Press. The New Press is a nonprofit, public interest publisher. New Press books and authors play a crucial role in sparking conversations about the key political and social issues of our day.

We hope you enjoyed this book and that you will stay in touch with the New Press. Here are a few ways to stay up to date with our books, events, and the issues we cover:

- Sign up at www.thenewpress.com/subscribe to receive updates on New Press authors and issues and to be notified about local events
- Like us on Facebook: www.facebook.com/newpressbooks
- Follow us on Twitter: www.twitter.com/thenewpress

Please consider buying New Press books for yourself; for friends and family; or to donate to schools, libraries, community centers, prison libraries, and other organizations involved with the issues our authors write about.

The New Press is a 501(c)(3) nonprofit organization. You can also support our work with a tax-deductible gift by visiting www .thenewpress.com/donate.